Montana
Fly Fishing Guide

Montana Fly Fishing Guide

by John Holt

Volume I

West of the Continental Divide

Drainages

Bitterroot
Blackfoot
Clark Fork
Flathead
Glacier
Nat'l Park
Kootenai
Swan

Greycliff Publishing Co.
Helena, Montana

For Dad and Rich

Maps by Marita Martiniak

Photographs of "special flies" by Doug O'looney

Printed in the U.S.A.
04 03 02 01 00 99 98 97 96 9 8 7 6 5 4 3 2 1

Publisher's Cataloging in Publication Data
Holt, John, 1951–
Montana fly fishing guide. Vol I, West of the Continental Divide / by John Holt.
p. cm.
Includes index.
ISBN 0-9626663-2-7

1. Fly fishing—Montana—Guidebooks. I. Title.
Sh456.H65 1995 799.1'2'09786
QBI95-225

ACKNOWLEDGEMENTS

This project wouldn't have been possible without the input of countless people, including members of the Montana Department of Fish, Wildlife, and Parks, the guides and outfitters of Montana, and the individuals quoted in these volumes. It wouldn't have been possible without the work of George Holton in compiling massive amounts of stream and lake data while with the Montana Department of Fish, Wildlife, and Parks; without the example of Dick Konizeski (who initially traveled these waters in his books); an understanding Jim Pruett of Pruett Publishing Company; Glenda Bradshaw, Stan Bradshaw, Bek Meredith, and Gary LaFontaine of Greycliff Publishing Company; friends Jake How, Tony Accerano, Tim Joern, Bob Jones; and my wife Lynda.

John Holt donates 10 percent of his royalties to benefit the Montana environment.

TABLE OF CONTENTS

Volume I—West of the Divide

Moral: Humility and open-mindedness sometimes catch far more fish than all the wise guys.

– Robert Traver
Anatomy of a Fisherman

INTRODUCTION

Montana offers all of us who love to fly fish more than a little bit of everything. For trout there is a touch of heaven on earth. For a large number of other gamefish and panfish there is also surprisingly fine angling.

From classic rivers holding trophy rainbows and browns to high country wilderness lakes filled with unsophisticated native cutthroats, on out to high plains reservoirs and their own wind swept version of our sometimes arcane pursuit, the land presents several lifetimes of angling experiences. Those who live here and are lucky enough to fish over a hundred days a season admit that they will see, at most, maybe a quarter of the water lying out there.

With so much to fish, and so little time to do so, the need for a guide written strictly for fly fishers becomes clear. Other guides are available, many giving much sound information and advice. But there is not a guide on the market written specifically for fly fishers, who, as a whole (admittedly, there are a number of twisted souls out there), are not overly intrigued by the idea of fooling a catfish on a stinkbait imitation (size 2, 4X long hooks work best).

Concise, accurate information for fly fishers dedicated to catching trout 99 percent of the time (chasing bass with deer hair poppers or northern pike with saltwater patterns has a certain, esoteric appeal occasionally) is not available. For out-of-state visitors, where to start can itself be a frustrating, mind-numbing dilemma. For those fortunate enough to live in Montana, information regarding quality waters waiting quietly over the next range of mountains or hiding in some out-of-the-way coulee provides the impetus to expand one's angling horizons.

I am one of the fortunate ones who lives in Montana and has the opportunity to fish 100-plus days a season. All the same, I doubt that I have fished a quarter of the waters that will be mentioned in these guides. Obviously, other reliable sources were consulted for information. Each river, stream, creek, lake, pond, reservoir, and ditch mentioned in both volumes of this guide has been cross-checked with the latest data available from the Montana Department of Fish, Wildlife and Parks. Additionally, dozens of guides, fly shop owners, fisheries biologists, and hard-core anglers have been interviewed about the current state of trout chasing affairs.

Does this mean that every water holding good numbers of fat trout (or bass or pike) is mentioned in this book? Hell no. There are so many unnamed lakes and streams tucked away in the mountains, that even fish-and-game personnel do not have data on many of them.

What the reader will find in here are listings and descriptions of hundreds of waters worthy of an angler's effort. Divided into sections by drainages, major rivers are described in detail at the opening of each section.

Tributaries and lakes that provide quality angling are then covered (in varying degree) in alphabetical order in each drainage section. Information includes the type of water, species present, abundance and size range of the fish, any fly pattern that is locally important, and other pertinent facts. Specific insect hatches may also be discussed.

All other waters too small to offer quality fishing, too small to sustain heavy pressure, closed for the most part to public access, or just plain lousy fishing are listed alphabetically with brief comments at the end of the chapter. These conclusions are often a matter of opinion, of course (almost any spot can be challenging and fun for the angler with the right attitude). For example, many tiny creeks hold a couple of decent fish that are fun to locate and fool, but that's it. The rest of the stream holds three-inch dinks that would drown if they connected with a size14 Adams. That is why each of us should fish where our curiosity leads us. That's part of the magic of fly fishing—finding trout where no one else has. In Montana this can be almost anywhere.

One of the best ways to navigate in unfamiliar territory is by using United States Geological Survey (USGS) topographical maps. These show in detail important features, including rivers, streams, tiny creeks, lakes, ponds, mountains, forests, dams, swamps, buildings, roads, etc. Anyone who can read a highway map can read a topo. They are an inexpensive means to finding waters discussed in the guides.

Because there are literally hundreds of topo maps for Montana alone, it would be cumbersome and costly to own them all. By ordering both the *Montana Index to Topographic and Other Map Coverage* (an easy-to-use pamphlet that shows all maps of Montana and in itself contains some fairly good maps of the state) and the companion *Catalog of Topographic and Other Published Maps* (giving names, dates, and prices of maps currently available), you can decide what maps to order with marginal effort; or if you are hopelessly addicted to maps and the treasures they reveal like I am, kiss an evening goodbye. Larger scale maps are also listed. The address to order these is: USGS, Box 25286, Federal Center, Bldg. 810, Denver, CO 80225. An excellent new publication for small scale topographic maps that show major highways, public access sites, and other points of interest is the *Montana Atlas and Gazeteer* by DeLorme Mapping. You can order it by calling toll-free 1-800-874-4171, or look for it in book stores.

There are also sections dealing with subjects ranging from stream etiquette to travel arrangements to fishing gear positioned after the chapters on river drainages. This information is not crucial to catching trout, but it does contain some intrinsic value that may make a trip easier and more enjoyable.

And because every river or lake can be destroyed in the course of a season by logging, agriculture, mining, or simply overuse by anglers, environmental problems affecting specific waters will also be mentioned. The fly fishing community absolutely must become involved with preserving and even enhancing the world-class trout habitat of Montana. If we do not, it all truly will be gone in the future. Sending a check to your local Trout Unlimited is nice but not enough anymore. Personal commitment is needed. To me that is one of the possible benefits of these guides—some new people will be introduced to what Montana has to offer fly fishers. Those that would destroy these fine waters in service of the almighty twisted dollar only listen to the heat generated by the outraged aggregation of an angry mob—in this case one clutching fly rods and wearing waders. I would much rather work a stream with an angler who shares my love of rivers and fish than watch helplessly as chainsaws and D-9s rip the guts out of both water and trout.

The environmental comments are not a declaration of doom. They are a call to join in these battles. The good news is that although some of those battles are temporarily lost, more are being won. Not only are waters being protected but many damaged fisheries are rebounding in productivity. The fact is that fly fishing for trout in Montana is better than it was twenty years ago—and with the help of people inside and outside who care about this state it will be even better twenty years from now.

Even with the swelling of our dedicated ranks, there is still a lot of unfished (or lightly fished) water. And fishing on crowded waters like the Madison is still superb. The action would be even be better if everyone exercised the maximum degree of courtesy and common sense. Learning to share the resource will be a valuable skill in the future.

Admittedly some lakes, especially those with brook trout, are overpopulated and produce stunted fish. Keeping a few of these for a campfire dinner may actually improve the health of the system. But for anyone to keep a trophy brown from the Beaverhead or a trophy rainbow from the Missouri is both selfish and destructive. Catch-and-release with barbless or debarbed hooks is the only way to travel most of our waters anymore.

Still, the bottom line with fly fishing is the feeling of a large fish running for freedom as the rod bends double and the reel's drag buzzes toward mechanical breakdown. That's all this book is really about . . . the water, the trout, and the angler.

Fall rainbows on the Bitterroot
Photo by Don Roberts

The Bitterroot has gained a loyal following of serious fly fishers in recent years. Anglers from around the country come to cast over the river's rainbow, brown, cutthroat, brook, and bull trout (and this is roughly their order of importance). The number and size of the fish in the Bitterroot may not quite equal the trout populations in some of the state's better known waters yet, but the river has been improving since the mid-1980s. A good day on the water means catching twenty to forty trout, most of them under 15 inches, but with the occasional brute up to four or five pounds.

The river has its beginnings in the Bitterroot Mountains on the west and the Sapphires on the east. From the confluence of the East and West Forks near Connor, the river falls a little over 800 feet during its leisurely 85-mile journey to the Clark Fork at Missoula. There are some fast runs, tricky bends, and a few nasty irrigation dams, but for the most part the river is easy going.

If you float the river from the West Fork down through Connor, past Sleeping Child, by Victor, onto Stevensville, through Lolo and down to Missoula, you can experience every type of trout fishing a Rocky Mountain river can offer. From shallow riffles near the headwaters to gravel-banked runs and on into deep pools and glides, past thick piles of downed trees and over slow-moving flats, the Bitterroot has all the faces.

Despite the additional flows from Painted Rocks Reservoir, the lower Bitterroot still suffers from dewatering problems in dry years.
Photo by Stan Bradshaw

The fishery suddenly changed for the better in the mid-1980s. The Montana Department of Fish, Wildlife, and Parks, using money from sportsmen's license dollars, bought 15,000 acre feet of water per year from Painted Rocks Reservoir on the West Fork, to be released downstream when it's needed. While this wasn't enough to keep the middle and lower sections of the river from getting low in midsummer, with a water commissioner checking the irrigation ditches, it has provided enough

BITTERROOT RIVER

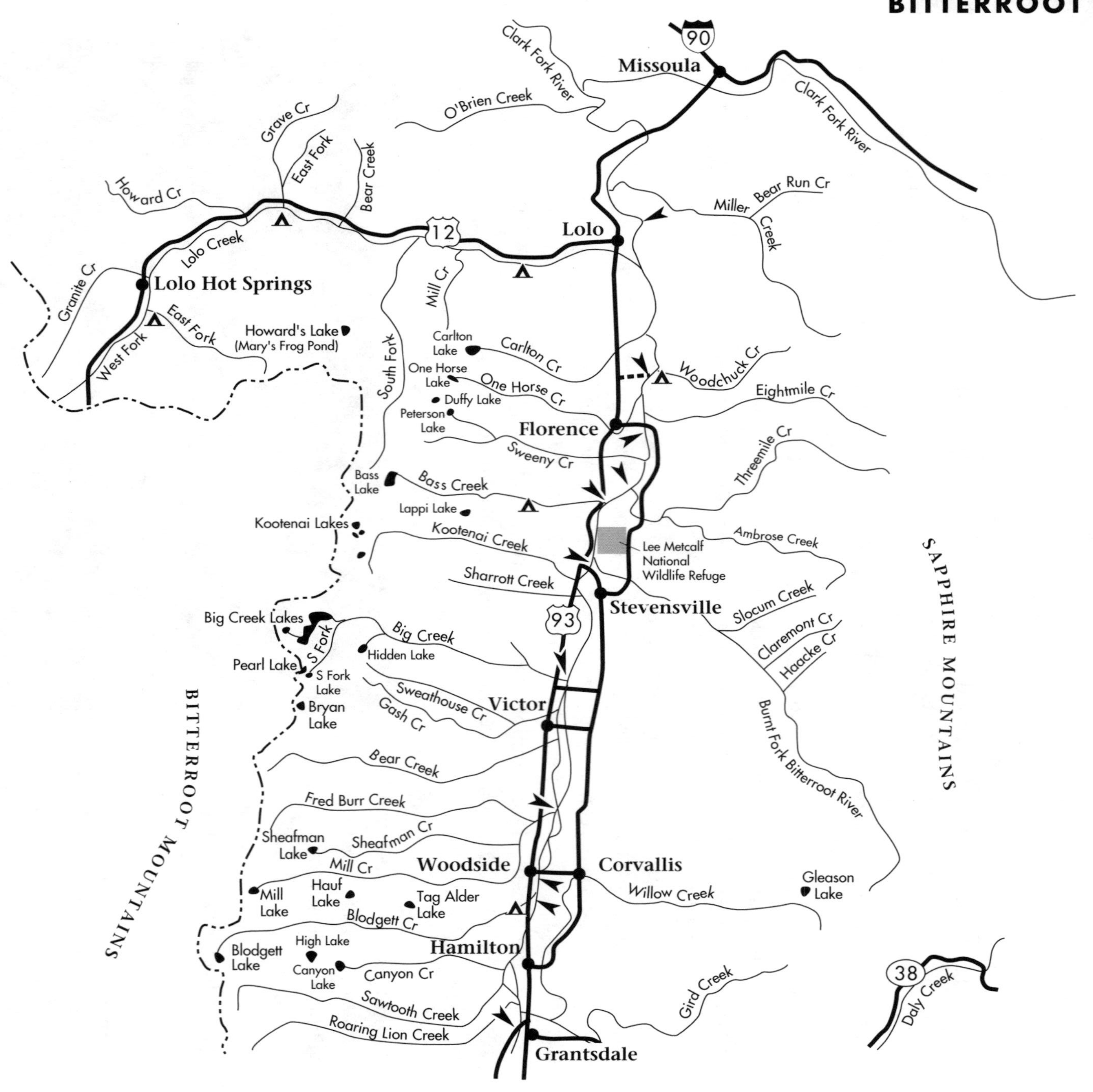

BITTERROOT RIVER

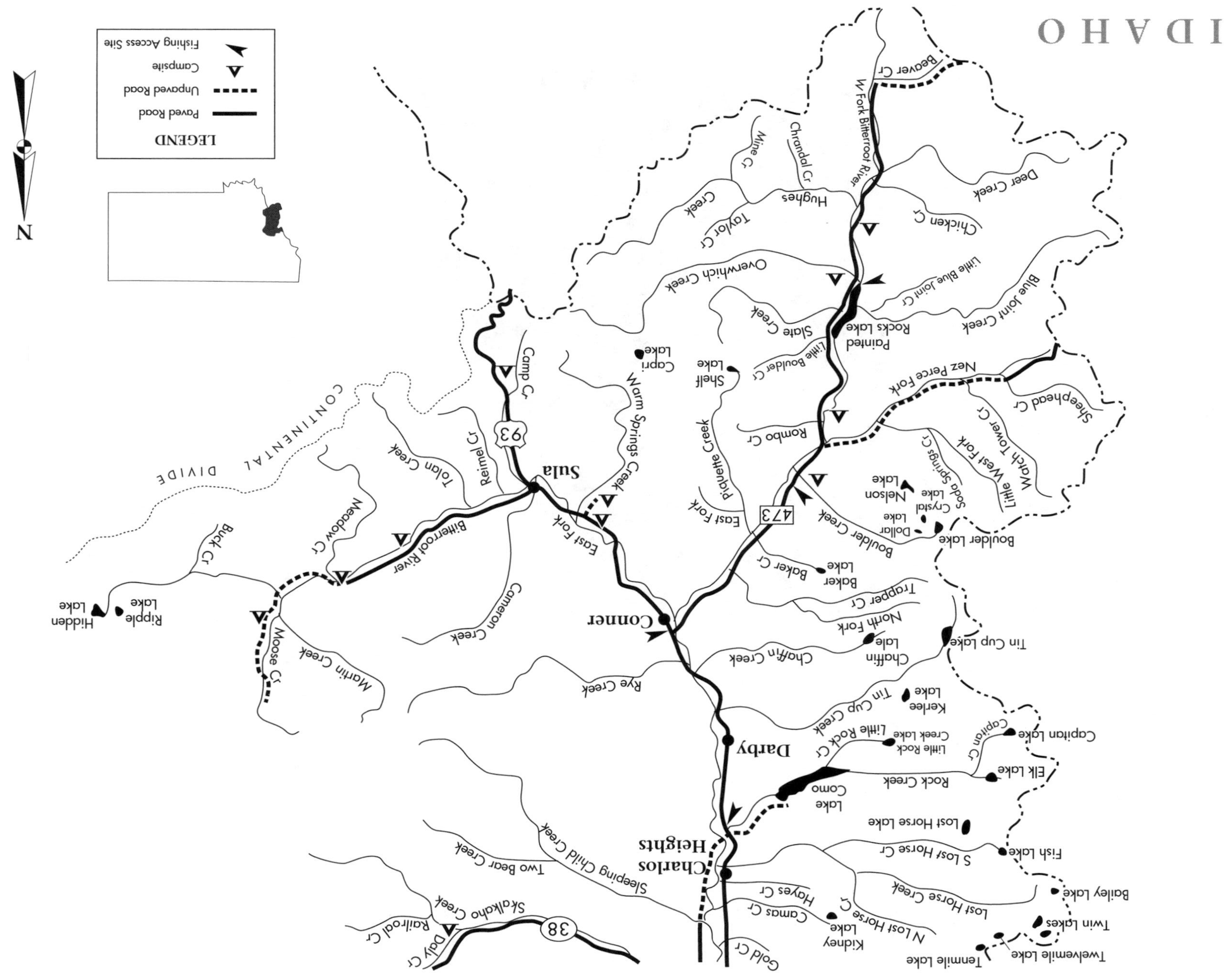

flow to keep the fishery healthy even through the drought years of the late 1980s and the early 1990s.

Conner to Hamilton—The first section, from the confluence of the East and West Forks just below Conner down to Hamilton, qualifies as a small river most of the year. Flows range from less than 100 cfs in February to over 2,000 cfs during the June-July runoff. The Bitterroot twists enough to dig holes and slots, but there are plenty of long, gentle riffles. The water from the Old Darby Bridge down to Wallace Crawford is an easy, short float, with no diversion dams—perfect for the visitor rowing his own boat. The fishing is consistent throughout the summer, mostly for smaller trout.

The Bitterroot south of Hamilton, at low water
Photo by Glenda Bradshaw

Hamilton to Victor—The second section, from Hamilton to Victor, still suffers in areas from channel destabilization. The river braids, creating numerous islands, and digs away at the unsecured banks. This part of the Bitterroot also gets hit harder by irrigation draw-down during the summer. The fishing, especially in the upper half, is still very good, and in the opinion of Woody Emrich, "if we can win a few more battles, this is going to be the best piece of the Bitterroot."

Maybe every fly fisherman's fantasy is to have a private trout stream. On the Bitterroot, from this section down, even if he can't get a deed to it, it's not hard for the angler to find a piece of water to call his own. There are side channels and oxbows with independent current from ground water or irrigation seepage. The heads of these cut-offs go dry or get low during the summer, so no boat traffic enters the channel. The angler can discover these "short pieces" by walking the shore a few miles. Many of them, with their sipping fish, look just like spring creeks.

Victor to Florence—The third section, from Victor to Florence, is slower water (none of this river is steep gradient anyway). There are deeper holes and longer flats. The trout feed steadily and fussily on the hatches. The river passes the Lee Metcalf National Wildlife Refuge, which covers 1,700 acres and stretches along 4½ miles of one bank. The fishing in this section slumps during midsummer in hot years, but it is a classic piece of dry fly water during the other three seasons.

On the Bitterroot, from this section down, even if he can't get a deed to it, it's not hard for the angler to find a piece of water to call his own.

Florence to the confluence with the Clark Fork—An interesting opportunity exists on the lower end of the Bitterroot. In the sloughs off the main channel between Florence and the mouth of the river there are good numbers of pike and largemouth bass. At the peak fishing times, from July through September, surface disturbers (size 1/0 plastic Sliders for the pike and size 6 deer hair bugs for the bass) produce fine top-water fishing. A major food item in this section of the Bitterroot is the crayfish, and in the slower, deep flats of the main channel a crayfish pattern catches not only bass but some really large trout.

Stone flies begin showing up on the river in March. The Skwala hatch is a time of high excitement for many anglers. Local guide John Adza claims that this period offers some of the best fishing on the river for those that know where and when the insects appear.

"On a warm day you can take browns that run well over 20 inches," says Adza. He describes the Skwala as a flat-shaped creature, dark olive and size 6 to 8, and adds that he has never seen them take to the air despite being winged. "There is a window of forty-five minutes to maybe an hour-and-a-half in the afternoon when the insects are really active and this triggers the trout. Even a brief period of sunlight is enough to get things going. The best spots are smooth runs near gravel banks. The bugs like the rocks to climb out of the water and dry themselves on."

Skwalas differ from their Salmon Fly relatives. Their hatching is not marked by wild, blizzard-like flurries that move steadily upriver day by day. Instead, the Skwala comes off in smaller numbers, hatching on a localized basis throughout the stream course in pretty much the same spots year after year. So, once the angler turns up a spot or two, he can return each spring and, with a little looking, wade into

A Special Fly for the Bitterroot

The Ugly Rudamus, developed in 1984 by John Foust, is a marvelous attractor, but it also works well during caddis fly and stone fly hatches on the river. It floats so high, the elk hair wing propped up at an angle, that it's a visible, easy-to-fish fly for drifting down riffles.

Howard West, president of Scientific Anglers, was watching John tie the new pattern one day and he blurted out, "That sure is an ugly fly," and that is where the first part of the name came from. Not even John knows where the second part came from.

UGLY RUDAMUS

Hook: standard dry fly

Thread: black Monocord

Tail: natural elk hair

Body: pearl flashabou

Underwing: mottled fly sheet

Overwing: natural elk hair (swept back in a bullet-head)

The Ugly Rudamus fishes especially well on broken water. It creates a broad enough outline on the surface to not only represent "food," in the general sense, to the trout but to also promise enough calories to make a trip to the surface worthwhile. The fly rests on that fine line between imitation and attractor, making it a very consistent fish catcher.

some good action. Rainbows will provide most of the fishing, with a few browns and maybe a cutthroat or two tossed into the mix.

The first flush of water from a combination of rain and snowmelt actually improves the fishing, but once the runoff begins, forget about fishing the main river. Millions of acre-feet of snowmelt pour out of the mountains and wash through the valley. Things often don't return to normal until July. Side channels and the mouths of feeder streams are the best locations at this time (tarpon fishing in Florida is not a bad idea, either).

Chuck Stranahan and Jim Hopkins started to collect insects one season, hoping to do the "complete" angler's hatch chart for the Bitterroot. They quit after finding fifty species. The important hatches include (besides the Skwala): the Chironomid midges, bringing up trout all winter; the Grannom Caddis, coming off heavily during the first weeks of May, especially on the upper stretch; the Salmon Fly, beginning in mid-June; the Golden Stone, a flurry in late June (John Foust says that they are great one in three years); the Green Drake and the Brown Drake, also starting near the end of June; the Spotted Sedge and the Little Sister Sedge, dominating the evening activity starting in late June; the Western Leadwing, beginning in late June (this is not an important dry fly insect, but the nymphs might explain the popularity of the Prince Nymph and the Leadwing Coachman wet fly on the river); the Pale Morning Dun, starting in early July; the Gray Drake, the spinners important in early July (this mayfly seems to flourish wherever there are slow, weedy canals around the river); the Trico, appearing over the flats in August, especially on the lower river; the Blue-Winged Red Quill, emerging midday from late August through mid-September; the Giant Orange Sedge, appearing in early September; and the Blue-Winged Olive, starting in mid-September and hatching the heaviest on overcast days.

If there is a "don't-miss" event on the Bitterroot, it is the combined blitz of the Green Drake and the Brown Drake. The spectacular flush of duns equals the hatch on any western river. Oddly, the larger Green Drake outnumbers the smaller Brown Drake (it's usually the other way around). On the prime stretches, like the loop around Hamilton (the float stretch from Angler's Roost to the Silver Bridge), rising trout and whitefish churn the surface all afternoon.

For the streamer fisherman there is an important difference between the upper and the lower stretches. In the upper river sculpins and suckers are the main forage species, and the best imitations and tactics mimic these bottom-clinging bait fish. But in the lower river squawfish and redside shiners dominate. The shiners, 3 to 4 inches long at maturity, become important during their spawning period in late June and early July, when male shiners turn especially bright, and red or even purple swimming streamers can be incredibly effective for large trout.

IMPORTANT HATCHES

Blue-Winged Olive
Blue-Winged Red Quill
Brown Drake
Chironomid Midges
Giant Orange Sedge
Golden Stone
Grannom Caddis
Gray Drake
Green Drake
Little Sister Sedge
Pale Morning Dun
Salmon Fly
Skwala
Spotted Sedge
Trico
Western Leadwing

Any selection of flies for the Bitterroot should reflect a strong local influence. Two fine pattern innovators, John Foust and Chuck Stranahan, operate fly shops right in Hamilton. A new fly from either of these men goes out on the rivers with guides and their clients, and in the simple, cold world of business, those creations succeed or disappear. For the Green Drake hatch the choice on the Bitterroot might be the Extended Body Polychute or the Brindle Hookup Dun, either of these imitations outfishing better known patterns.

Paul Inamoro, after a great day on the amazing 1992 Green Drake hatch (a year when many fish over 20 inches were caught), wrote, "It was easy to compare the Extended Body Polychute with the Green Drake Wulff. The Polychute took one trout after another and the Wulff got snubbed completely."

For mayflies the parachute-style imitations dominate on this river. That preference extends even to general searchers, the size-12 to size-20 Adams Parachute the most popular all-around pattern. Compara Duns, in appropriate color schemes (especially the Slate/Olive for the Blue Winged Olive), effectively match the smaller insects.

One local pattern that has achieved national recognition, the Ugly Rudamus, serves as a general caddis/stone fly imitation. The standard, popular flies, such as the Elk Hair Caddis and the Emergent

Sparkle Pupa, are often altered to match the various caddis hatches (both are tied with a dark wing and an orange body in size 8 for the Giant Orange Sedge).

The Baler Hopper is another local creation. With a body of evazote foam and legs of baling twine, this is an unsinkable and realistic fly. It floats low on the water, wobbling like a half-drowned grasshopper.

The Bitterroot is a good river for popping a dry fly attractor on the riffles. The Madam X, a downwing, rubber-legged fly born in this area, ranks with the Renegades, H & L Variants, Trudes, Humpies, and Wulffs in popularity. All of these patterns work consistently from sizes 18 to 8, with the smaller ones better in midsummer.

The most common nymphs for the Bitterroot are the Bomber Nymph (especially in a Green Drake version), Gray Nymph, Gold Ribbed Hare's Ear, Red Squirrel Nymph, Woolly Worm, Prince Nymph, Peeking Caddis, Matt's Stone and Pheasant Tail. Most people fish medium sizes, 8 to 16, but at least one person, T. C. Yale, disagrees. "You pick up too many whitefish on regular-size nymphs in the Bitterroot. I use #4 hooks, for all the popular patterns, and while I still get a whitefish occasionally, they're always real big."

POPULAR FLIES

Adams Parachute

Baker Hopper

Bomber Nymph

Compara Duns (SLate/Blue)

Extended Body Polychute

Gold Ribbed Hare's Ear

Madam X

Matt's Stone

Peeking Caddis

Pheasant Tail

Prince Nymph

Ugly Rudamus

Woolly Worm

You can get on the Bitterroot along its entire length at a number of bridges crossing the river and through various parcels of public land. There are also several clearly marked state fishing accesses along the river.

Anyone floating the river should be aware of the diversion dams, weirs, and downed trees that make the river hazardous for the inexperienced. Weirs are not too difficult to negotiate, but a trip over a diversion can be deadly.

Fishing Waters in the Bitterroot Drainage

Baker Lake: To get to this alpine lake just under Trapper Peak, drive to the trailhead up the West Fork Highway and then take the gravel road at Pierce Creek. The hike in is an easy 2½ miles, making Baker a popular spot. It is often good for cutthroats that are measured in inches, not pounds.

Bass Creek: The outlet stream for Bass Lake tumbles over a bed of nutrient-poor, igneous rocks, never scouring holes deep enough to shelter large fish. It comes into the Bitterroot a few miles north of Stevensville. This is typical of many west-side streams that look wonderful but tend to yield small fish. There are plenty of small cutthroat, rainbow, and brook trout to fill a day on the wilderness section. The lower few miles are dewatered for irrigation. This is a common problem for not only west-side, but east-side streams as well. Irrigation damages both the resident fishery and the spawning runs out of the Bitterroot.

Bass Lake: This deep lake in the Selway-Bitterroot Wilderness is 100 acres when full. Bass Lake is one of the old, man-made water storage projects in the region. Reached by a tough, 7-mile hike, it has a number of fat 10- to 20-inch rainbows, remnants from previous airdrops. The lake is not rich in nutrients, with insect samplings showing low populations of mayflies, caddisflies, and damselflies. Midge larvae and pupae are the main food source, with a healthy portion of terrestrials—beetles, grasshoppers, and ants—thrown in. Wind is a common companion up here, so take a six-weight outfit. Wet patterns such as the Halo Midge Emerger and String Midge Larva in sizes 16 to 22, or small generic imitations such as the Hare's Ear, Pheasant Tail, and Twist Nymph in olive (always a good lake color) work well. Flying Ants (especially patterns with a clear Antron wing), Foam Beetles, Gartside Hoppers, and the Deer Hair Hornet are deadly on flat, calm water. A diligent, competent angler has a shot at twenty to forty trout on a good day.

Big Creek: This classic mountain stream begins way back in the Bitterroots and flows quickly from Big Creek Lakes down to the river near Victor. The lower reaches are sucked dry for irrigation. The upper runs, followed by trail, are easy fishing for brooks and cutts that love Wulffs, Humpies, Trudes—all the sophisticated stuff. In the canyon, 4 to 5 miles below the lakes, the trail skirts the stream and hikers stare down into green pools so deep that the bottom isn't visible. This a good spot for the fly fisherman to get specific, drifting nymphs that naturally sink fast, such as Bead Heads or Tear Drops, for the cutthroats, or even swimming small streamers, such as a Baby Cutthroat or a Muddler, for the bull trout. The streamer fishing requires a longer, heavier rod, a 9-foot, six-weight; otherwise a 7-foot, two-weight is ideal for dry fly popping.

Big Creek Lakes: In high country, these glacial-cirque waters are at the head of Big Creek in a basin edged with pine and talus slopes. At high water these lakes are actually one body of water totaling close to 250 acres and maybe 100 feet deep. Plenty of 8- to 14-inch Westslope cutthroats and rainbows swim here (the larger cutthroats stay around the inlet cove at the upper end). As in most high country lakes of size, there are also a few picky trout in the three- to four-pound range. And as always, a nymph like the Gold Ribbed Hares Ear, cast well ahead of the cruising fish and then moved ever so slightly, produces consistently. Time your strike to the flash of white jaws.

The west side of Big Creek Lake
USDA–Forest Service

Montanans use their wilderness areas. Even though it's an 11-mile trek into this area, on a normal July weekend in 1992 a troop of thirty Boy Scouts, a horse outfitter with a half-dozen clients, and eight other pairs or groups of backpackers camped around the lake.

With this kind of pressure, if everyone keeps a trout or two for a camp dinner it doesn't take long for the larger trout along the accessible shoreline to get cropped down. And this is exactly what happens each season on Big Creek Lakes.

Jay Gaudreau used an inflatable kick-boat to fish across the lake. "The trout were a bit finicky. They didn't take just anything. The hot fly during the day was a size-8 Joe's Hopper and during the evening it was a size-12 Dancing Caddis. On the near side, along the trail, the fish averaged 8 to 10 inches, but on the far side, against a bank so overgrown that no one could reach it on foot, the cutts and bows averaged 12 to 14 inches."

Using small water craft is the simplest key to success on high mountain fisheries.

Bitterroot Irrigation Ditch: On the east side the Ditch is fishable mainly during the growing season when ranchers need water. The artificial flow is paralleled for its 80-mile length by two-lane road. Some very big rainbows, brooks, and browns, recruited in the spring from the river, are caught in this thing each season. It's a strange fishing spot that sometimes resembles a spring creek and at other times looks like the Los Angeles River. Light tippets and precisely matching patterns, especially during the heavy hatches of Trico, Gray Drake, and Blue Winged Olive mayflies, fool these trout. Hopper and beetle imitations also work in the heat of the summer. Creeping tactics are required for these spooky fish. The whole place is short on aesthetics, but a five-pound trout is a five-pound trout.

The secret is knowing precisely where to fish along the canal. The irrigators periodically kill the weeds with chemicals, wiping out insects and fish in the process. Some stretches of the ditch run barren for weeks after this cleanup, and any angler casting the water blind may very well be wasting time. Your best bet is to walk and hunt for risers.

According to the Chaffin family, one of the early ranching outfits in the valley, it wasn't always done this way. The owners considered the ditch a valuable recreational outlet for their families. When the weeds grew too thick, impeding water flow, everyone went out with hay forks and pitched the mats of vegetation out of the canal. The Ditch was one of the finest fly fishing waters in the valley at the time.

Blodgett Creek: Entering the river near Hamilton, Blodgett has cutthroats, brooks, and the raging bulls of autumn. The lower section is dewatered. A campground sits at the end of the road. Blodgett is ridiculously fast fishing for 6- to 10-inch fish once you get a half- mile up the trail. Seven miles up, past old logjams and sheer cliffs, there are beaver dams where you can get a 16-inch cutthroat. Two patterns, a

Looking west up Blodgett Canyon
USDA–Forest Service

Light Caddis Variant and a Hare's Ear Trude, cover just about any situation, but this is also the perfect spot to try the odd flies that never work anywhere else.

Marshall Bloom, a volunteer worker on a fry-loss study on Blodgett Creek led by Fish, Wildlife and Parks biologist Chris Clancy, provided the following data:

Trout fry, hatched in the creek, drifted down towards the river from mid-June to mid-July. They only drifted for three to four hours each night, probably to avoid predators, and spent the days in the shallow stream margins.

Workers set drift nets at three sites—above an irrigation diversion, in the irrigation canal, and below the irrigation diversion. Above the canal 900 fry were collected in one session, over 500 immature trout were captured in the canal itself, and only 200 fry were recovered below the canal.

This represents a tremendous loss of fry to the Bitterroot in just one ditch. Multiply this loss by all the ditches in all the dewatered tributaries in the system. And this is just one way that ditches affect the trout population.

Blodgett Lake: You can see hints of the cirque country that holds this water as you drive along U.S. 93. Even if it weren't full of healthy cutthroats, the lake would be worth a long walk, especially in early autumn. The top three flies recommended for Blodgett are the Twitch-Pause Nymph, Otter Shrimp, and Zug Bug.

Blue Joint Creek: A fine little stream that pours into Painted Rocks Lake, Blue Joint is easily fished along the 20-mile trail for some nice cutthroats up to 14 inches, as well as lesser numbers of other species. The trout here take either the Royal Humpy, with its red and white color scheme, or the Coachman Trude, with its green and white color scheme, preferring one over the other at any given moment.

Blue Joint Creek
Photo by Gary LaFontaine

Boulder Creek: A typical Bitterroot mountain stream (and like many, it gets better as you go up a way), the Boulder joins the West Fork of the Bitterroot several miles upstream from the confluence of the West and East Forks of the Bitterroot. Four miles up the trail, through aspen groves and huckleberry patches, there's a waterfall with a large pool at the bottom. That hole has the greatest variety of trout species, with the biggest specimens of each (for example, cutts up to 14 inches instead of 8 inches).

Boulder Lake: This glacial cirque lake has a few cutthroats to 18 inches that are finicky feeders. Bring long leaders and small nymphs (preferably something matching a midge—a size-18 Serendipity is a good choice). Reached by 10 miles of relatively easy trail from the end of the Boulder Creek Road, Boulder Lake is dammed at the outlet and holds 20 acres at full pool.

Burnt Fork Bitterroot River: Located in the Stevensville area, this is a nice, easy-to-fish stream pouring out of the Sapphire Mountains that is followed by dirt and gravel road and then trail to Burnt Fork Lake. The lower reaches dry up from irrigation, but the upper reaches vary from open, meadowland pools and runs to forested stretches filled with brushy banks and logjams. An Elk Hair Caddis and an Adams are as fancy as you normally need to be on this creek. It has good numbers of cutthroats and brookies, some over a foot. A few bull trout wriggle up to spawn in the late summer and early fall.

Burnt Fork Lake: Reached by several trails, the most obvious being the one at the end of Burnt Fork Road, this lake is really excellent right after the ice goes out. Relatively nutrient-rich due to the surrounding limestone formations, the lake is drawn down quite a bit for irrigation but it is 30 acres when full and good fishing for bull, cutthroat, and rainbow trout averaging less than a foot. Damselfly nymphs and Woolly Worms, bigger flies than are usually successful in these high mountain fisheries, handle the subsurface action. Caddis, mayfly, midge, and terrestrial imitations work on top. Don't forget some sort of a skittering caddis pattern.

Camas Lakes: Way up the Camas Creek drainage, getting to Camas Lakes is, in the words of Terrell Mortensen, "a hell of a hike. You can't get a horse into them. There's a stretch where you have to climb over, jump over, and squeeze between boulders ranging from car-size to house-size."

The upper lake is better than the lower lake. There are still a lot of small cutthroats there, but at least on this one you have the chance to hook a big fish. Right after ice-out in 1989, Bruce Bair took pictures and released three nice fish, all over 18 inches, caught near the inlet on a Stub Wing Bucktail.

Cameron Creek: This seven miles of good, small-water fishing unfortunately is mostly on private, posted land. It enters the East Fork near Sula. This is a brook, bull, cutthroat, and rainbow stream.

Carlton Lake: Reached by the Carlton Lake Road south of Lolo, this lake, at 7,700 feet, sits exposed in scrub timber just below Lolo Peak. The wind always blows; any air coming off the snow is chilling. Carlton is 40 acres when full, but during summer drawdown it is an ugly, 20-acre bowl. There are small cutthroats, rainbows, and hybrids, all of which do a neat disappearing act at times.

In spite of all this Carlton is a popular day trip with hikers and four-wheelers, probably because it so close to Missoula. Anyone who makes the trip up here should visit the truly spectacular waterfall a few hundred yards below the outlet.

Como Lake: Fifteen miles southwest of Hamilton on Rock Creek and easily reached by country road, Como is over 1,000 acres when not drawn down for irrigation. There is a public campground and this place is well known and overrun with happy visitors as long as the weather remains warm. Water-skiers hatch here in the summer. It's a beautiful lake when full and irrigation-ditch ugly when sucked down 50 feet or so. Como is planted with thousands of 8- to 10-inch Arlee rainbows, and also some tired brood stock from the hatchery. Working the north shoreline away from the crowds is the best bet, especially around the mouths or tributaries. A float tube or canoe helps. There is currently a project underway to expand the storage capacity on Como Lake to provide more water for irrigation and instream flows.

Lake Como
Photo by Stan Bradshaw

Daly Creek: Seventeen miles up the gravel Skalkaho Highway east of Hamilton, this swiftly flowing water is ice-cold, clear, and small, but fun fishing for small cutts and rainbows and even a few resident bull trout.

Until recently Daly was closed to all fishing because deposits of the mineral cinnabar, in a disturbed area, were poisoning the stream with mercury. Don't drink the water.

East Fork Bitterroot River: Forested in the upper reaches and open in the lower reaches, this stream runs for 37 miles to Sula and under U.S. 93 to join the West Fork. Irrigation really does a number on the lower section and some of the middle section. In the northwest part of the state the streams are silted up from logging. Down here they just suck the life out of them. The hell with the fish.

All the same, there are cutthroats and rainbows in entertaining numbers to maybe a touch over 12 inches, plus minor concentrations of brown, brook, and bull trout. In the spring rainbows finished with spawning hang around long enough for the Salmon Fly hatch in the second week of June. The stream usually runs clear during the hatch, making it good water for large dry flies (an Evazote Salmon Fly, buoyant and flush floating, is a good pattern). There are no dams on this fork to pump up the summer flow and it gets low, sending the fishing into a funk after July. In the winter, the mountain whitefish love nymphs if you get a serious case of cabin fever.

Chuck Stranahan says about the East Fork, "It used to have a healthy population of cutthroats, up to 16 inches, natives adapted to the river. Now it has mostly small rainbows. Without some protection from the crowds it will remain just another roadside fishery that doesn't live up to its potential."

El Capitan Lake: A very popular backcountry lake above Lake Como, El Capitan sees both backpacking and horse traffic, but still has decent action for foot-long-or-so cutthroats in its 15 acres of dark water. Very small Woolly Worms, sizes 12 and 14, tied with fluorescent chenille, work especially well here.

Gleason Lake: Go up Willow Creek Road, then walk the last mile in the Sapphire Mountains to this nutrient-rich water. It has plenty of healthy Westslope cutthroats that love leech patterns and damsel nymphs. Try fishing a Purple Bunny Leech over the weed beds with a sinking line (this tactic took trout after trout here one afternoon).

Hauf Lake: Another small dammed high-country pond, this one lies around the western side of Printz Ridge in the Bitterroots. It's not hit much and reports on it are sketchy. This is the type of lake that needs constant updating. It is over 7,000 feet in elevation and, if it hasn't been hurt recently by irrigation demands, may offer good fishing for fat cutthroats.

Hidden Lake: At nearly 7,000 feet in the Big Creek drainage, Hidden Lake is managed for cutthroats (planted with 1,000 four- to six- inchers yearly) that do well due in large part to the lack of fishing pressure. Easy to fish—remember, they are, after all, cutthroats.

Hughes Creek: In the West Fork drainage, this small stream is followed by gravel road and trail for nearly 20 miles. Plenty of simple pleasure here for 7-inch cuttthroats and brookies amid the pine forests. A size-16 nymph—maybe a Deep Sparkle Pupa or a Flashback May—something bright, dangled on a taut line in any pool nearly always gets a quick, jolting strike.

Kootenai Creek: Entering the river near Stevensville, Kootenai is dewatered below (of course), a good mountain stream above. The way it tumbles, in a pool-and-fall sequence, makes buoyant dry flies, maybe a foam Air Head or a deer hair Irresistible, especially efficient for the hordes of pan-size cutthroats. This is worth the walk just to fish under the "hanging canyons," those walls extending out over the stream.

Kootenai Lakes: Three lakes lie at the upper end of the Kootenai drainage. Middle Lake was planted with goldens many years ago, but they're history. North Lake has some nice rainbows and South Lake is packed with stunted brookies. Almost all high country lakes now are managed for cutthroats, so look for rainbow-cutthroat hybrids (or even golden-rainbow hybrids). In lakes stuffed with small brookies, any fly will catch fish (except for the Stu Apte Tarpon pattern). Catch a bunch for a lakeside meal and do the lake (and the trout) a favor.

Little Rock Creek: One of the numerous pretty and productive mountain streams that runs into Como Lake, a set of waterfalls just up from the mouth stops any spawning run coming out of the lake. But there are resident cutthroats up 10 inches living in the small pools and pockets. For some reason the ticks (more dangerous than a lot of better known terrors of the woods) are especially bad here in the spring.

Little Rock Creek Lake: Located about 5 miles above Como Lake, this water is swampy and fertile for a high country lake. There are lots of easy-to-catch, 12-inch cutthroats. It's a rough hike in spots, the stream and the trail often becoming one.

Lolo Creek: Lolo flows alongside the Lewis and Clark Highway (U.S. 12) for 30 miles to the town of Lolo and is accessible for much of its length from the road. There is a famous hot springs, with a resort where a tired angler can soak in a pool after a hard day of flogging. The stream is heavily hit by both residents and travelers who cannot resist the look of the water. In the upper section Lolo runs through dense pine forests. In the middle it flows through open meadow, including a lot of former pasture land now getting chopped up into homesites. There is a little bit of everything in the drainage, most commonly brookies, cutts, and rainbows, but with browns moving up from the river in the fall.

Eastern fly fishermen especially like the lower section, from a mile above the Lolo bridge down to the Bitterroot, because the stream reminds them of home waters. Cottonwoods nearly join in a canopy over the pools and runs. The water digs deeper, providing hiding spots for nicer fish. The stream rewards the angler who casts accurately, giving up only small trout, mostly brookies, from the open areas but much nicer fish from the dark, shaded holds.

Pat Ruge provided a list of his best trout from the lower reaches of Lolo in the past few years: a 14-inch brook on a size-12 Quill Gordon in November, an 18-inch rainbow on a size-8 Bitch Creek nymph in July, and a 19-inch brown on a size-18 Slate/Olive Compara Dun in October. He noted, "Fish like these are the exception, not the rule."

Lolo isn't a stream where the fisherman can always ignore the hatches. It's rich enough in this lower stretch to get not only well-known mayflies and caddisflies but also strong numbers of some real oddities. A professional entomologist should collect this water—there are undoubtedly significant populations of "relict species" because of the springs flowing into it. In early November there is a surprising hatch of one large, stunning mayfly, the gray-flecked duns riding like little sailboats. And this insect doesn't fit any of the descriptions in any of the angling entomologies. Trout relish these mayflies, feeding on them any day the weather is decent.

Good hatches include the Spotted Sedge, coming out in good numbers through June, and the Ginger Quill, appearing in early July. These are both big enough insects, popping in enough quantity, to get the larger trout looking at the surface.

Lost Horse Lake: Nearly 70 acres, Lost Horse is typical of many of the backcountry lakes (like Twin Lakes, Ten, and Twelvemile Lakes) in the Bitterroots. There are boggy sections along the shoreline with clumps of rock rising above the water. It is managed for native cutthroats that do well in this environment. The fishing is often easy for trout averaging 12 inches and maybe on rare occasions reaching a pound or two. Warm valley winds often curl along the slopes, carrying grasshoppers, ants, and beetles out onto these lakes in the afternoon. The trout have keyed to this phenomenon, so take a selection of terrestrial patterns on trips to this alpine country.

Warm valley winds often curl along the slopes, carrying grasshoppers, ants, and beetles out onto these lakes in the afternoon. The trout have keyed to this phenomenon, so take a selection of terrestrial patterns on trips to this alpine country.

Martin Creek: The huge fire that swept through this area of the East Fork in the early 1960s decreased both the size and number of trout in this mountain stream, but the drainage is finally healing itself. There are enough small cutthroats in the riffles, pools, and pockets, all ready to flash to a size-16 Trude or Double Wing, to make this fun fishing.

Mine Creek: Really nothing great as a trout stream, Mine Creek has some interesting beaver ponds about a mile above Hughes Creek with cutthroats and rainbows in them. The largest and deepest pond in the system holds the best fish, but the beavers are very active so anything may change. The fly fisherman should climb to a high vantage point and study the entire complex for a while before starting to fish.

Vincent Thome, with a 16-inch rainbow to his credit here, explained his favorite tactic: "To take the better rainbows, you have to 'sneak fish' these waters. I get up to the base of the dam, stay out of sight, and cast the fly as delicately at possible. This is not an unusual approach to beaver ponds. My equipment might be more delicate than normal. It includes a two-weight outfit and a 16-foot, 6X leader, generally with a size-18, light-wire Partridge and Olive soft hackle fly.

"I let the fly sink and just watch the line tip for a sign of a strike. If it gets all the way to the bottom I let it sit there for at least a minute, which gives the fish time to forget the line splash, and then start a slow, deep, hand-twist retrieve."

Mitchell Slough Complex: This old channel of the Bitterroot starts above Tucker Crossing between the towns of Corvallis and Victor. This complex is fed by irrigation water from the river and numerous spring seeps. At one time Mitchell Slough was just like most of the ranch-land streams in the state—trampled, overgrazed, and dewatered. Various owners began a very expensive rehabilitation project in 1981, hiring a private consulting firm to work on the problems. The fishery bounced back quickly in the spring-fed branches, producing an eight-pound brown in 1988.

It's interesting to compare the fishing in a "natural" stream, one where cattle do not graze the banks, to a beaten-down stream. Along Mitchell the grass grows high and the first jump of a grasshopper carries the insect four to five feet into the air. Any breeze catches the grasshopper, and if the wind is blowing out over the water, it dumps him onto the flow. On any summer day the trout in Mitchell key on grasshoppers, more so than on most creeks, rushing out from the banks like sharks on a chum line.

The dilemma on Mitchell Slough is that the owners, after taking what was nothing and creating a great spring-creek fishery, do not want the public on it. They deserve the respect of all anglers for the effort they put into rebuilding the fishery (and, in the process, helping the Bitterroot). Maybe it is enough if it stands as an example of what could be done for all the streams and rivers of the state.

Nez Perce Fork: Followed by road for 20 miles from the West Fork to the headwaters, Nez Perce Fork offers very good fishing for cutthroats and brookies, along with some browns and bull trout late in the season. There are little Yellow Sally stone flies fluttering around all summer, enough to make a size-16 Chuck's Yellow Trude a main fly. The specific pattern becomes important here for big (up to 16 inches) and choosy fish.

One Horse Lakes: Not far from Carlton Lake southwest of Lolo; there are small rainbows and cutthroats here.

Flows from Painted Rocks Reservoir have become a factor in the high quality of the upper Bitterroot trout fishery. Photo by Gary LaFontaine

Overwhich Creek: This creek enters the West Fork of the Bitterroot River just above Painted Rocks and provides (or did provide) average action for small cutthroats for 14 miles to the barrier falls.

In 1992 a large slide after a heavy rain storm buried this stream in sediment. The Forest Service, stung by the public outcry, rushed to the area to study the situation and quickly determined that the problem was caused by an old fire and not by the excessive logging and road building right in the slide area. They said this with a straight face.

It will take four or five years for this stream to recover.

Painted Rocks Lake: This reservoir provides four miles of waterskiing bliss in wooded country along the west side of the West Fork Highway. It's hard to say which hurts the fishing more in the summer, the irrigation drawdown or the passing speedboats (put up a warning flag if you're bobbing around in a float tube).

Generally there are plenty of better places to cast a fly in the Bitterroot Valley, but there are enough cutthroats to make this lake worth a visit early in the season when the lake is full, the boaters are still in winter shock, and the fish cruise the shorelines in the cold water.

Peterson Lake: Go up Sweeney Creek Road south of Florence, then on logging road to reach Peterson Lake at the head of the north fork. The lake offers good fishing for small rainbows, cutthroats, and hybrids. There is usually a strong inverse correlation on these high mountain lakes between the size of the trout and the pace of the fishing action.

Ripple Lake: Some big trout swim here that are not often caught. The small lake lies up the East Fork in the Anaconda-Pintlar Wilderness and has both cutthroats and rainbows.

John Foust says, "Don't fish any of these mountain creeks too early. The water out of the snowfields is just too cold for good fly fishing. But they come into their own in the summer."

Roaring Lion Creek: This small canyon stream washes out of the Bitterroots south of Hamilton, home to good numbers of small cutthroats. John Foust says, "Don't fish any of these mountain creeks too early. The water out of the snowfields is just too cold for good fly fishing. But they come into their own in the summer."

Rock Creek: A real pretty, forested mountain stream, not far from Darby, Rock Creek flows swiftly over smooth shelves and short drops. The lower stretch is ruined by irrigation, but some fair-sized brookies, cutthroats, and rainbows hold out in the upper sections.

Sheafman Lakes: Seven miles of trail, starting at the mouth of Sheafman Canyon north of Woodside and twisting into the Bitterroots in rugged, timbered, and steep-walled country, take you to these high mountain waters. The lower, 6-acre lake is managed for cutthroat trout that do not grow large but are fairly abundant. The upper lake is barren.

Shelf Lake: Hike 6 miles of trail from the lower end of Painted Rocks Reservoir to reach this 7,600-feet-high lake that offers average fishing for 12-inch cutthroats.

Skalkaho Creek: Pretty name—it means "place of the beaver." This is one of the last unspoiled drainages in this part of the country, flowing clear and swift towards the Bitterroot near Hamilton. Plans to clear-cut much of this drainage would spell disaster for the excellent numbers of medium-sized cutthroats (beautiful, oddly colored fish with dark, purplish-brown backs) and the occasional brown, brook, and bull trout. Forested mountains stretch off in all directions. The water runs over a golden, coppery-colored streambed. Fishing this easy and this enjoyable purifies a cluttered mind. It's not a trophy trout stream, but it is beautiful water that would be ruined by siltation from the logging. Maybe it won't happen here. Care to place a bet?

Skalkaho Falls
USDA–Forest Service

John Foust recommends the Gray Hackle Peacock and the Renegade, but he adds, "On these streams the size of the fly is just as important as the color and shape. Most people use size-10 and size-12 dry flies, but size-14 and size-16 patterns almost always work better. It's important to adjust the fly size to the lip size."

Sleeping Child Creek: This stream joins the Bitterroot south of Hamilton and is heavily fished for various salmonid species which, except for the transient spawners, never reach great size. In the lower reaches, however, those spawners turn this creek into a wonder. For some reason, the browns in the fall really use Sleeping Child, starting their upstream push as soon as there is enough water. A favorite tactic is to fish a Schroeder's Hopper as a dry indicator and a heavily weighted Feather Duster as a nymph, working the deeper runs and pools. The whole exercise of reading the water changes, and you should look for spawners in holding areas.

In the upper reaches the stream is followed by a good trail to its mountainous headwaters on the east side of the valley. The water is so clear that you have trouble judging the depth. The flies have to be fished in and under the wood snags, but at the same time a fine leader, at least a 5X, increases the number of strikes. You get broken off in Sleeping Child by some of the spring and fall spawners that linger even in this tumbling section.

A favorite tactic is to fish a Schroeder's Hopper as a dry indicator and a heavily weighted Feather Duster as a nymph, working the deeper runs and pools.

South Fork Lolo Creek: Mainly a cutthroat stream, this creek crosses private land in the lower reaches but is decent angling in the upper runs.

South Fork Skalkaho Creek: A down-sized version of the main creek, the South Fork has cutthroat and bull trout. It is reached from the Skalkaho Highway some twenty minutes (and 10,000 hairpin, blind curves) above Hamilton.

The bull trout throughout the Bitterroot drainage are not big fish that run up from the river, but instead smaller resident fish. The large waters in western Montana with bull trout populations, Rock Creek (in the Clark Fork watershed) or the South Fork of the Flathead, produce ten-pound-plus specimens for streamer fishermen, but if a riverine strain like that ever existed in the Bitterroot, it is lost. The smaller stream bulls, a 15-incher a monster, still eat mainly baitfish, but the patterns for catching them aren't the "tarpon flies" popular for bull trout on other Montana streams.

A study by hydrologist Gary Decker and biologists Chris Clancy and Rick Swanson showed that bull trout are a better indicator species for watershed health than even the cutthroat. There is a strong positive correlation between good bull trout populations and watershed health. In degraded streams bull trout, very sensitive to sedimentation, are pushed out by brook trout.

Threemile Creek: Three Mile joins the Bitterroot just north of the Lee Metcalf Wildlife Refuge. There must be hundreds of creeks like this that come wandering down out of the hills and then cut their narrow way through pasture and meadowland to main rivers. There are usually some small cutthroats up above and some bigger brooks or rainbows in the middle sections. All too often these streams are hurt by grazing and irrigation in the bottom reaches.

Too often these little buggers aren't worth fishing, but the kid in me makes passing them up impossible. Dapping nothing but the leader while lying on my belly, the sight of a little trout sucking in a size-20 Adams is as much fun as anything. The mind of a child at work here, thankfully.

On Threemile, at least, this creep-and-crawl fishing is safe for the moment. There is a major riparian restoration project going on in the lower few miles of this creek. It might provide even better fishing for "kids" of all ages in a few years.

Tin Cup Lake
USDA–Forest Service

Tin Cup Creek: Reaches the river just north of Darby. The glaciated geology of this drainage blesses Tin Cup with a variety of terrains. There are spread-out bog reaches, meandering meadow stretches, and tumbling runs, all inhabited by excellent numbers of slightly larger-than-average cutthroats and brookies.

Tin Cup Lake: Why one high mountain lake in an area is richer than its neighbors is always a mystery. Tin Cup, fairly fertile despite its 9,000-foot-plus elevation and seasonal irrigation drawdowns, has lots of stunted westslope cutthroats—the kind with moray eel-shaped heads and rattlesnake bodies—that will hit anything. But at the inlet, especially off the shallow shelf on the southwest side, there are 16- to 20-inch fish. These bigger trout don't hit just anything. As a matter of fact, they can get downright uppity, cruising along the edge picking something from the bottom. They won't do more than glance at a Woolly Worm or a bait-fish imitation, but they will take a small nymph, a size-18 Pheasant Tail or Zug Bug, if it is sitting right in front of their noses.

Twin Lakes: Both Upper (40 acres) and Lower (65 acres) nestle in glacial cirques right below the mountain tops at the head of Lost Horse Creek. The land, rocky and exposed, has no fertility of its own to contribute to the lakes. The 8- to 10-inch cutts and rainbows accept like a gift from heaven any fly that hits the water.

Warm Springs Creek: Near the Idaho border, upstream from Connor, this little stream is in country so nice that it reminds you of what western Montana was like fifty years ago. There are cutt, rainbow, brook, and bull trout, with some of the better ones hanging in the big, sandy holes.

The easiest way to cover those deep pools is to "milk" the fly downstream, in the words of Harry Merritt, "not just letting it hang but waving the rod tip side to side, with a downwing dry, such as a Picket Pin, for the cutthroat or a small streamer, such as a Dark Spruce, for the bull trout, covering the water."

West Fork Bitterroot River: This fork heads along the southwestern border of Montana, flowing through Painted Rocks Reservoir to join the East Fork near Connor. Above Painted Rocks the water holds fair numbers of brook, cutthroat, and rainbow trout. Below the lake, you will find a smaller-scale version of the upper Bitterroot, open and rocky banks alternating with brushy shores. This is excellent dry fly water for browns, rainbows, and cutthroats. It fishes very well through the summer because of the cool releases from the dam.

Private land blocks much of the water, but roads and Forest Service land provide adequate access for non-floaters. This stretch is floatable, but it is a tight squeeze in spots and big logjams appear suddenly around corners—this stream is dangerous enough to discourage the inexperienced boatman.

The West Fork has roughly the same insects as the main river, but the timing is a little different for the hatches. The water, with the dam moderating runoff in early summer and adding flow in midsummer, also fishes better than the main river for some hatches.

Here are quick notes on what to watch for in the West Fork:

Skwala Stone— start looking for it in March; better on the lower six miles of the river.

Salmon Fly— pops a little earlier on the West Fork, and this is the one time that 20-inch rainbows come to the surface.

Golden Stone— some years it overshadows the Salmon Fly up here.

Spotted Sedge— provides excellent surface action in the evenings from May through early July.

Green Drake and Brown Drake— certain sections have heavier hatches of these mayflies than others.

Yellow Sally— ubiquitous; and with the river fishing well in hot weather, this makes a good imitation, such as Chuck's Yellow Trude, important.

Blue-Winged Red Quill— this pretty mayfly appears in August, emerging from 11 a.m. to 3 p.m. each day.

Giant Orange Sedge— early September; just enough insects for trout to really key on them in the lower part of the river.

One special, midsummer terrestrial to look for on the West Fork is the Spruce Moth. Some streams get infestations and some don't. The West Fork has the right forest composition for this insect. The Spruce has a long cycle, building up over the years to peak abundance.

The angler can drift popular attractors, such as the Kolzer Orange and H & L Variant, or popular searchers, such as the Caddis Variant and Hare's Ear Parachute, all summer on the West Fork and catch cutthroats and rainbows to 15 inches steadily. It is an easy-to-wade and easy-to-read stream.

It is not just a small-trout fishery, however. The fisherman who runs a streamer or a nymph aggressively under and through the logjams hits big trout on the West Fork (like the fish caught by Bill Lucoff, a 24-inch brown on a George's Brown Rubberlegs Nymph; by Justin Baker, an 18-inch brook on a Muddler Minnow; and by Marshall White, a 19-inch cutthroat on a Birds Nest Nymph.

West Fork Lolo Creek: Followed by the Lewis and Clark Highway from Lolo Hot Springs to Lolo Pass, this is small water that gets hammered by passing motorists for small cutthroats early in the year.

Willow Creek: From Willow Lake this stream flows towards Corvallis. It is dewatered in its lower reaches, but heavily fished by area residents for the remainder of the creek's 17 miles for cutthroat and brook trout. It drops from pool to pool, creating easy-to-fish holding water.

Willow (Fool or Sage Hen) Lake: Located in Skalkaho country, Willow is at the end of a poorly maintained trail (which discourages visitors). There are plenty of average rainbows and a few very big ones. Willow Lake is surrounded by meadows. This makes the lake shallower and richer than most mountain lakes, with an abundance of aquatic plants. The weeds change the fly selection, making imitations of damsel nymphs, mayfly nymphs, and caddisfly larvae more important. The trout cruise and take whatever is along the bottom instead of rushing up to grab any speck of food.

Try, as Tim Moss recommends for Willow, "looking rather than casting, waiting for the fish that cruise parallel to the shoreline because those are the active feeders."

Other Waters

Ambrose Creek: Cutthroats.

Bailey Lake: Rainbows and cutthroats.

Baker Creek: Too small.

Bear Creek (Victor): Small fish.

Bear Creek (Lolo): Small fish, but spawning cutthroats come into it from Lolo Creek in the spring.

Bear Creek Lake (Victor): Barren.

Bear Run Creek: Too small.

Beaver Creek (Big Creek): Cutthroats.

Beaver Creek (West Fork): Brookies and cutthroats.

Bryan Lake: Rainbows.

Buck Creek: Cutthroats.

Butterfly Creek: Cutthroats and rainbows.

Calf Creek: Too small.

Camas Creek: Hit by hikers on the way up to the lakes. There is a mix of rainbows, cutthroats, and brooks (a 6-incher is a brute).

Canyon Creek: Cutthroats. There is a spectacular waterfall, and above that waterfall there is a mountain that looks like a miniature replica of the Matterhorn.

Canyon Lakes: Rainbows and cutthroats.

Capri Lake: Cutthroats.

Carlton Creek: Cutthroats and rainbows.

Cedar Creek: Too small.

Chaffin Creek: Cutthroats.

Chaffin Lake: Rainbows.

Chicken Creek: Cutthroats.

Chrandall Creek: Cutthroats.

Christensen Creek: Cutthroats. It just drops too fast for any decent trout to hold.

Claremont Creek: Cutthroats and rainbows.

Clifford Creek: Cutthroats.

Coal Creek: Cutthroats and rainbows.

Crystal Lake: Nice cutthroats. If you're not totally exhausted after walking 11 miles to Boulder Lake, you can scramble up a steep but short trail to this one.

Deer Creek: Cutthroats and rainbows.

Dick Creek: Too small.

Divide Creek: Too small.

Dollar Lake: Part of the Boulder and Nelson complex of lakes. Worth fishing for willing cutthroats if you're in the area.

Duffy Lake: Rainbows.

East Fork Camp Creek: Brookies and cutthroats.

East Fork Grave Creek: Too small.

East Fork Lolo Creek: Cutthroats.

East Fork Piquette Creek: Cutthroats and rainbows.

Eastman Creek: Too small.

Eightmile Creek: Cutthroats.

Elk Lake: Cutthroats. Nothing spectacular about the fishing, but there are good camping spots and good horse grazing areas. This is a popular site with elk hunters in the fall, and they often fish it.

Fish Lake (Martin Creek): Cutthroats.

Fish Lake (Lost Horse Creek): Rainbows.

Fred Burr Creek: So brushy that, in the words of Richard Brautigan (Trout Fishing in America), "you had to be a plumber to fish it."

Gash Creek: Cutthroats and rainbows.

Gird Creek: Brooks, browns, and rainbows; occasionally a big one.

Goat Lake: Cutthroats.

Gold Creek: Cutthroats and rainbows.

Granite Creek: In a beautiful area of the forest; accessible by logging roads off the highway above Lolo Hot Springs. The fish aren't fat and the fish aren't big, but everytime you do something right with the fly you get a strike.

Grave Creek: Brookies and cutthroats.

Haacke Creek: Too small.

Hackett's Pond: Private.

Hayes Creek (Charlos Heights): Brookies and cutthroats.

Hayes Creek (Missoula): Too small.

Hidden Lake: Cutthroats and rainbows.

High Lake: Cutthroats and rainbows.

Holloman Creek: No access.

Hope Lake: Cutthroats.

Howard Creek: Too small.

Howard's Lake (Mary's Frog Pond): Cutthroats, rainbows, and mosquitoes; very small but deep, almost impossible to find but I did once—never saw or heard any frogs.

Jack the Ripper Creek: Cutthroats, rainbows, and violence.

Johnson Creek: Too small.

Kerlee Lake: Cutthroats; only tiny fish.

Kidney Lake: Rainbows.

Lappi Lake: Barren.

Larry Creek: Too small.

Lavene Creek: Too small.

Legend (Faith) Lake: Cutthroats.

Little Blue Joint Creek: Followed up the canyon by a good trail; fun pocket-water fishing in the first few miles for the same mix of cutthroats and rainbows that are in Blue Joint Creek.

Little Boulder Creek: Too small.

Little Burnt Fork Creek: Too small.

Little West Fork Creek: Cutthroats and rainbows.

Lockwood Lake: Barren

Lost Horse Creek: Seven miles south of Hamilton and 4 miles up Lost Horse Road. It is so rough and brushy that casting is tough. At the lower end there are waterfalls that drop up to 15 feet, and in the spill pools below these there are concentrations of 8- and 9-inch cutts.

A good Bitterroot brown trout
Photo by John Holt

Lyman Creek: Too small.

Maude Lake: Barren.

McClain Creek: Too small.

Meadow Creek (Sula): Bull and cutthroat trout. With the added protection bull trout habitat will get if that species is declared endangered, all of these small waters will return to a more natural state of flow. That in itself may not be important to the angler, but the improved condition of all the small tributaries affects the main river.

Meadow Creek (Lolo): Too small.

Mill Creek (Lolo): Brookies and cutthroats.

Mill Creek (Hauf Lake): Full of feisty 6-inch to 9-inch trout, mostly rainbows, with an occasional whopper of 12 inches. In the words of Chuck Stranahan, "It's a great place to be nine years old again."

Mill Lake: Cutthroats.

Miller Creek: Poor access.

Moose Creek: Cutthroats.

Mud Creek: Too small.

Nelson Lake: A brutal 4½ mile hike, but the fishing for cutthroats up to 16 inches is excellent at times.

North Fork Bear Creek: Too small.

North Fork Granite Creek: Too small.

North Fork Sweeney Creek: Cutthroats and rainbows. Want a tip on these mountain streams? Fish an upstream dry fly with a short leader, six feet at the longest, with no more than a foot or two of line outside the top guide. That will help you strike quick enough to hook these lightning-fast little buggers.

North Fork Trapper Creek: Cutthroats.

O'Brien Creek: Cutthroats and rainbows.

One Horse Creek: A real skinny horse. Fair for small cutthroats in the upper reaches.

Pearl Lake: It takes two hours to climb up to it from the head of Big Creek Lakes and only twenty minutes to climb down on a wicked trail. The cutthroats are easy, numerous, and on average a few inches longer than the ones in Big Creek Lakes. If you are already camping at Big Creek Lakes, this one is worth a trek.

Pierce Creek: Too small.

Piquette Creek: More fun than the lake, with some good spill pools in the canyon that hold hungry cutthroats and rainbows.

Piquette Lake: A high cirque lake with sparse timber and talus slopes (these are not my favorite high mountain spots—too exposed and not very rich). The fishing is spotty for small cutthroats.

Porcupine Creek: Too small.

Railroad Creek: Cutthroats.

Reimel Creek: Poor fishing because there's no real holding water.

Rombo Creek: Too small.

Rye Creek: Cutthroats.

Salt Creek: Too small.

Sawtooth Creek: Cutthroats and rainbows.

Sears Lake: Barren.

Sharrott Creek: Cutthroats and rainbows.

Sheafman Creek: Cutthroats. It's so steep that you're always casting uphill.

Sheephead Creek: Cutthroats and rainbows.

Signal Creek: Too small.

Silverthorn Creek: Too small.

Slate Creek: Too small.

Slocum Creek: Cutthroats and rainbows. It's a meadow stream instead of a riotous mountain cascade. It's accessible by county road.

Smith Creek: Too small.

Soda Springs Creek: Cutthroats and rainbows.

South Fork Bear Creek: Too small.

South Fork Big Creek: Brookies, cutthroats, and rainbows.

South Fork Big Creek Lake: Reported to be barren, but a hiker on the trail to Big Creek Lakes swore to me that there were fish in there. The old, decrepit dam leaks, ruining the spawning grounds, but the lake itself is deep and rich. The few rainbows left in a spot like this might be really decent. Any volunteers to check on this one?

South Fork Lost Horse Creek: Seven- to nine-inch cutthroats; access to the bottom is reached by a good road from Charlo Heights. Try nymphing with a size-14, weighted Montana Stone in the deeper pools for an occasional nicer fish (they don't come up often for dry flies for some reason).

Spud (Charity) Lake: Not all that charitable even for the small, 8- to 10-inch cutts. Two days of fishing around this boggy, two-acre lake never produced any of those two- to four-pound trout that rumor puts here.

Stuart Creek: Too small.

Sweathouse Creek: Brookies, cutthroats, and rainbows.

Sweeney Creek: Brookies and cutthroats.

Tag Alder Lake: Rainbows. There's no trail into this one, just a cross-country bushwhack, and that alone tells you something about the fishing.

Taylor Creek: Cutthroats and rainbows. Hughes Creek has a number of tributaries, like this one, that are worth a few casts in the better pools.

Tepee Creek: Too small.

Tenmile Lake: Cutthroats.

Tolan Creek: Cutthroats.

Trapper Creek: Cutthroats and rainbows.

Twelvemile Lake: Cutthroats. Certain lakes are perfect for the serious backpacker who wants to go there just because so few do.

Two Bear Creek: Cutthroats.

Watchtower Creek: Cutthroats.

West Fork Butte Creek: Too small.

West Fork Camp Creek: Brookies and cutthroats.

Wiles Creek: Too small.

Woodchuck Reservoir: Rainbows.

Wornath Reservoirs: No access.

■ *Special thanks to John Azda, Bruce Bair, Justin Baker, Marshall Bloom, Woody Emrich, Elna Foust, John Foust, Jim Hopkins, Paul Inamoro, Jay Gaudreau, Harry Merritt, Terrell Mortensen, Tim Moss, Pat Ruge, Chuck Stranahan, Vincent Thome, and T. C. Yale for their help on the Bitterroot drainage.*

Blackfoot River near River Junction
Photo by Stan Bradshaw

The Norman Maclean novella, *A River Runs Through It,* with the Blackfoot River as its setting, begins with the best known sentence in angling literature, "In our family, there was no clear line between religion and fly fishing."

That book mirrors what the Blackfoot was in the first half of this century. The development of mining, logging, and ranching in the drainage finally overwhelmed the ability of the river to heal itself (biologists call these "cumulative impacts"). In 1992 the respected watchdog group, American Rivers, put the Blackfoot on its list of the Top Ten Endangered Rivers. The river was so different from the picture painted by Norman Maclean that the movie, produced by Robert Redford, of *A River Runs Through It* was filmed mostly on the Gallatin.

Of those Four Horsemen of the Trout Stream Apocalypse—mining, ranching, logging, and subdivision developing—there is no doubt about the prime culprit on the Blackfoot. Logging of the forests on private lands in the basin, and ranching, with the gross overgrazing of national forest lands in the Alice Creek drainage, exacerbated the sedimentation problems, but as bad as they are, they cannot approach the damage caused by mining. Abandoned workings in the headwaters ooze a brew so acid, so laden with heavy metals, that it wipes out life as it slowly creeps downstream year after year.

"In our family, there was no clear line between religion and fly fishing."

The worst mines are the Mike Horse and the Paymaster in the Heddelston Mining District. The current owners, ASARCO and the Atlantic Richfield Co. (ARCO), refused for years to do anything at all about these sites. Finally the Montana Department of Health and Environmental Sciences (DHES) coaxed ASARCO to look at the problem. As of this writing, ARCO and ASARCO have made some minor overtures at cleanup, but the jury is still out on whether DHES has the will to insist on a complete and lasting restoration of these headwater areas.

A proposed mine of huge dimensions is in the works for the upper Blackfoot River eight miles northeast of the small town of Lincoln. If completed, the mine, originally planned by the Phelps Dodge Corporation, would have devastating effects for both Lincoln and the river itself. The gold deposit—possibly as much as 5.2 million ounces with a potential value of $2 billion—is one of the largest in

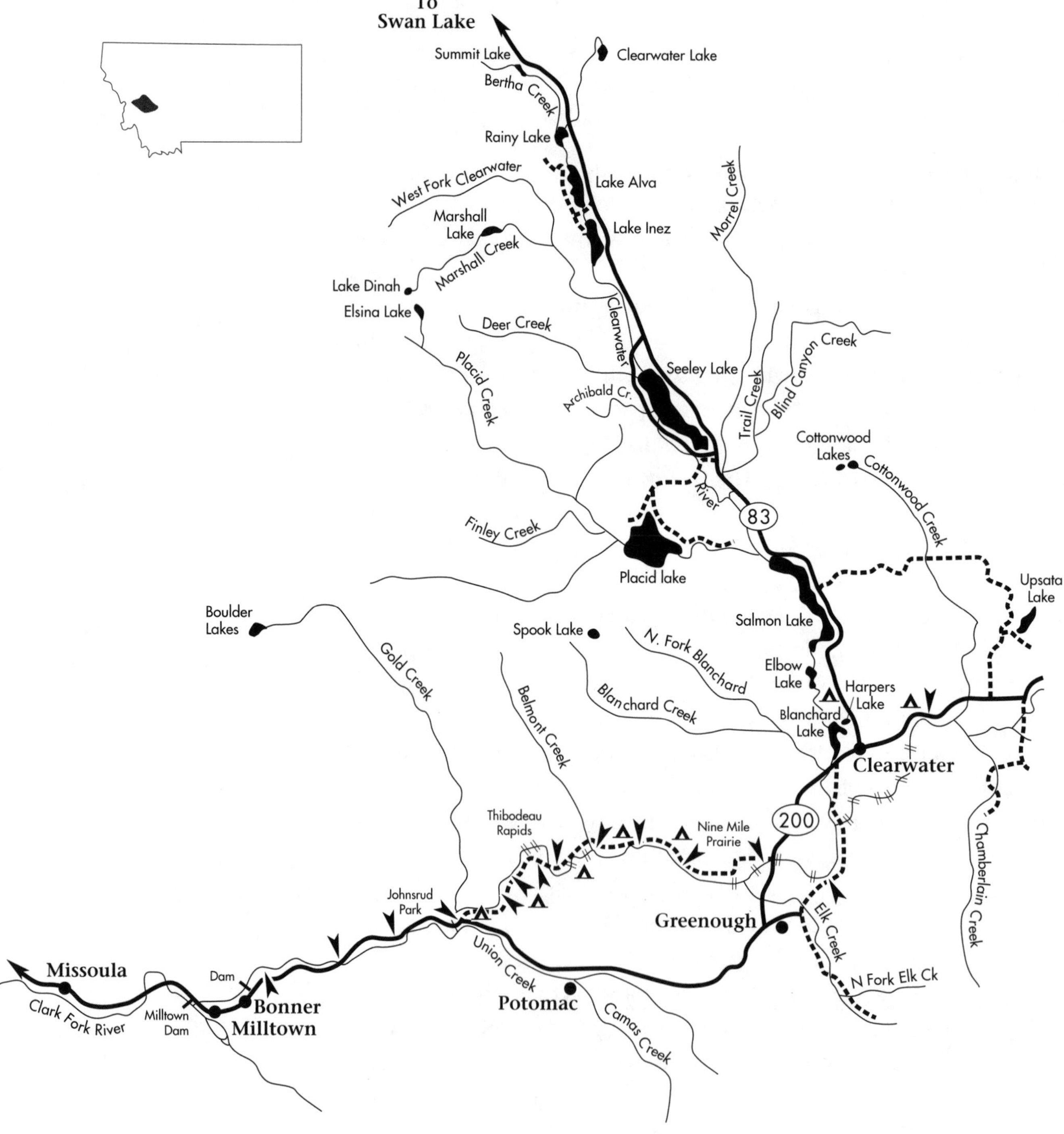
To
Swan Lake
Summit Lake
Clearwater Lake
Bertha Creek
Rainy Lake
West Fork Clearwater
Lake Alva
Marshall
Lake
Lake Inez
Morrel Creek
Marshall Creek
Lake Dinah
Elsina Lake
Deer Creek
Clearwater
Placid Creek
Blind Canyon Creek
Seeley Lake
Archibald Cr.
Trail Creek
Cottonwood
Lakes
Cottonwood Creek
River
83
Finley Creek
Placid lake
Upsata
Lake
Boulder
Lakes
Spook Lake
Salmon Lake
N. Fork Blanchard
Gold Creek
Elbow
Lake
Harpers
Lake
Belmont Creek
Blanchard Creek
Blanchard
Lake
Clearwater
200
Thibodeau
Rapids
Nine Mile
Prairie
Chamberlain Creek
Johnsrud
Park
Greenough
Elk Creek
Missoula
Union Creek
N Fork Elk Ck
Dam
Bonner
Clark Fork River
Milltown
Dam
Milltown
Potomac
Camas Creek

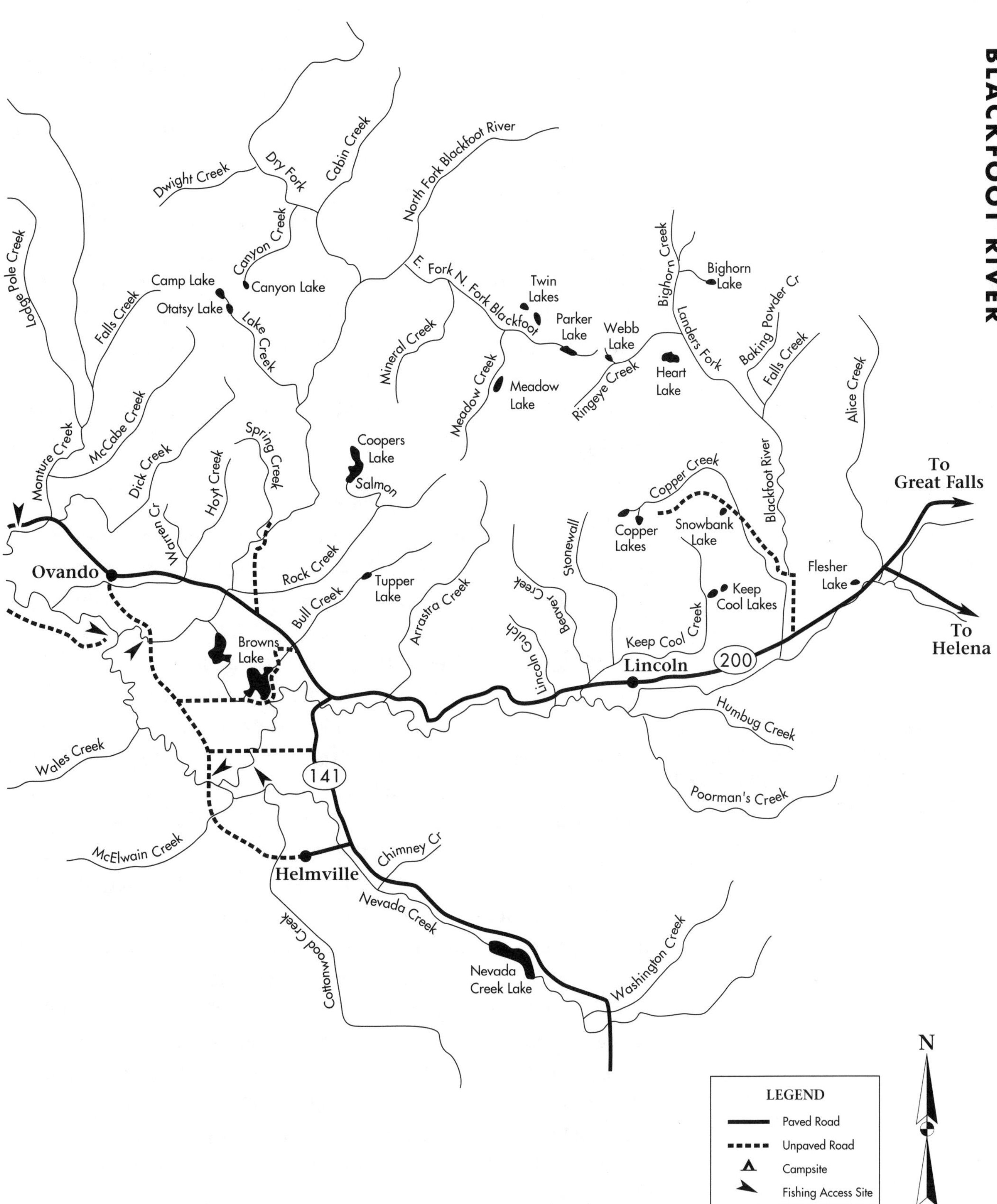
Dwight Creek
Dry Fork
Cabin Creek
North Fork Blackfoot River
Lodge Pole Creek
Canyon Creek
Canyon Lake
Camp Lake
Otatsy Lake
Lake Creek
Falls Creek
E. Fork N. Fork Blackfoot
Twin Lakes
Parker Lake
Webb Lake
Bighorn Creek
Bighorn Lake
Baking Powder Cr
Landers Fork
Falls Creek
Heart Lake
Ringeye Creek
Mineral Creek
Meadow Creek
Meadow Lake
Alice Creek
McCabe Creek
Monture Creek
Dick Creek
Hoyt Creek
Spring Creek
Coopers Lake
Salmon
Warren Cr
Copper Creek
Copper Lakes
Snowbank Lake
Blackfoot River
To Great Falls
Ovando
Rock Creek
Bull Creek
Tupper Lake
Arrastra Creek
Beaver Creek
Stonewall
Lincoln Gulch
Keep Cool Lakes
Keep Cool Creek
Flesher Lake
To Helena
Browns Lake
Lincoln
200
Humbug Creek
Wales Creek
141
Poorman's Creek
McElwain Creek
Helmville
Chimney Cr
Nevada Creek
Cottonwood Creek
Washington Creek
Nevada Creek Lake
N
LEGEND
Paved Road
Unpaved Road
Campsite
Fishing Access Site

the country. The giant cyanide heap-leaching gold extraction process could pollute both ground water and the river, killing off a number of species of trout and char now residing in the main river and its tributaries. In addition, the influx of nearly 400 hard-rock miners into the area would change its character for decades, at least.

In a curious turn of events, Phelps Dodge has agreed to sell its majority interest in the proposed mine to another large company. As of this writing, it is not clear whether the sale will go through. If the sale goes through and a permit is issued for the mine, it would level a mountain less than one-half mile from the Blackfoot, force the relocation of part of Highway 200 approximately 1000 feet closer to the river, and threaten the river corridor downstream from the mine with pollution (see "Moving Mountains in Montana," by John Holt, *Fly Fisherman*, March 1994).

The Big Blackfoot Chapter of Trout Unlimited, the Clark Fork Pend d'Oreille Coalition, the Orvis Company, the Montana Department of Fish, Wildlife, and Parks, and others have waged a strong fight over the last few years to restore the Blackfoot's quality trout fishery. If the proposed mine on the upper Blackfoot comes to life, the overriding sentiment is that this resource would suffer significantly.

The devastation visited on the Blackfoot by mining is rooted, in part, in the 1872 Mining Law.

The devastation visited on the Blackfoot by mining is rooted, in part, in the 1872 Mining Law. Under the provisions of this law, mining companies can explore and remove precious ores from federal lands (your lands). They can buy these lands, thousands of acres in a major project, for $5 per acre (yes, $5 per acre). They do not pay a single penny in royalties on the billions of dollars of minerals removed. There are no provisions in the law for environmental protection or reclamation. And to date, state regulation of hard-rock mining has offered precious little protection from mining abuse.

The recounting of these problems is not meant as a horror story—just the opposite. All of the publicity from the book and the movie helped create a strong coalition of conservation groups, led by the efforts of the Big Blackfoot Chapter of Trout Unlimited. The effort to restore the Blackfoot began in the late 1980s and by 1992 the trout were rebounding from River Junction, at the mouth of the North Fork of the Blackfoot, down to Bonner. The fishing was so good that year that the fly shops in Missoula sent more trips here in August than to any other river.

The Blackfoot may end up being the sacrificial river that finally mobilizes the American public. The people may put enough pressure on their congressmen and senators to change the mining, grazing, and logging practices on federal lands (all of the current laws are under attack). With luck and a lot of hard work, this fabled river may yet end up as the symbol of responsible resource management.

Outside of spring runoff, when the river rages with a vengeance from late April into early July (much to the consternation of Salmon Fly devotees everywhere), the Blackfoot flows very clear and deep-emerald green. The structure and the trout themselves are frequently visible through several feet of water.

The river drains the Garnet Range to the southeast, a good piece of the Scapegoat Wilderness rising to the northwest, and numerous drainages pouring out of the timbered mountains rolling on either side of the water.

The Headwaters to Lincoln—The Blackfoot is pretty but somewhat sterile above Lincoln. Parts of it dry up completely in the winter, and the poison of the Mike Horse and Paymaster mines enters the river east of Lincoln, just below Rogers Pass. The contaminated mine sediments are creeping downstream at a rate of six-tenths of a mile per year.

Lincoln to the Helmville Bridge—From Lincoln to the Helmville Bridge the river looks like designer brown trout water, with thick brush and trees lining undercut banks. Brown trout are by far the dominant species in this section, in part because of their ability to survive in tougher conditions than other trout. The few cutthroats, brookies, and rainbows hold around the mouths of tributaries that add clean flow. The current picks up, oxygenating the water and cleaning the streambed somewhat. This stretch is not difficult to wade, except for climbing over, under, and around logjams. Those obstructions make floating very tough, even dangerous, but it is possible for those who do not mind dragging their craft over downed trees. This section fishes best from the end of June into early July.

This is prime streamer water. The numbers of trout might not be outrageously high, but there are good fish in the holes and runs.

A Special Fly for the Blackfoot

It was surprising how often local fishermen mentioned the Picket Pin as one of the best flies for the Blackfoot. Older anglers, men such as Gene Bell, insisted that it was still the most effective pattern on the river.

The modern version of the Picket Pin certainly possesses all the characteristics of a good Blackfoot River fly. It has the downwing that matches the silhouette of a stone fly, probably the most important order of insects in the drainage. It has the bulk of all good attractor patterns, promising the calories that bring fish up in fast water. And it has a peacock herl body and head, the "green" that many fishermen say is the best color on the Blackfoot. The Picket Pin can be fished as a dry fly, wet fly, or streamer.

Jack Boehme, a famous fly tier in western Montana from the 1930s into the 1950s, developed many patterns, but the only one that gained national recognition was the Picket Pin. He developed flies not for the Clark Fork, which ran right through Missoula but was totally devoid of life because of mine waste from Butte, but for Rock Creek, the Bitterroot, and the Blackfoot.

Woolly Buggers, Spruce Streamers, and Muddlers (Yellow Marabou Muddlers are a great variation for browns), blasted bank-tight, then danced and shimmied in the current, pull trout out from cover. In this smaller water, floating lines and weighted flies give a better action than sinking or sink-tip lines. The opposite is true on the bigger, faster water of the lower river. Watching a 24-inch brown chase your streamer like an out-of-control ski-jet is exhilarating. Maintaining enough self-control to keep from jerking the fly out of the water is another matter.

Helmville Bridge to the mouth of the North Fork—For roughly two-thirds of the distance from the Helmville Bridge to the mouth of the North Fork of the Blackfoot the river slows down. This terrain is scenic enough, but floating this section borders on boring. This is due, not just to the lack of pace, but to the twisting nature of the river. Paul Roos insists, "You can say good-bye to Mineral Hill twenty times."

There are adequate numbers of browns, some of fair size, hanging beneath the brushy, undercut banks and bends of the river. One great spot, which always holds a number of larger fish, is the mouth of Nevada Creek. This is good hopper water at midday, but in the morning and the evening trout line up in the bankside runs and sip mayfly duns and spinners.

Carlton Urquhart fishes this stretch frequently. "There are not great numbers of any single mayfly species, a few Pale Morning Duns, a few Tricos, and a few Blue-Winged Olives appearing over the course of the season. The best hatch may be the *Callibaetis*.

"One morning was special. I only caught six browns, but every one was sipping *Callibaetis* spinners and refusing any presentation that was dragging. Every fish was a triumph. Two of them were over 18 inches, the rest over 13 inches. They took a size-14 Gray Clear-Winged Spinner."

One thing that makes these fish so tough is the lack of fishing pressure. They are not used to humans flogging away with fly rods. A sloppy cast (the kind that comes so naturally to so many of us) usually puts the browns down fast.

The mouth of the North Fork to Clearwater Junction—From the confluence of the North Fork of the Blackfoot down to the junction with the Clearwater, the main river changes into beautiful rainbow trout water, with some nice browns and cutthroats thrown in for good measure. There are long riffles, runs, and deep glides; below Sperry Grade Access there is a spectacular canyon stretch. The big three—mayflies, Caddisflies, and stone flies—are present in healthy numbers in the cold, well-oxygenated water. This is a beautiful float, especially through the looming cliffs of 5-mile-long Box Canyon, but there's a dangerous rapid at the bottom of the canyon that inexperienced boatmen should portage around.

The dry fly fishing settles into a midsummer pattern. During the middle of the day large attractors, sizes 4 to 10, floated on seams and slots out in the river, take the best fish. The drifts have to be long and drag-free. The fly, oddly enough, has a much better chance if it's green.

Five different sources, Gene Bell, Ed Massey, Dalton Palin, Paul Roos, and Joe Wigley, some speculating on the reason and some not ("green-tinted water"—"green mudstone bottom"—"a lot of green stone flies"), independently said that green attractors are the key. The patterns they liked are the H & L Variant, Lime Trude, Olive Stimulator, Picket Pin, Lime Double Wing, Renegade, Green Humpy, and Turk's Tarantula—and the only thing in common with this assortment is the color.

Grasshoppers, reaching plague numbers in this valley some summers, plop onto the water in abundance. A good grasshopper imitation (green-bodied, of course—and this advice came separately from Forrest Schaeffer) makes even the old, cautious browns rush up to the surface. The fly should be drifted away from the bank. The rule of thumb during the day seems to be that the water should be at least two feet deep.

Early in the morning or late in the afternoon the angler can match the hatch and work the shallows. Bigger trout move close to the shore to feed with the lower light, sipping whatever insects happen to be kicking around. The fish don't get real fussy about the imitation, maybe because there aren't many heavy hatches, just a smattering of everything, but the presentation still has to be drag-free.

This piece is such fun water to cover. The rainbows and the whitefish can often be seen, their tails and sides flashing as they nose the

PICKET PIN

Hook: 2X long dry fly
Tail: brown hackle fibers
Body Hackle: brown hackle
Body: peacock herl
Wing: gray fox squirrel tail
Head: peacock herl

This dressing, listed in many recent books, isn't the original Jack Boehme recipe. The Picket Pin had a body of flat gold tinsel. Another variation, the Bloody Butcher, had the peacock herl body, but instead of brown it had red and yellow body hackles.

To compound this mystery there was a sheet at Jack Boehme's shop in the Turf Bar in Missoula dated 1949 that recommended flies for the Blackfoot. The Picket Pin was on this list. In the stock bins, left at the Turf after his death, there were variations labeled Picket Pins with peacock herl bodies and brown body hackles.

substrate for nymphs. Walking the riffles on a hot July afternoon, drifting a Zug Bug, qualifies as world-class decadence. The hell with arthritic ankles and knees. This is the time to wade wet and enjoy life.

Clearwater Junction to Johnsrud Park—From Clearwater Bridge down to Johnsrud Park, a section entirely within the 26-mile-long Blackfoot River Recreation Corridor, the river flows swiftly, studded with boulders that make floating challenging. This is a very popular white-water area, the canoes, rafts, drift boats, kayaks, and inner tubes going by like an unending parade on a warm day. At least half the people yell, "How's fishing?" My policy is not to answer unless they toss me a beer.

This angler fished the confluence of the Clearwater and Blackfoot, probably in the 1890s.
Photo courtesy of Photograph Archives, Montana Historical Society

The fishing is typically in deep pocket water in and around the large rocks. There is not much time here for trout to decide on what to eat and the calories-expended to calories-gained ratio is instantly factored in by the fish. Large nymphs and wets underneath or bushy caddisfly and stone fly drys on the surface will draw more strikes than the size-20 Pheasant Tail Nymphs or size-20 Olive Compara Duns in this fast-paced environment. Goddard Caddis and Parachute Caddis, buoyant and visible flies, fish well in the rough water.

Wading this stretch is difficult, but working to get to the good water is often the most important part of the presentation. The fly drifts a lot better if you don't have to mend continually to avoid a belly in the line. The trout are opportunistic but not foolish.

Johnsrud Park to Bonner—From Johnsrud down to the diversion dam above Bonner, the river is a series of long runs, boulder-strewn white water and deep holes. The dry flies need to be big and bushy. In the pools try pulling a buoyant pattern, such as a Deer Hair Woolly, under and then letting it pop back to the top. Sometimes it takes a "trigger" movement like that to make these trout come to the surface.

Here is where the "down and dirty" fly fisherman shows up well. Probing the deep pools takes at least a 10-foot, sink-tip line and often some lead above the nymph. The fly itself is weighted. It is tough to keep track of the pattern and to control the inevitable belly in the line. You have to use enough weight to get the fly to the bottom, without draping on so much that the nymph drags along like a doorknob. You'll lose flies if you're doing this right.

The fall is always Woolly Bugger time. The big trout, browns in particular, cannot resist a black or olive Bugger cast bank-tight, snaked and danced through the rocks and boulders, and then zipped into the clear water. Pause occasionally in your retrieve and let the bugger drift a bit.

POPULAR FLIES

Deer Hair Woolly
Goddard Caddis
Green Humpy
H & L Variant
Lime Double Wing
Lime Trude
Olive Stimulator
Parachute Caddis
Picket Pin
Renegade
Spruce Streamer
Turk's Tarantula
Woolly Bugger
Yellow Marabou Muddler

The Blackfoot never developed a nationally famous series of original patterns. In the 1930s the flies created in Missoula were fished on all the surrounding rivers. The Franz Pott's woven-hair flies, Norman Means's balsa bugs, and Jack Boehme's hair-winged flies were popular, but even they never supplanted the older, classic wet flies. These Missoula patterns were thick-bodied and heavily hackled

In his angling shop, actually a corner of the Turf Bar in Missoula, Jack Boehme left a handwritten list of the "flies for the Blackfoot." They included the Mosquito, Black Gnat, Gray Hackle Peacock, and Red Ant (which looked nothing like an ant), the samples in his fly case running from sizes 6 to 12.

Maybe this lack of a legacy stems from the generous nature of the river. It is seldom necessary to exactly match any hatch. There are lots of aquatic insects, but rarely a blizzard of any one species. The Blue-Winged Olive, both in the spring (March) and in the fall (September), emerges in good numbers, especially on the lower water around Johnsrud Park. During the Salmon Fly hatch the heavy runoff, with its brown flood, wipes out any surface fishing four years out of five. There are still a few straggling Salmon Flies during a normal year just as the water drops, and a good adult imitation, like the locally popular Maki Salmon Fly, catches fish. The Golden Stones, coming at the end of the runoff and after the Salmon Flies, might be the single most important hatch on the river. A flush imitation, like a size-6 to size-10 Elk Hair Golden Stone, works better than a high-riding pattern on the Blackfoot. There are Pale Morning Duns and Tricos during the summer. The little Olive Stone Flies hang around the river. Caddisflies, especially the Green Sedge, a fast-water fly, flutter in small swarms on summer evenings. A sparse hatch of the Giant Orange Sedge shows up in September, and trout always seem to notice this big insect.

Salmon Fly—maybe the single most important fly on the Blackfoot
Photo by Dan Abrams

Of course, you can always collect specimens and perfectly match whatever happens to be hatching in size, color, and shape. You can pick out the newest creation, a CDC Caddis or a Duck Butt Dun, and catch trout. There is no law against this, even if such fussiness seems a little out of place on the river. Hatch matching is one of those rights (implied if not specifically mentioned) that is guaranteed in the Constitution. It is just that an exact imitation is usually not critical for catching trout on the big Blackfoot.

State fishing access sites dot the river from Johnsrud Park up to Brown's Lake, and reaching the river from Montana 200 is not difficult. There is a good gravel road that runs through the Recreation Corridor, skirting the river, from Johnsrud Park to the Roundup Bar (the bar burned in the early 1990s, but the name lives on) access.

The Blackfoot does not have the reputation of many other rivers in Montana, but if this stream was located in, say, Wisconsin or Pennsylvania, it would be nationally famous. Such is the quality of fly fishing in Montana. The river is a fine fishery that is slowly improving—a challenging, diverse piece of water to cast a fly over.

Fishing Waters in the Blackfoot Drainage

Alice Creek: Alice begins below Rogers Pass, flowing out of the Alice Mountains south to Montana 200. It is a small stream, with not a lot of water to begin with, and years of drought in the late 1980s have shrunk it even further. The trout are still there, mostly cutthroats from 6 to 10 inches, but Alice is fished quite a bit and, as a result, it is an average creek at best. To escape the crowds, and find slightly bigger trout, go into the canyon stretch, about 5 miles above the highway.

Bertha Creek: Swampy and brushy, this stream flows from Summit Lake down to Rainy Lake in the head of the Clearwater drainage for several miles of extremely frustrating (casting is a bitch) fishing for small cutthroats. Superb terrain for masochists.

Bighorn (Sheep) Lake: As with most mountain lakes in the area, it now receives periodic plantings of Westslope cutthroats instead of rainbows and Yellowstone cutthroats. But there are still a few old—and large—rainbows hanging on in Bighorn.

It's hard to get to these fish. A poorly maintained, 2-mile spur off the Bighorn Creek trail goes nearly to the Continental Divide. The best last part of the trek is a steep, ankle-busting drop down to this 10-acre, bowl-shaped lake.

Byron Mitshkun thinks that the fishing is worth the effort. He is a high-lake specialist, always using a 13½-foot, two-handed graphite rod in the backcountry. He can roll cast 70 feet, and doesn't have to worry about the trees or the rocks behind him (a handy trick at Bighorn because there are pines around most of the shoreline). He recalls, "I went up there in October of 1991, probably the only year, with its long, warm autumn, when I could have gone in that late. The trout were spread all around the edge of the lake. The fishing was fast enough, with a cutt every few minutes, up to 16 inches but most closer to 12 inches, and an occasional rainbow over 20 inches Maybe I was lucky, or maybe the lake, cradled in a steep valley, is sheltered, but it wasn't very windy the four days I was there. I caught all of my fish on dry flies, mostly a size-14 Gray Bivisible."

Blanchard Lake: A large beaver pond on the Clearwater River not far from the Seeley Lake turnoff at Clearwater Junction, Blanchard covers 10 acres when the rodents are industrious. Jeff Milks reports on Blachard: "I hit it twice, in June and late August, and it fished much better the first time. The brook and cutthroat trout were in the deepest water in the center. The perch were all over. A bass of four or five pounds nearly ripped my arm off. It's fun casting for a smorgasbord of species, including trout up to 10 inches."

Boulder Lake: You can't get there from here. You have to go over to another drainage, the Flathead, drive up a logging road off the South Fork of the Jocko Road, and then hike 2 miles over the hump into the Blackfoot watershed. It's popular for a backcountry lake, but scramble over to the talus slope, away from the beaten path, and the size of the cutthroats jumps from 8 to 10 inches to 11 to 13 inches.

Brown's Lake: Five hundred acres in open, often windy country, it's about fifteen minutes by good gravel road from Ovando. There are boat ramps, public toilets, and camping sites. This is not a wilderness experience. There's no truth to the rumor that the trout have seen so many bait fishermen that they feed selectively on corn and marshmallows.

Is this any place for a self-respecting fly fisherman? It is if he wants to catch trout up to ten pounds. The state stocks Brown's Lake with both Arlee and Kamloop strain rainbows. The Arlee plantings get taken out fast both summer and winter (a very popular lake for ice fishing), but any survivors quickly balloon to two to four pounds. The Kamloop planters are not so easy to catch. The Kamloops don't swell to the "stuffed" appearance of the Arlees in their early years, but live and grow much longer, reaching the double digit weights occasionally. Trollers take a greater toll on the Kamloops than the bait fishermen (and this should tell the fly fishermen something).

Brown's fishes best early in the season, before the weeds bloom and the picnickers sprout in profusion. The inlet and outlet (both Bull Creek) are shallow and inconsistent fishing. The best place for a fly fisherman in a float tube or a boat is the center basin, about 20 feet deep but with humps as shallow as 10 feet Those humps hold concentrations of fish. The nymph or streamer fisherman with a sinking line and a lot of patience can pick up trout all day.

The best time for the angler limited to bank fishing is during the June and July damsel hatches. He is in the right position, pulling his fly back towards the shore, to mimic the incoming, swimming naturals. The peak of this migration usually happens early in the morning—a good time to beat the regular crowds to the water.

Curt Turner, who loves this scrubby looking lake out on the sagebrush flats sends reports on the fishing:

> June 1990—6 rainbows one morning, even the 10-inchers were bulbous, best fish of 3½ pounds, all on a size-8 Timberline Emerger.
>
> July 1991—no damsels, and damsel nymphs didn't work today, but I caught 12 rainbows on a size-12 Cased Caddis Larva, best fish almost 3 pounds.
>
> September 1992—fished the inlet, a place I usually pass by. I made one cast and caught a fish. I kept casting. I have never seen such a concentration of trout on Brown's. These were Arlee rainbows, fall spawners, and maybe they were stacked up at the mouth of the creek. Best fish was just over 2 pounds, 26 trout in four hours, most of them on a size-6 White Bunny Leech.

Brown's also gets hatches of Traveler Sedges, large caddisflies matched by a size-8 fly in late June, and *Callibaetis* mayflies in late August. The fishing quality of both of these hatches depends on the weather, the lake getting warm and scummy during a hot summer.

Camp Lake: It's nearly 10 miles above Cooper's Lake, up the Lake Creek Trail, and has rainbows and cutthroats. The trout grow well, nice and plump, until about 15 inches, and then they start to get skinny between 16 inches and 20 inches. This is a clue that food forms are small, probably a good base of midges, but there aren't enough larger insects or forage fish. The best flies are small, too. The pressure is pretty intense on Camp for a backcountry lake.

Canyon Creek: This is a good cutthroat stream for small fish that average 8 inches and take almost any dry thrown in their direction. It is part of the Dry Fork of the North Fork of the Blackfoot River drainage in the mountains north of Ovando.

Clearwater Lake: Over 100 acres and 40 feet deep, Clearwater is only a few miles by a good trail off a logging road east of Montana 83. Maybe it's those steep drop-offs that intimidate fly fishermen, but many of my friends who haunt the high mountain lakes all summer avoid this one, even though they all know that it has big, two- to four-pound cutthroats. The trout are here, but they don't get giddy over the simple tactics that fool hungry fish in less fertile mountain waters.

Tom Messer and his English friend, John Creviston, portaged a canoe up to the lake in September 1989. John fished a team of three flies, an Orange Asher on the "bob," as they drifted right across the middle. He concentrated on the flat lanes in the choppy water, lifting and dropping his rod to keep the flies dancing. On four passes across the lake, a full day of fishing, he caught 15 cutthroats, all over two pounds.

There are great stillwater tactics, refined on the reservoir trout fisheries of the United Kingdom, that cover an entire lake, not just the edges. When the wind is blowing enough to riffle the surface, those methods work wonderfully on the big, daunting lakes of Montana, too.

Clearwater River: In its upper reaches, this is an easily worked stream for cutthroats, brookies, and rainbows. There are lots of logjams, riffles, and small pools. Plenty of people hit this water as it flows through Rainy, Alva, Inez, and Seeley Lakes.

Between Seeley and Salmon Lakes the river winds and twists through thick tag alder. There are plenty of deep gravely pools and runs, a good bit of which is visible from Montana 83. This is very difficult water to wade and cast to properly, but there is a transient population of browns (and a few bull trout) in the fall and in the spring. The fun comes with the hook-up because there's not a lot of room to play a good fish.

Does the name of this river provide a clue to great fishing? The Clearwater doesn't muddy up during runoff. The level may rise, but the lakes settle out any mud. When every other river is a brown flood, this one is at its absolute best. The down side is that, with the water flowing off the top of the lakes, the lower river gets real warm by early July, and the fishing drops way off.

The fly fisherman who uses normal dry fly and nymph tactics isn't going to hit the bonanza on the Clearwater. The browns move into the river from the lakes (natural, glacially formed waters) and spawn in the fall. These fish stay in the river over the winter and into the spring, until it warms up too much, usually in late June, and then they migrate back into the lakes. These big trout eat minnows.

Clearwater River below Seeley Lake
Photo by Gary LaFontaine

Rich Anderson, who fishes the stretch between Seeley and Salmon, recommends, "Girdle Bugs, in olive and black, for stripping fast, and a Grove's Bullhead for working deep and slow. The flies have to be worked tight to the brush."

The water between Salmon and the confluence with the Blackfoot is good in the spring, too. It gets rainbows up from the main river. There are stone fly hatches, especially the Goldens, that bring trout to the surface. Smaller streamers work in this section.

Cooper Creek: Cooper Creek has some average fishing for cutthroats in the upper reaches, with some bull trout down below. It is followed by a good road that equates to good access and heavy pressure. This stream is not the outlet of Cooper's Lake, but rather a tributary of the Landers Fork.

Cooper's Lake: Nearly 200 acres, it's deep and not very fertile. It is 18 miles from Ovando on a good road that skirts and then crosses Rock Creek. It is planted regularly with cutthroats that are hit hard and rarely last long enough to reach any size. The ones that do are shell-shocked and skittish.

Copper Creek: This is fished more than it deserves by people driving up to Snowbank Lake. "Thirty-five years ago," Paul Roos recounts, "there were 18- and 20-pound bull trout caught out of this little stream. The logging and the road building dumped sediment into it, hurting the native species."

There are still cutthroat and some nice bull trout in Copper, but no more 20-pounders. The hope is now that the Forest Service is on a tighter leash, especially around bull trout habitat, the stream will get better.

Cottonwood Creek: Cottonwood flows through open meadowland to the Blackfoot not far above Sperry Grade. Two miles of it wander through the Blackfoot-Clearwater Game Range. The water does not look like much here, and it's often muddy and difficult to wade, but for the quiet, accurate caster there are brown, brook, rainbow, and bull trout. Seven-foot rods and stooped postures are called for. There is brush and undercut banks, and you could work this stretch of water for days. This one is fun, tough and frustrating at times.

Tim Stroup found one way to fish it. "I just staked out a few holes and stayed on the creek that night. I slapped a size-8 White Deer Hair Moth and caught not only browns in the dark but rainbows and brookies, too. The biggest fish landed was an 18-inch brown, but something bigger broke off my 1X tippet."

Cottonwood Lakes: These are a 9-mile drive from the Seeley Lake Campground up the Cottonwood Creek Road. These waters have cutthroat, rainbow and some brook trout that grow nicely in the fertile water. Of course, the bigger ones, up to four pounds, are not the village dummies. They cruise the shoreline, nosing for insects (try matching the *Callibaetis* nymph with a size-12 Gold Ribbed Hares Ear). The large trout seldom rise, even when there are insects on the surface, but they gently take slowly retrieved nymphs.

Dry Fork of the North Fork of the Blackfoot River: Go up the North Fork Trail, then up past the lower 3 miles that go dry every summer. The upper reaches, 12 miles of classic water, are full of 10- to 15-inch cutthroats. The fish are easy; the country is scenic; and a little walking gets you away from civilization. A small box of dry flies —a few Wulffs, Double Wings, and Humpies, rough attractors that cover the three main situations—upwing, downwing, and just plain fat insects—is all that you'll need here if the water is warm enough. Sometimes, with the river running from 40 to 50 degrees Fahrenheit, nymphs near the bottom are necessary.

East Fork of the North Fork of the Blackfoot River: This one is up a trail that starts at the North Fork Guard Station. The East Fork is somewhat similar to the Dry Fork, except for an abundance of beaver dams and ponds. Some of these are well past their prime and silted up. Others are not bad for smallish cutthroats. The country is forest and moist meadow and the creek is followed by good trail (popular with horse packers).

Flesher Lake: It is right next to Montana 200 outside of Lincoln. This one is planted with 5,000 small rainbows each season and the fish that don't go airborne early on grow well and provide some sport for float tubers of less than discerning tastes.

Gold Creek: This enters the Blackfoot almost across from Johnsrud Park. So close to Missoula, it gets hard hit by local fishermen and these small streams can't give up too many limits. It used to be much better in years gone by, but logging and mining have hurt the cutthroat, rainbow, brook, and bull trout. The bull trout especially cannot spawn in silted areas and, with the loss of the clean gravels, they have almost disappeared. The other species are holding their population levels, if not their size, at the moment.

Belly boating on Harper Lake
Photo by Stan Bradshaw

Harper's Lake: Harper's is a strange place to my way of thinking. There are some fat cutthroats in this 18-acre, 28-foot-deep pond sitting out in the open south of Montana 83, just a mile or so up from Clearwater Junction. Rainbows, including big, old, sluggish brood stock, are dumped here every year.

Match the crayfish. The water is full of these (and you can catch enough to have your own shellfish extravaganza). A Clouser Crawfish or a Bug Skin Crawfish, retrieved with a stop and run-run-run strip (a "run" lasting five feet with short pauses in between) over the bottom, isn't going to pick up the small stockers, but who cares? The big fly can get a half-dozen 15-inch-and-up trout on Harper's in a day.

Heart Lake: Up the trail at the end of the Landers Fork Road, Heart is just jammed with beautiful, 8- to 16-inch grayling that are easy to catch. There are trout here, too, often the kind measured in pounds instead of inches, but they are the rare treat. Depending on the snowpack, this country is not usually fishable before July, but the lake is prime if you can get into it as soon as possible.

Keep Cool Creek: After joining with Stonewall Creek, it enters the river just below Lincoln. Here is a shining example of good management. The riparian habitat is in great shape. The stream, running at 35 cfs during the summer, meanders in a deep channel through meadow cover. The fishing for rainbows, brookies, and cutthroats, most in the 8- to 10-inch range, is excellent.

Dalton Palin provided comments on flies, "The fish are not fussy, but they don't like a splashy presentation. So a hopper, if that's what someone picks, should be cast so that it lands with a soft plop."

Keep Cool Reservoir: Managed on a yearly basis for Eagle Lake rainbows that grow well, this is locally popular right up Keep Cool Creek, not far from Lincoln.

Lake Alva: Three hundred thirty acres, it's just upstream from Inez in the Clearwater River chain of lakes next to Montana 83. It is plagued by hordes of small yellow perch (unless you're one of the people who know how delicious perch are—and then it's blessed with them). The trout, cutthroat and bull, compete badly. There are largemouth bass in some of the coves, but this is not a great bass lake either.

The Montana Department of Fish, Wildlife, and Parks used to poison out both Alva and Inez regularly, and for three to six years afterward the cutthroat fishing would be spectacular. Then the rough fish would take over again. It was a hopeless battle.

Lake Inez: A summer-home lake just downstream from Lake Alva, it has lots of boat traffic and a public campground. It is also infested with yellow perch, but there are some cutthroat trout and kokanee salmon.

Landers Fork of the Blackfoot River: Upriver from Lincoln, the lower water on this one is not much. It is scoured, all the cover washed out. The stream gradually improves for small brook, bull, and cutthroat trout as you move upstream. The riparian habitat is recovering and the fishing is getting better. It is still not great.

McCabe Creek: As small cutthroat streams go, it's pretty good for colorful, 9-inch trout. It runs below Spread Mountain and merges with Monture Creek. The upper stretches are the best fishing.

Meadow Creek: A tributary of the East Fork, it gets hit hard at the bottom, in large part due to two campgrounds, but there are 8 miles of fine fishing along the trail for rainbows and cutthroats.

Michael Schott notes, "Up high it's a typical mountain stream, but there's a wonderful meadow stretch in the wilderness. The trout are bigger there. My best was a 2½-pound rainbow on a dry Hornberg, but my son caught a 4-pound rainbow just before dark one day on a Bucktail he tied out of his dog's hair. There are good numbers of fish here, too."

Monture Creek: Like many waters, Monture is named after a person, French-Canadian fur trader Nicholas Monteur; since he did something of note—traveling in Blackfoot Indian territory long before most white men would risk it—he at least deserves the honor.

Monture is crossed by Montana 200, the Blackfoot Highway, 2 miles south of Ovando and enters the big Blackfoot just above Scotty Brown Bridge. The stream is large enough, especially early in the season, to float from the highway down to the river in a small craft. The distance is only a couple of miles, but a boat gets you away from convenient access points and into better trout water. In this lower section the stream twists and digs through glacial gravels, creating one deep hole after another, every pool seemingly holding its share of rainbow, cutthroat, and brown trout.

Early in the season, until at least July, Monture, like other mountain streams, runs cold. Dry flies do not pull fish up from the bottom well, so unless the trout are already looking up at a hatch of insects the best choice is usually a nymph. The technique is as important as the fly. Gary Katz explains, "I floated and stopped, fishing maybe five hours total, and caught thirty-four trout, all of them under 14 inches except one 17-inch brown, and eleven whitefish. The best nymphs were weighted, a size-12 Bead Head Zug Bug and a size-10 Natural Drift Stone the most consistent, but it wasn't enough to have lead just on the fly. There wasn't enough room for long drifts and slow sinks, so I put split shot every twelve inches for four feet up the leader. This dragged the nymph deep right away and covered the pools efficiently."

Monture Creek can be productive for small cutthroat even at the height of summer. Photo by Stan Bradshaw

Later in the summer both the winding water below the highway and the tumbling water above it get plenty of grasshoppers. A good hopper imitation does well for any angler brave enough to slam the fly into the darker patches under logs and brush. The trout still aren't big, averaging 10 inches on a good day, but they rush the fly courageously.

The angler can follow Monture upstream on 12 miles of gravel road and then 18 miles of good (and well-used) trail to the headwaters. There is a maintained camping area, Monture Creek Campground, just below the Blackfoot Highway crossing. It is a nice place to base for the entire Blackfoot drainage.

Morrell Creek: This flows past the Double Arrow development up into the southern reaches of the Swan Range. Water levels drop quite low and the fishing in the lower sections is slow for cutthroats and brookies. There may be a brown or two and some kokanee in the autumn up from the Clearwater River. The wild reaches above the falls are barren.

Nevada Creek: This one is on the Helmville cutoff from Montana 200. This small stream has plenty of sweeping bends, grassy and brushy undercut banks and, despite siltation, dewatering, and overheating, some good browns. The stream is followed by the highway here and there to the reservoir. Try dry flies in the evening and maybe a Woolly Bugger or two against the banks for good measure. There are some bull trout here, too. The upper reaches are followed by an old logging road and hold small cutthroats and rainbows. With restoration of the riparian area, this stream could be a lot better.

Stream bank grazing has taken its toll on parts of Nevada Creek.
Photo by Stan Bradshaw

Nevada Creek Lake: Ten miles south of Helmville on the Nevada Creek Road, this 100-acre reservoir is drawn down many feet much of the year. The water, clouded by blooms of algae, contains rainbows (numbers depend on the stockings and fishing pressure at any given moment). Aesthetically this lake stinks, but some fat fish cruise the weeds.

North Fork of the Blackfoot River: If wilderness areas ever need a symbol to justify their existence, the North Fork can be that reminder.

Imagine the alternative—the trees strip-logged from the edges, banks pounded down by cattle, the flow a summertime trickle after dewatering, water sterilized by the weeping discharge of a few abandoned mines. In this drainage all of these things would not be a probability—they'd be a certainty. The very existence of this classic trout water must gall the rape-and-pillage mentality.

The North Fork has its own gateway above Ovando, the Harry Morgan Access. The stream flows lazily in open meadow in the lower stretches, and bull trout to 24 inches swim with the rainbows and cutthroats. The bull trout's migration is stopped by a waterfall several miles up from the end of the road.

Above the falls this is primarily a cutthroat stream. The water flows over clean, light-colored gravels, digging slots against banks and tumbling into deep riffles. There are insects hatching all summer, but never enough to get the backcountry cutts in a fussy mood. Generally buggy-looking flies, the ones that represent a whole group of insects, are effective if they match the predominant form in size.

Dwight Missildine's box of flies has only two patterns in various sizes, a Dark Cahill and a Light Cahill. "A light pattern and a dark pattern," he says. "But I tell you, any dry fly works better on this river if its fished on a light, soft tippet, at least a 4X, because it's important in such clear water to get a good drift. If you're missing strikes, a lot of times it is because of drag on the fly."

The river is just as easy to fish with nymphs as it is with dry flies. Little stone fly patterns, in sizes 14 through 10, match an important insect and catch a lot of trout in the North Fork. Good patterns include the Golden Stone Nymph and Ted's Stone Fly Nymph.

It is really important to release all fish on the North Fork. It gets enough pressure, enough trout killed for camp meals, that the average size of the cutthroats is down to 13 or 14 inches. Old records show that the population levels out at 16 or 17 inches with minimal human harvest.

Otatsy Lake: Swampy on the north and timbered the rest of the way around, Otatsy sits in a cluster with other good backcountry lakes (Camp, Canyon, Heart, Parker,and Webb) and as a result it is on a popular circuit. It's filled with 9- to 13-inch cutthroats and rainbows.

The North Fork of the Blackfoot
Photo by Stan Bradshaw

Parker Lake: This isn't a big lake, only 12 acres and 15 feet deep, but at only 6,000 feet elevation it doesn't winterkill. The springs at the inlet provide adequate spawning habitat. It is in the East Fork drainage, a 3-mile hike up from Webb Lake (which is 9 miles from the end of the Landers Fork Road), in the forested, mountain country. Parker is an average fishery as far as the number of trout, but the cutthroats are large, averaging 16 inches There is a campground on the lake.

Placid Lake: Not a direct link in the Clearwater lake chain, it is only a few miles off the chain, up Owl Creek by good road. This is a summer-home madhouse that looks like it escaped from a Chevy Chase movie. Lots of 4-inch rainbows are planted here each year. There are also trash fish, some largemouth bass, kokanee salmon, and several species of trout (unfortunately, in declining numbers). It's not worth

Salmon Lake on the Clearwater
Photo by Stan Bradshaw

bothering with, but some of the little creeks that dump into the lake are fun fishing for small brookies and cutthroats. The mouth of Placid Creek especially holds some nicer fish.

Rainy Lake: A good lake for cutthroats that average less than a foot, it is on Montana 83 north of Seeley Lake. It's about 70 acres and best fished from a float tube or a boat. Trout seem to rise continuously on it.

Salmon Lake: Right next to Montana 83 south of Seeley Lake, Salmon is an attractive piece of water (except for the huge log monument to a local resident's ego on one of the islands). All kinds of trout live here, including cutthroats, rainbows, bulls, and browns, along with kokanee salmon and various warm-water species. The best trout water is along the south shore and the best largemouth bass water is near the marshes at the inlet. There is serious boat traffic on the lake in the summer.

Seeley Lake: Seeley is a true madhouse in the summer with boats, water-skiers and landing float planes. It is over 1,000 acres and reached by roads all over the place. The resort town of Seeley Lake is on the east shore. Despite all the recreational craziness, there is some good fishing for cutthroat and rainbow trout. The north shoreline, where the Clearwater dumps in, is the best place to work streamers (rainbows especially are a good play in the spring here), but give any loons (the bird, not the boaters) a wide berth. They nest on the north side of the lake in the spring. The state biologists are trying to find some strain of trout that can coexist—if not compete—with the warm-water species. The latest attempts include stockings of McBride cutthroats.

Snowbank Lake: Up a road near the Copper Creek Campground and planted with cutthroats that grow *slowly,* this lake is worth a visit for anyone interested in geology—a classic glacial kettle.

Spook Lake: This one has been good at times for cutthroat trout of several pounds or more, but the summer tourist crowd hits the place pretty hard and catch and release is not a regular part of the action. A float tube helps. Spook is not far from Placid Lake.

Summit Lake: This is a beautiful lake right next to Montana 83. The view into the Mission Mountains is spectacular. Tag alders and willows surround the swampy shoreline. You need a float tube to cast dry flies to the free-rising cutthroats that run from 10 to 12 inches No one fishes here much except for a few loons.

Upsata Lake is good for largemouth bass.
Photo by John Chisholm

Twin Lakes: These are in the East Fork Drainage in the Scapegoat Wilderness. Upper Twin is planted with cutthroats. It is only 6 acres, but the trout grow big. Lower Twin is 16 acres and it is managed for rainbows that don't grow nearly as large. Nice country—worthwhile fishing.

Upsata Lake: An open-country, pothole lake near Ovando that is 85 acres and up to 40 feet deep it's popular with area residents for good numbers of rainbows that sometimes hit 20 inches, largemouth bass up to a couple of pounds or so, and some perch. It's best in the spring right after ice-out. The angler can work from a float tube, throwing bright, weighted streamers into the shore and quickly retrieving them along the bottom. The trout are in there busting the heck out of rough-fish fry.

Warren Creek: Flowing to the Blackfoot not far from Ovando, it's not bad fishing for cutthroats and rainbows. The landowners, in cooperation with the Big Blackfoot Chapter of Trout Unlimited, are doing extensive work on the riparian zone of Warren.

A number of small streams near Ovando are good fishing, some of them for brook trout up to a couple of pounds. They are crossed here and there by dirt and gravel roads, allowing limited access. When in doubt, though, check around and ask for permission. Trespassers really nailed some of this fine water in the seventies and a few of the property owners are still mad as hell. Nymphs down deep take the brookies, cutthroats, and rainbows under the brushy banks. There are even a few browns of size in these little creeks.

Webb Lake: In the Lander Fork drainage, Webb is reached by trail 9 miles back in timbered country. This 18-acre lake, really a large beaver pond, has the Yellowstone strain of cutthroat trout in it.

Water snakes are a common sight on Montana's rivers and streams. Photo by Glenda Bradshaw

West Fork Clearwater River: Tumbling out of the mountains through very thick forest, this is a small stream with some nice holes and pockets containing small cutthroat and brook trout. This fishing is more for "wandering in the woods" than anything else.

Other Waters

Archibald Creek is too small and too warm, but its mouth at the Clearwater is a hotspot for largemouth bass.

Arrastra Creek: Cutthroats.

Baking Powder Creek: Cutthroats.

Beartrap Creek Reservoir: Private.

Beaver Creek (Placid Lake): Cutthroats and rainbows.

Beaver Creek (Lincoln): Little access.

Belmont Creek: Has brooks, cutthroats, and rainbows. Take the Blackfoot Recreation Corridor Road down from Nine Mile Prairie to this creek. It's fun because of the variety of species, although a 10-incher will be a whopper.

Blanchard Creek: Brookies, cutthroats, and rainbows.

Blind Canyon Creek: Small cutthroats.

Boles Creek: Brooks and rainbows. It's a tributary of Placid. There's a logging road following the stream to the headwaters.

Bull Creek: Private.

Cabin Creek: Cutthroats.

Camas Creek: Brookies. There is good access near Potomac and fast fishing for 6- to 10-inch trout.

Camp Creek: Cutthroats.

Canyon Lake: Cutthroat and bull trout.

Chamberlain Creek: Cutthroats.

Chimney Creek: Too small.

Cold Creek: Too small.

Colt Creek: Too small.

Colt (Bertha) Lake: Cutthroats.

Colt Creek Reservoir: Ephemeral water. It exists only during runoff when the creek overflows, but for those few weeks it's hot for small cutts.

Conger Creek: Too small.

Copper Lakes: Cutthroats. The fish are nice, but Jeff Milks reports, "They rise all the time, but these are tough cookies. In three trips I only caught two, about 16 inches. It's going to take a better fisherman than me to figure out these trout."

Cottonwood Creek (Helmville): Brooks, browns, and cutthroats.

Deer Creek: Brooks and cutthroats.

Dick Creek: Browns, rainbows, and cutts. This is a meadow stream near Ovando. I took an Eastern friend here and after a day of twenty fish, including a 13-inch brown, he was babbling something about heaven. Do we get spoiled out here?

Dinah Lake: Rainbows up to five pounds. It's right under the Clearwater-Jocko divide. The overfed slobs are real discriminating. There's just a lot of natural food for them.

Douglas Creek: Poor fishing.

Dwight Creek: Cutthroats.

East Twin Creek: Too small.

Elbow Lake: Poor fishing for trout—better for bass and perch. Elbow is a bulge in the Clearwater River.

Elk Creek: Mostly 7- to 8-inch cutts and brookies. The old gold camps of Coloma and Garnet sprang up here in the 1860s. Garnet is a popular ghost town.

Elsina Lake: Small cutthroats and rainbows.

Falls (Landers Fork): Cutthroats.

Falls Creek (Monture Creek): Cutthroats and rainbows.

Fawn Creek: Cutthroats.

Finley Creek: Obscenely fast fishing for small brooks, cutthroats, and rainbows. It is a tributary of Placid Creek (which flows into Placid Lake).

Fish Creek (Nine Mile Prairie): Too small.

Fish Creek (Salmon Lake): Poor access.

Fish (Big Sky) Lake: Private.

Frazier Creek: Too small.

The Blackfoot's white water attracts lots of boaters in the summer.
Photo by Stan Bradshaw

Geary Pond: Rainbows.

Hogum Creek: Brooks and rainbows.

Horsefly Creeks: Brooks, browns, and cutthroats.

Hoyte Creek: Brookies.

Humbug Creek: Posted. Not really worth asking to fish.

Jones Lake: No trout. Private.

Kliendschmidt Spring Creek: A tributary of Rock Creek (which enters the North Fork of the Blackfoot near Ovando), this stream is so battered that no trout were found in a 1985 survey by state biologists, but with a flow of 15 to 17 cfs this could be a fine spring creek with rehabilitation.

Krohn Creek: Brookies.

Lake Creek: Cutthroats.

Lincoln Gulch: Brookies.

Liverpool Creek: Too small.

Lodgepole Creek: Cutthroats.

Marshall Creek: Bull, cutthroat, and rainbow trout. This one dumps into Marshall Lake and at the mouth, starting in late August, the bull trout stack up waiting for the fall rains.

Marshall Lake: Brook and bull trout. It is reached by a county road up from Lake Alva.

McElwain Creek: Too small.

Meadow Creek Lake: Cutthroats.

Middle Fork Landers Fork Creek: Too small.

Moose Creek: Too small.

Morrell Lake: Cutthroats and rainbows. There is poor fishing in this shallow mudhole, but it is a great place to get the bejabbers scared out of you by a grizzly. It's in the Clearwater drainage above Seeley.

Mountain Creek: Too small.

Mud Lake: Cutthroats.

North Fork Blanchard Creek: Brooks and cutthroats.

North Fork Elk Creek: Cutthroats.

North Fork Placid Creek: Brooks and cutthroats.

Owl Creek: Brooks and cutthroats. This is the stream that connects Placid Lake with the Clearwater River, and it's not bad fishing in spite of easy access, because everybody up here is out waterskiing.

Placid Creek: Bull and cutthroat trout and kokanee salmon. The kokanee come out of Placid Lake to spawn and really stack up thick in the lower section. Don't believe the locals when they say you have to snag the little devils. They'll take a red or yellow egg pattern, a size-16 Glo Bug or Marabou Single Egg, drifted dead near the bottom.

Poorman Creek: Brooks, cutthroats, and rainbows. There were some fresh, good beaver bonds on it in 1992.

Ringeye Creek: Too small.

Rock Creek: This private stream on the North Fork of the Blackfoot, entering the river just above Montana 200, is potentially a wonderful spring creek, with a flow of 22 cfs. One of the ranches on the lower end has started a restoration project that shows some promise for the restoration of spawning habitat. While this creek isn't generally accessible to the public, the landowner's restoration efforts are benefitting the North Fork with more fish because of increased spawning.

Salmon Creek: Cutthroats and rainbows. This is a meadow tributary of the North Fork near Ovando. It gets nice rainbows and cutts up from the river early in the season.

Sauerkraut Creek: Too small.

Seven Up Pete Creek: Poor access. Cutthroats.

Shoup Creek: Too small.

Shoup Lake: Private.

Silver King Lake: Private.

Spring Creek: Brookies and cutthroats.

Stonewall Creek: Brown, brook, bull, and cutthroat trout.

Swamp Creek: Too small.

Tobacco Valley Creek: Cutthroats.

Tupper Lakes: Private.

Uhler Creek: Cutthroats.

Union Creek: Mostly small brookies. It enters the Blackfoot near Johnsrud, one of the meadow streams, but it's not as rich as many of the others in this valley.

Vaughn Creek: Too small.

Wales Creek: Cutthroats and rainbows.

Wales Reservoir: Limited access.

Washington Creek: A small tributary of Nevada Creek that you cross here and there while driving the Helmville-Avon Road. This water doesn't look like much and it isn't. Don't bother finding access to this one.

West Fork Cold Creek: Too small.

West Fork Marshall Creek: Cutthroats.

West Twin Creek: Too small.

Willow Creek: Too small.

■ *Special thanks to Rich Anderson, Gene Bell, Gary Katz, Ed Massey, Tom Messer, Dwight Missildine, Jeff Milks, Byron Mitshkun, Dalton Palin, Paul Roos, Forrest Schaeffer, Michael Schott, Tim Stroup, Curt Turner, Carlton Urquhart, and Joe Wigley for their help on the Blackfoot drainage.*

Gary, Chester, and friend on Rock Creek
Photo by Don Roberts

THE UPPER CLARK FORK

To many fly fishers viewing the upper Clark Fork while buzzing along I-90, the mile upon mile of brushy undercut banks, wide gravel riffles, and deep runs look like ideal big-fish habitat. From Warm Springs down to Milltown the nearly 100-mile drive can take on the trappings of Chinese water torture for those who love to fish, but who must race on to meet other commitments. The angler just knows that there are hundreds, no thousands, of big browns under those banks or up on the rocky shelves sucking in insects. Not to wet a line is cruel—life at its harshest.

It is good water to dream about. No other river in Montana is a better example of the fate that awaits all of our streams if avarice and neglect dominate in this state. But no other river demonstrates the ability of our waters to bounce back from past abuse. The Clark Fork at this moment is teetering between two possible futures—magnificence or ruin.

So which will it be? It is important to understand the past and the present of the Clark Fork. Even now a person cannot drink the water. It probably wouldn't kill him, but it would most certainly make him feel a bit out of sorts.

Montana is nicknamed the Treasure State because of its mining past, personified by Butte's Berkeley Pit. Copper, silver, and gold were dug, hammered, and blasted from the earth in staggering quantities. The wastes from this hardrock labor were flushed untreated into Silver Bow Creek, the headwater tributary of the Clark Fork, the tailings accumulating in the riparian corridor of the river. There are millions upon millions of tons of the stuff, extending all the way to Milltown Dam, and the sediments are loaded with deadly concentrations of heavy metals. From before the turn of the century, until the 1950s, mining waste turned the water red, destroying all life (even stopping the growth of algae). The smelter in Anaconda also delivered toxins into the drainage.

This situation changed with the creation of a waste treatment system. The most important element in the plan was a series of "settling ponds," shallow potholes where the tainted water from Silver Bow Creek was treated with lime salts to precipitate out the heavy metals. This left the flow at the outlet of the ponds, the official starting point of the Clark Fork, clean enough to support trout.

UPPER CLARK FORK RIVER

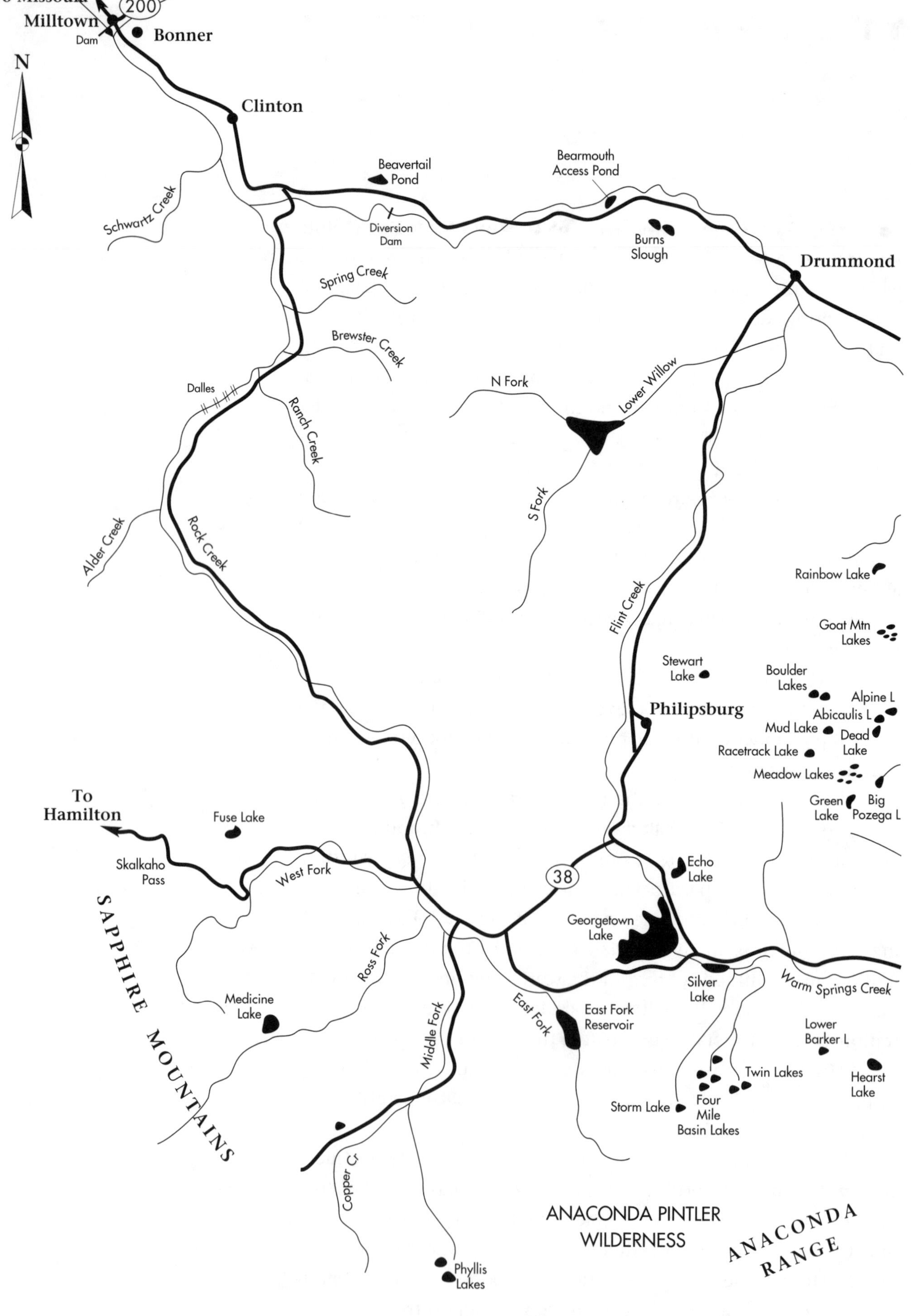

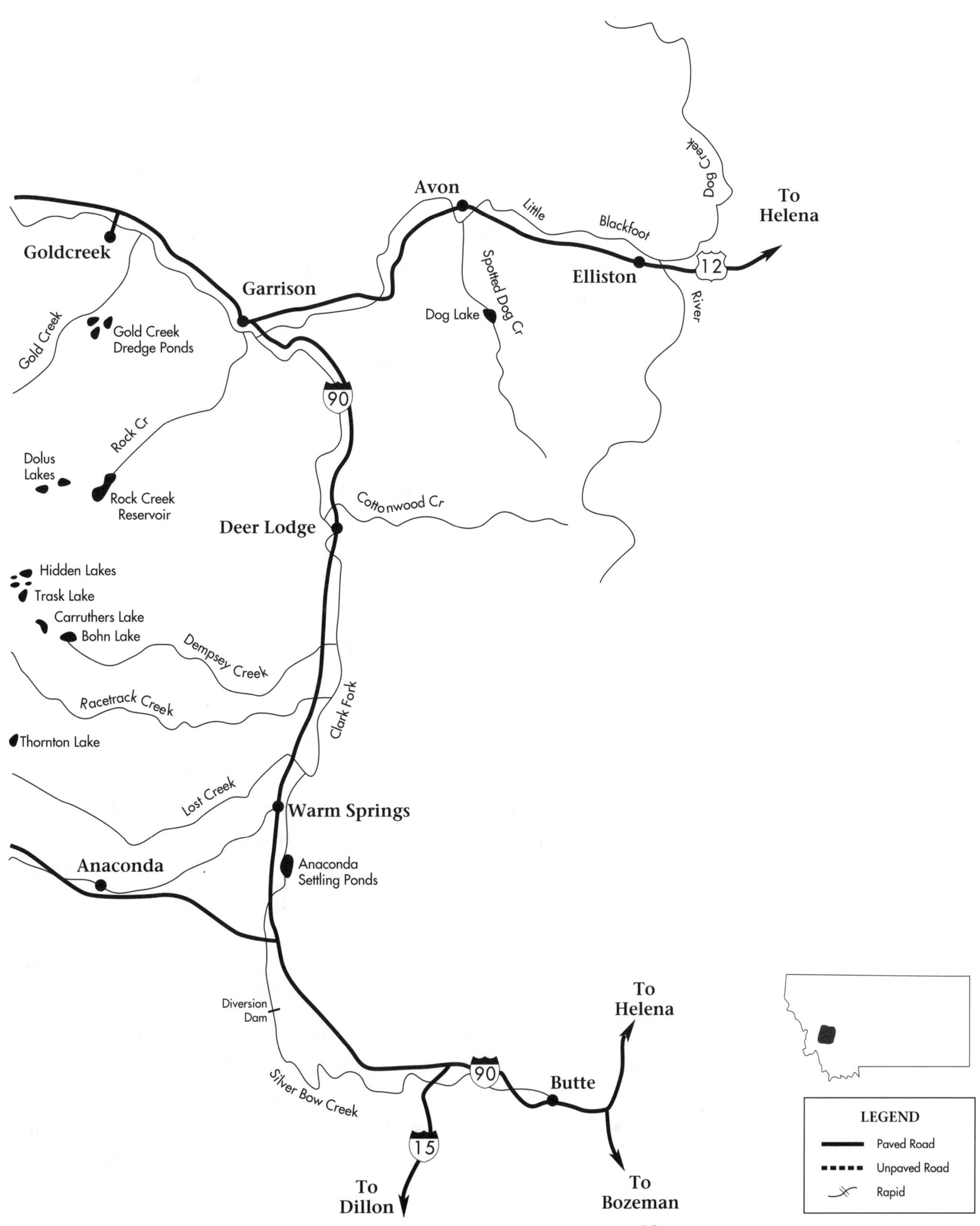
Avon
To Helena
Little
Blackfoot
River
Dog Creek
Goldcreek
Garrison
Elliston
12
Spotted Dog Cr
Dog Lake
Gold Creek
Gold Creek Dredge Ponds
90
Rock Cr
Dolus Lakes
Rock Creek Reservoir
Cottonwood Cr
Deer Lodge
Hidden Lakes
Trask Lake
Carruthers Lake
Bohn Lake
Dempsey Creek
Racetrack Creek
Clark Fork
Thornton Lake
Lost Creek
Warm Springs
Anaconda
Anaconda Settling Ponds
Diversion Dam
To Helena
Butte
90
Silver Bow Creek
15
To Dillon
To Bozeman
LEGEND
Paved Road
Unpaved Road
Rapid

And support trout it does—in incredible numbers. In the 5-mile special management section, beginning at Warm Springs, brown trout in the 12- to 16-inch range, with a few weighing several pounds or more, swim in good health. Biologists' surveys indicate a population of catchable-size brown trout between 1,900 to 2,400 per mile, an astounding figure considering the hammering the water still takes from a quality standpoint.

The Clark Fork, in this upper stretch, is not a large river (a decent long jumper could leap across it). This makes the 2,400 trout per mile figure truly astonishing. The Madison, with ten times the water volume, has 4,500 catchable-size trout per mile; the Missouri, with twenty times the water volume, ranges from 2,000 to 4,000 catchable-size trout per mile.

So is everything perfect on the Clark Fork? Hardly. This drainage, all the way from Butte to Milltown, has been declared the nation's largest Super Fund site by the Environmental Protection Agency (EPA). The massive task of removing or capping the tailings deposited for nearly a hundred years in the flood plain is just beginning.

In the meantime, every few years a heavy rainstorm washes deposits from surrounding areas into the Clark Fork. The sudden flush of heavy metals kills thousands of trout. The carnage is this gruesome simply because even in a short stretch there are so many browns to kill. Such incidents are localized and do not destroy the river, but they are symptoms of a lingering disease in the watershed.

Wayne Hadley, the Montana Department of Fish, Wildlife, and Parks (FWP) biologist for this area, predicts that despite a "big-time effort" now underway to clean up the tailings around Warm Springs, work in the rest of the drainage will drag on into the next millennium and contaminated areas will slowly flush metals into the river for all that time.

The Clark Fork's past was one of incredible destruction. The present, however, is surprisingly good. The upper river really is one of the richest trout streams in the state. The Clark Fork is still threatened, however, this time by cattle ranches. Its future is still uncertain.

The Deer Lodge valley is a microcosm of an economic war raging over the western half of Montana. In the past, the extractive industries—mining, logging, and ranching—operated with no concern for the environment. Their excuse for every action was the sacred word, "jobs." They could legally destroy any river.

Now, however, one of the largest industries in the state is tourism; and this part of the economy is fueling growth even though a key component of tourism, our rivers, still have no "right" to exist as trout fisheries. Even though it is likely that the Clark Fork fishery eventually will be the center of the economic revival of the upper valley, state law does not recognize its existence as a valuable use of water.

Old attitudes die hard. The FWP filed an application for an instream flow reservation on the upper Clark Fork. This reservation would would give the department the opportunity to object to any new depletions of water from the river. It would not "steal" any older, existing claims on the flow of the Clark Fork. Any rancher could continue extracting "his" water from the river.

A group of cattlemen in the Deer Lodge valley banded together to fight the reservation application. Their motivation? Their fear that somehow FWP would use their reservation to interfere with irrigation. There is nothing in the department's past behavior to support that reaction. Just paranoia.

The irrigators preach more storage as the panacea to cure all our water shortage woes. But under current state law, it's not clear that sportsmen could even create their own storage facility on a river for flow protection (a dam on a tributary, for example, to hold back runoff). And most irrigators, while wanting anglers to ante up for new storage projects, would sooner die than suggest that you be allowed to send water down the river for fish.

The situation is not entirely hopeless, however. In 1991 the irrigators agreed to work jointly with fisheries and other environmental interests to try and develop a management plan for the Clark Fork above Milltown Dam. The legislature passed a bill placing a moratorium on any new uses of water while the management plan takes shape. That planning effort, completed in December 1994, proposes closing the basin's surface waters to new depletions. Not a complete answer, but a step in the right direction.

But the question remains: What will happen to the Clark Fork?

A Special Fly for the Upper Clark Fork

The upper Clark Fork, with its heavy caddis hatches and selective browns, was the testing ground for the Emergent Sparkle Pupa. Once the pattern passed muster on this tough river, it was ready to catch fish anywhere in the country.

This was the first fly to use Antron yarn, the sparkling, multi-sided Dupont nylon. The brightness and translucence of the clear filaments matched the air bubbles carried by emerging caddisflies inside their transparent sheaths.

EMERGENT SPARKLE PUPA

Hook: standard dry fly

Overbody: Antron yarn (drawn over the underbody in a sheath)

Underbody: Antron yarn and fur blend (dubbed sparse)

Wing: deer hair

Head: dubbed fur

The Emergent Sparkle Pupa, created in 1972 by Gary LaFontaine, is one Montana fly that has become popular across the country. It is tied in many sizes and colors to match the natural insects. From the Gun Powder River in Maryland to the Sacramento River in California, it is the proven answer for caddis hatches. It is the standard imitation for emerging pupae on most Montana rivers.

Butte to Warm Springs—This section of the river, known as Silver Bow Creek, is still unable to support trout. Maybe, after the Super Fund cleanup, this water will rebound, but the best estimates are that this won't happen for thirty years.

Anaconda Settling Ponds (at Warm Springs) to Deer Lodge—The first five miles of the Clark Fork are under special regulations (artificial lures and flies only). The river is naturally rich, sitting on the bed of limestone that underlies the entire Deer Lodge valley, and in true spring-creek fashion it meanders tortuously. It cuts and digs between willow- and alder-choked banks, creating the fabulous habitat that harbors such a high population of brown trout.

The trout grow very quickly to the 15- to 18-inch range and the average size catchable fish is a healthy 14 inches, but they don't have the food base to get much larger than this. The exceptions are a few big cannabilistic browns. There are no sculpins and very few whitefish for the trout to eat. The upper Clark Fork is, as Wayne Hadley calls it, "a caddisfly economy."

The major caddisflies are two net-spinning genera, the Spotted Sedge and the Little Sister Sedge. As larvae they are filter-feeders, capturing food from the current in their nets. The populations of these insects are incredible, over 2,000 larvae per square yard in the river, and when they emerge, peaking from late May through July, there are evening blizzards that trigger a trout feeding frenzy.

It would seem that this early summer period should be easy fishing with this combination of wall-to-wall trout and heavy hatches. The truth is that the only trout in the upper river are browns (no other species can survive the concentrations of heavy metals), and browns are seldom easy.

Wayne Hadley notes, "There are often complex hatches with more than one species coming off at one time. The browns will key to one and if you are not catching fish, you'd better re-think your strategy. I've also fished during intense surface feeding activity just at dark and never taken a fish. I haven't figured it out, yet. It's humiliating to know you're fishing over so many trout."

This section of the Clark Fork was the birthplace of some important caddisfly imitations. Gary LaFontaine developed the Deep Sparkle

Pupa and the Emergent Sparkle Pupa to fool the hypercritical trout of the river. The Emergent especially, with its reputation, became commercially popular nationally (fishermen are such hidebound traditionalists that only three new patterns, the Emergent being one of them, have cracked the list of top-ten bestsellers in the last twenty years).

During the heavy caddis hatches the choice is simple. When the browns are rolling on the surface, taking pupae struggling in the film, the Emergent in matching size and color catches fish. The best variations are a size-14 Brown and Yellow for the Spotted Sedge, and a size-16 or size-18 Ginger for the Little Sister Sedge. Grease the fly with floatant, so that it rides half in and half out of the surface film, and fish it either dead drift or with twitches over rising trout.

So much emphasis (and dogma) has been placed on drag-free drifts that a good deal of quality action is missed when it comes to caddis. The insect is not known for taking sedate, stately rides downstream as though on a regal tour of its riverine world. When emerging and egg-laying, the bugs bounce and sputter all over the place. Giving the fly a little action or even using the dreaded "drag" judiciously will many times outperform the accepted methods.

There are other insects in the upper river. The Clark Fork rivals the Beaverhead as prime cranefly habitat. The cranefly larvae, semi-aquatic insects that burrow in the damp muck of the banks, get washed into the river with the first flush of snowmelt in April and trout gorge on these chunks of food (matched by a size-8 Cranefly Larva nymph). Also important to fisherman are the midsummer flights of adult craneflies. So many insects hover over and dip onto the flats at dawn in July and August that the river surface is an orange haze. Trout leap and slash at the dancing insects (matched by a size-12 Orange Skating Spider).

Emergent Sparkle Pupa

There are Blue-Winged Olive mayflies, the early season (March and April) and late season (September and October) broods of *Baetis* making the trout rise. Tricos appear in August, but the spinner flights aren't heavy enough to get the bigger fish working. There are some stone flies, both Salmon Flies and Goldens hatching sporadically in early summer. All of these hatches seem to be getting better as the water quality improves.

Grasshoppers are important during midsummer. There are a lot of hopper patterns out there, but my favorite is still the old Joe's Hopper. The more chewed up the thing gets, the better it works, especially dragged in or just below the surface film. Gartside's, Jacklin's, Dave's, Jay's, and Juanita's hoppers also work well.

The river has its seasonal moods. It fishes best for rising trout right before and right after runoff. By midsummer it gets warm and low (irrigators hit it hard), and unless the area receives early rains the river slips into a funk. It's still possible to catch trout, but the best times are from 1:00 a.m. until 6:00 a.m. There is a dedicated group of night fishermen who slap size-8 White Deer Hair Moths on, or swim size-4 Muddlers through, the deep pools. Autumn, when the browns are moving and aggressive, is really streamer time. They especially like yellow and brown or orange and brown patterns, such as the Marabou Muddler, Golden Demon, Mansfield, and Dark Edson Tiger, but since the average-size trout far outnumber the behemoths, a smaller fly, a size-4 to -10, does much better than a tarpon pattern.

The trout populations start declining below the 5-mile special regulation section. The banks are more open, cattle graze and trample the riparian vegetation, and diversion dams pull off the water needed to dilute the heavy metals and moderate the temperatures. By the time the river reaches Deer Lodge the trout numbers are down to three hundred catchable-size trout per mile. This sounds dismal, especially when compared to the numbers of fish in the upper water, but this is still a small river and there are enough trout to make it a good fishery. It's not unusual during prime months to catch twenty browns on an afternoon right in the middle of Deer Lodge.

Deer Lodge to Drummond—The trout numbers, mostly browns but with a few rainbows and cutthroats around the mouths of the tributaries, are good, not great, all the way to Drummond. Guides begin floating the Clark Fork at the confluence with the Little Blackfoot, especially right after the tributary's runoff. There are probably more large trout in this part of the river, and it's not unusual to catch a number over 18 inches on a good day.

Reports of nice fish include:

- Dennis Osada—Sixty-one trout, almost all browns, best of 19

The upper Clark Fork just below Gold Creek
Photo by Gary LaFontaine

inches, on various flies during a two-day float from Gold Creek to Drummond in June.

- Ron Beck—Seven large browns, best of 22 inches, on a size-6 Muddler just above the Jens bridge in September.
- Jeff Bird—A 17-inch cutthroat, a 19-inch brown, and a 24-inch brown on a size-8 Gartside's Hopper below the mouth of Gold Creek in October.

This is a good stretch to dead-drift larger nymphs, sizes 6 to 10, tight to the brush piles and undercut banks. Girdle Bugs, Bitch Creeks, Woolly Buggers, Deep Sparkle Pupas, and Prince Nymphs are proven flies on this stretch. At the end of the drift, it's always wise to allow the nymph to wiggle in the current for a few seconds and then, with a slow, steady retrieve make it swim right up past the obstruction. Even discerning browns have their weak spots.

Wayne Hadley comments on this section, "People think that below every tributary there are more trout. I've found that there is no truth to this in my samplings, and that includes below the Little Blackfoot River. Yes, way down stream, below Rock Creek, there is a noticeable improvement in fish populations, but otherwise there is no difference below the tributaries. The new water coming in does not seem to make much, if any, difference. The trout are spread out.

POPULAR FLIES
Bitch Creek
Cranefly Larva Nymph
Dark Edson Tiger
Deep Sparkle Pupa
Emergent Sparkle Pupa
Girdle Bug
Golden Demon
Halo Mayfly Emerger
Joe's Hopper
Mansfield
Marabou Muddler
Orange Skating Spider
Outlaw Hopper
Prince Nymph
White Deer Hair Moth
Woolly Bugger

"There are some dead stretches because the tailing problem is handled in Band-Aid fashion with berms down to Drummond. If the cleanup is done correctly there will be a noticeable improvement in numbers throughout this part of the upper river."

Drummond to the mouth of Rock Creek—This stretch quickly deteriorates into dead water. The populations around Beavertail in midsummer are thirty trout per mile (and these aren't big trout). The river is hurt in part by numerous hot-water springs emptying into the river, but if the flow wasn't sucked down for irrigation there would be enough volume to moderate those high temperatures.

In the fall, with cooler weather, browns, and rainbows run upstream into the lower few miles of this water. These trout hold here over the winter, until the river heats up again the following summer, and at least as far up as Beavertail the fishing can be good in the spring.

Mouth of Rock Creek to Milltown Dam—The Clark Fork comes alive again at the mouth of Rock Creek. This tributary, pouring out of the high mountains and running most of the way undefiled through U. S. Forest Service land, more than doubles the midsummer flow of the main river. Suddenly there are more rainbows and cutthroats mixed into the trout population, and suddenly there is a full spectrum of insect hatches.

The Clark Fork comes alive again at the mouth of Rock Creek.

On the upper Clark Fork it is possible to do well with matching flies in the longer flats and in the side channels. This section gets the same sequence of hatches as the lower Clark Fork (below Milltown Dam), but the main river is such a splendid series of deep holes and runs that the bigger trout in the heavy current don't rise well during most hatches.

The exceptions to this general indifference are the big insects. Paul Koller says, "There is typically a three-day spurt of Salmon Fly activity between Clinton and Turah. It doesn't move upstream in any pattern. Instead it just pops throughout that section. Trout key on it quickly. It happens two weeks before the hatch starts on Rock Creek, usually in the last week of May."

In late June, right after runoff, there is a good, mixed hatch (probably the best in the whole Clark Fork) of Green Drakes and Brown

Drakes. Golden Stones, a number of species ranging from size 6 to size 12, are abundant and important. These bugs are meaty enough to get big trout feeding regularly on top.

Normal dry flies, even big bushy attractors, are usually less than spectacular on this part of the Clark Fork. A floating pattern must have inherent buoyancy from balsa or foam, or it will get sucked down by the undertow.

Powell Swanser, who fishes the river in the Turah area as much as anyone, has a pattern named the Outlaw Hopper. He calls it the "John Deere tractor of the fly world," and says, "More than once I've tossed it into the middle of the Pale Morning Dun hatch, with the 10-inch trout gobbling frantically and locked tight to a size-16 image, only to have a 24-inch granddaddy brown try to slam my big bug into the sunset."

A floating pattern must have inherent buoyancy from balsa or foam, or it will get sucked down by the undertow.

Powell carefully approaches the holding spots of big fish, but he doesn't fish his pattern with a great deal of delicacy. The idea is to throw something in front of the trout that looks big and good to eat, making sure to get his attention by skip casting, twitching, or even retrieving the fly. The approach works on this river.

One problem in midsummer, during the irrigation season on this stretch, is that the returning water often flushes loose large concentrations of green algae. The gunk floats downstream, tangling your fly. The fishing is borderline impossible, but some big trout are turned on because plenty of food also is freed. One tactic that works (and is work) is to use a weighted Yellow Marabou Muddler and strip the thing quickly through the crud. You will be constantly cleaning the fly, but the browns love yellow and you will take fish if you exercise diligence.

One special spot worth noting is the estuary area above the Milltown Dam. The small lake behind the dam is poor fishing, but biologists do find the occasional big brown swimming here with the hordes of rough fish. At the head of this lake the river braids and meanders, and in this slow, silky water nice trout, mostly browns up to 25 inches, sip on the hatches of small insects (especially the Pale Morning Duns and Blue-Winged Olives).

Bill Dudley wrote about one day during the Pale Morning Dun hatch, "For some reason the duns were a size smaller than usual this year, and the fish were especially critical about the imitation. The

The upper Clark Fork has ample access. Photo by Stan Bradshaw

answer was a size-18 fly and a long, 6X leader. I'm ashamed to admit it but I only landed four of the ten fish I hooked. The other six cleaned my clock. The biggest fish I beached was a 22-inch brown, taken on a size-18 Chartreuse Halo Mayfly Emerger, but two of the ones that I lost were much bigger."

Fishing access sites, county roads, and several bridges provide access all along the upper Clark Fork. Many ranchers along this section will grant access, also, if you ask permission politely.

If we as a society are ever judged on our treatment of rivers and the Clark Fork is part of the sampling, we'll all get the electric chair. Despite all of the pollution and abuse we have rained down on it, the upper Clark Fork is still a solid piece of damn fine fly fishing water. It cannot stay this way. There is a battle raging over this stream that has to destroy the status quo. The Clark Fork is either going to get better or it is going to get worse.

Fishing Waters of the Upper Clark Fork Drainage

Abicaulis Lake: You'll find this 17-acre lake nearly 8,000 feet above sea level up the Racetrack Creek drainage. It's about an 8-mile Jeep-track drive from the campground to good fishing for rainbows and rainbow-cutthroat hybrids, especially around submerged logs near the shore. The wind usually blows up here, and thank goodness it does. When the lake's surface is calm these are the spookiest trout around. Flat water means 16-foot, 6X leaders and long casts.

Alder Creek: This small, rapidly flowing tributary of Rock Creek enters the river from the west, near Bitterroot Flat Campground. Followed by trail, this stream has plenty of small cutthroats that don't receive much pressure. Dapping a small Madame X in the pockets and riffles will net you a thousand trout in a day. As with most Rock Creek tributaries, spawning rainbow and bull trout use the lower reaches.

Alpine Lake: Poor road above Abicaulus Lake will take you to Alpine Lake. At about the same altitude as Abicaulus, it is dammed for irrigation and sees large water-level fluctuations. There are plenty of 16-inch-long rainbows here, along with a few much bigger.

Anaconda Settling Ponds: Located on the west side of I-90 near Warm Springs and just west of the Mill-Willow Bypass, these ponds have some truly huge trout in them—browns up to fourteen pounds and rainbows up to eleven pounds. The Settling Ponds have attracted a national cadre of devotees to large trout. Four-pound fish are common and skilled anglers may catch a dozen of these and larger in a day's fishing (the key word here is "skilled").

What lends a sense of the absurd to this fishing is the fact that the structures were built to settle wastes out of mining discharges. The inflow was (and still is) treated with lime salts to precipitate out the heavy metals. Sediments containing these mine leachings fortunately get covered by thick beds of aquatic weeds, the overlay of vegetation providing ideal habitat for insects, leeches, snails, and scuds.

Because of their origin and appearance, no one comes here for aesthetic reasons. The area is an ugly, scarred moonscape, mounds of dirt and rock covered with thistle and spurge. Patches of copper tailings, so toxic even weeds can't grow in them, pockmark the area. Skeleton forests of dead trees litter the skyline. Fishermen come here to catch and release (strictly enforced with artificial lures only) large browns and rainbows—not to drink in the scenery.

The upper Clark Fork below the Anaconda Settling Ponds, near Warm Springs
Photo by Gary LaFontaine

Taking trout is a matter of matching the food. Anyone flogging away with general attractors is usually in for a long day. The water fishes best early or late in the season or during prolonged spells of cool weather. The ponds become too warm in the dog days of summer and the trout take an extended siesta. Like many fertile, still-water fisheries, the ponds are on one moment and off the next. Patience, observation, then a careful presentation are the keys to success. Use whatever rod and line combination allows you to make consistently long, accurate, and quiet casts. Leaders over 12 feet long don't hurt either.

The only fly fishermen who catch a lot of trout (and a "lot" means between six and twelve a day) are the stalkers. They crouch behind a bush, staring into the water for cruising fish. These trout are usually 18-inch to 21-inch rainbows, but browns occasionally hunt the weed edges, too. The fish don't move for a fly. The imitation has to cross right in front of them. And the pattern has to be a great still-water fly to get consistent strikes—a good one won't do.

The best pattern on the Settling Ponds for cruising fish is probably the Rollover Scud. It is tied with a strip of lead on top of the hook shank. On the retrieve it rides normally, with the hook down, but as soon as the retrieve stops the fly flips over. For some reason, that quick roll by the Scud makes even reluctant cruisers flash to the fly.

Catching the really large trout is a time-consuming game. Try working a big leech pattern, size-2 isn't too big, in the deepest holes over the weed beds. Vary your retrieves, as much to fight boredom as to entice trout, and cast time after time in search of a behemoth in the mood to eat something.

Pond 3, besides trout, is also planted with kokanee salmon. Ponds 1 and 2, Island Pond, East Pond, and all canals are open from August 15 through September 30. The Hog Hole is open from May 25 through June 30, and Pond 3 is open from May 25 through September 30. These regulations are subject to change and the visitor should check them each year.

Bearmouth Access Pond: Located right next to I-90 by the Bearmouth Rest Area, its stocked rainbows see everything known to man in the way of lures, flies, and bait, including small dogs and polished license plates. The trout are jerked out of here in a hurry, but the ones that survive and wise up grow big and fat feeding on the freshwater shrimp. Scud imitations worked very slowly through the aquatic weeds will take fish, but you must experiment with depth and retrieval speed (this holds true for any water filled with freshwater shrimp). This isn't the place to hone your still-water techniques—truck fumes, crying babies, adults overcome with the joys of summertime trips, and armed robbers (what's an unemployed writer to do?) hang out at these places of roadside madness.

Beavertail Pond: Thirty miles east of Missoula right next to I-90, highway construction crews created this pond by taking gravel for the roadbed. There is a public fishing access site on it. It is shallow, weedy, and warm. It's not great trout water but the state does stock it regularly with 9-inch hatchery rainbows. There are scads of sunfish, none seemingly bigger than 4 inches, and there are good numbers of beautiful, two- to six-pound largemouth bass. How long the population of bass can hold up is questionable. With hordes of egg-eating sunnies around, it must be difficult for the bass to bring off a successful spawn. For this reason catch and release on the bass is especially important on this pond.

Big Pozega (Deep) Lake: Dammed and 52 acres lying in the Modesty Creek drainage, you get to Big Pozega on a four-wheel-drive road. There are cutthroats and cutthroat-rainbow hybrids that survive the severe water fluctuations caused by irrigation demands. It is an interesting lake to fish because the trout don't look like they're stamped out of a cookie cutter. They are a range of sizes, averaging 10 to 12 inches, with bigger fish cruising the edges of the downed timber.

Big Thornton Lake: This is a 30-acre mountain cirque piece of water in the Racetrack Creek headwaters reached by trail and containing some small rainbows.

Bohn Lake: Located in a glacial cirque in the Dempsey Creek headwaters, this 25-acre lake at 7,100-feet elevation is fertile, growing plenty of cutthroats in the 16- to 20-inch class. You can motor right to it with a four-wheel-drive rig. The fish are fed well enough to demand the more sophisticated tactics and flies of the rich ponds in the valley—the Rollover Scud and the Floating Damsel Nymph are effective patterns here, too. The only thing missing on Bohn might be a ghillie dressed in tweeds, some cheese and crackers, and a little bubbly.

Boulder Lakes: These three small lakes in the Boulder Creek drainage (no kidding?) have been planted with westslope cutthroats in the past and now provide average fishing for average cutthroats. The lowest lake, the biggest, is the best.

Brewster Creek: A tributary of Rock Creek with good access from a forest service road, it's brushy and small, but offers fast fishing. Every species of trout that exists in the Rock Creek drainage is in Brewster, including a few that outgrow their 6- to 9-inch bretheren.

Burns Slough: Lots of swampy water and acres of cattails lie on both sides of the railroad tracks up past Bearmouth. There are largemouth bass here and the water is planted with Arlee rainbows. The bass aren't big, but they're eager (locals call this area "Bass-a-Matic"). Fishing beneath the powerlines is a hair-raising experience.

Carruthers Lake: Hike to this pretty mountain lake on 3 miles of trail west of Bohn Creek up the Dempsey drainage. There are good numbers of small cutthroats here. A 9-incher is a brute and even he will be skinny. The fishing here is typically monotonously repetitive and fast. A few trout kept for an evening meal wouldn't hurt the situation too much—it almost qualifies as mercy killing.

Copper Creek: This easy-to-fish stream drops out of the Anaconda-Pintlar Wilderness to the Middle Fork of Rock Creek. Cutthroats and a few brook and bull trout take small attractors, Wulffs and the like, especially in the middle reaches where the banks have some cover. The stream is followed by a good trail to the headwaters.

Cottonwood Creek: Flowing into the Clark Fork at Deer Lodge, Cottonwood is followed by road and then trail for 12 miles to its headwaters. This one could be a little gem, but in town it has been straightened and walled-in for flood protection. Storm drains empty directly into it. Houses crowd alongside it. Garbage is dumped into it. In spite

Cottonwood Creek
Photo by Stan Bradshaw

of all this the spring creek runs over thick beds of aquatic vegetation. Brook trout up to 10 inches and the occasional brown trout up to 14 inches hang in the holes right in town. Instead of being a tribute, protected in a park setting, to the city of Deer Lodge, it is just another tradgedy—and the people of the area are not even aware enough to be ashamed.

Because the main river once ran thick with mining sludge, most of the tributaries in the valley are drained to meet irrigation demands for valley farms and ranches, particularly for hay crops. Natural flows have often been altered by dams in the mountains that store spring runoff and then dribble out the resource during the summer. Still, some of the streams dry up in sections during years of poor snowpack and rainfall.

On many Deer Lodge Valley creeks (and those in similar areas), the best way to locate quality fishing is to follow them upstream, above the agrarian flat lands where the water is withdrawn. There are pools, riffles, and pocket water in the foothills even higher up. During the summer, when the valley ponds and the main river warm to the point where fishing hits the skids, the little, cold, sparkling streams offer entertaining action for cutthroat, rainbow, and brook trout.

Dead Man's (Dead) Lake: A small cirque lake just down the hill from Abicaulis, Dead Man's has some decent cutthroats up to 16 inches This is beautiful, high mountain country and that alone makes it worth the visit.

Dempsey Creek: This tributary flows through canyon, timber, and pasture to the Clark Fork, providing habitat for 6- to 8-inch cutthroats. It is dewatered in the lower reaches.

Dog Lake: An 11-acre pond in the Dog Creek drainage with brookies, cutts, and some browns up to 14 inches, Dog Lake is a dark-water lake—nasty looking actually—and fluorescent or reflective nymphs and wet flies work best. Drive south of Avon to get to it.

Dolus Lakes: From the trailhead at Rock Creek Lake, hike in to these alpine cirque lakes northwest of Deer Lodge. Dolus Lakes have mainly cutthroats, some hybrids, and a few browns. Located in a tight chain, between 7,800 and 8,000 feet in elevation, it's easy to fish all four of them in a day. They offer good fishing for trout up to 15 inches.

Dutchman Creek: This little spring flow runs between Warm Springs Creek and Lost Creek. The stream itself is small, but there is a diked pond for water storage that has brown trout to eight pounds (every puddle in the valley floor gives up fish like this).

East Fork Reservoir: In the Rock Creek drainage about ten minutes by road from Georgetown Lake, the reservoir covers 500 acres and is 75 feet deep when not drawn down. Brook trout, bull trout to some size, and rainbow trout with delusions of grandeur are taken along the drop-offs with streamers. This lake fishes well early in the season, before irrigation demands.

East Fork Rock Creek: This small water flows into the East Fork Reservoir and is followed by Highway 38 and then trail to the headwaters. This is an easy stream to fish except for the willows and tag alders that guard the banks much of the way. Grasshoppers are thick up here as is the smell of sage after a warm rain. The cutthroats and even crazed brookies, 8- to 12-inch fish with more ambition than intelligence, slash and race after a hopper pattern spinning in the current. This stream is a lot of fun over cold beer and casual conversation.

Echo Lake: This 75-acre summer-resort lake, not far from Georgetown

Lake, is replete with a public campground, vacation homes, domestic disputes, and water-skiers. Lots of 4- to 6-inch rainbows are dumped in here each year and as they mature they are fools for leech patterns and damselfly nymphs. There are wild brook trout in the lake and they react the same way to these patterns.

Flint Creek: This classic, small, brown trout stream winds through mostly private land, though the landowners have been kind enough to grant access to those who ask. There are also cutthroats, brooks, rainbows, and whitefish. Parts of the stream are accessible from U.S. 10A. Some lower sections go dry during drought years, so the visiting angler, lacking local knowledge, should drive up to Philipsburg and work that area.

Wading carefully (read: crouched and quiet) along the willow-and-grass-lined banks, working a Gartside's Hopper during the day and a Goddard Caddis in the evening (brown trout like flies that "plop") work all summer. In the fall the mouth of the stream (just go to the city park in Drummond and walk the quarter mile up the Clark Fork) gets a great run of browns from the river. The first mile of Flint Creek, and the first pool in the Clark Fork itself, get crammed with spawners. Streamers (yes, this means Woolly Buggers at ten paces), swept under the banks and through the runs as soon as the days noticeably shorten and cool, is what fly fishing is all about at this time.

Flint Creek above Maxville—the land surrounding it is heavily posted, so make sure you have permission. Photo by Gary LaFontaine

Four Mile Basin Lakes: According to a 1984 study by the Montana Department of Fish, Wildlife, and Parks's Pat Marcuson, lake number 4 in the Warm Springs Creek headwaters basin was stocked as recently as 1983 with goldens. Lake number 5 was also planted up to at least 1977. Not many of the beautiful little creatures have been seen since then. They are tough to catch in the lakes. When they head for the spawning inlets, a weighted Muddler worked across their noses a few times often turns the trick. The big male goldens look like sunsets on a planet from another star system. The females are emerald and blood red. These are fantastic fish, but then, so are all trout. These lakes lie over the hill west of Twin Lakes, a couple of miles by trail from the end of the Twin Lakes Creek Jeep road.

Fuse Lake: A 2-mile hike off the Skalkaho highway just east and north of the pass, this cirque lake is overpopulated with skinny-and-getting-smaller grayling that are desperate for attention. Any size 16 or smaller dry will take fish. A very few fish over 8 inches remain.

Georgetown Lake: Almost 3,000 surface acres lie right next to Montana 10A, with summer homes, resorts, public access, boat launchings, waterskiing, and campgrounds. So what? This lake in the early season and again in the fall has some of the nicest brook trout in the state, along with a lot of fat rainbows. The brookies take Olive Zonkers and Damselfly nymphs fished with sink tips along the eastern shore (there

Georgetown Lake
Photo by Stan Bradshaw

are spring holes here). A fly has to get right down to the tops of the thick weed growth before the fish will pay attention to it. Float tubes work best but there'll be company from boaters bait fishing for the trout.

Georgetown stands right now as an unabashed success story. In the 1940s this was one of the finest trophy trout lakes in the country, the fish averaging over four pounds. But incredibly the Montana Department of Fish, Wildlife, and Parks stocking policies turned this rich, relatively shallow (maximum depth of 38 feet) water into a put-and-take fishery. Bait fishermen from nearby cities would come up to take limits of 9- to 12-inch hatchery rainbows, the gullible Arlee strain, on worms, corn, and marshmallows. This was often a family activity, a fine way to spend a day with children, but it was silly to ruin the finest lake in the state when there were many beautiful, but infertile, waters nearby that would be perfect for hatchery-truck, dump stocking.

One man, biologist Wayne Hadley, started working to change the old policies when he was transferred to the region in the 1980s. Slowly, after a lot of jawboning with sportsmen's groups in the area, he gained support to lower the kill limits. Even the initial results, with the average size of the trout rising, were so exciting that it became easier to exact more changes.

Instead of stocking only Arlee strain rainbows, Wayne began adding Kamloop fingerlings to the plants. In 1991, just three years later, an angler caught a ten-pound Kamloop rainbow. Even the regular rainbow stock, with the new regulations, were surviving and growing within a few seasons to three and four pounds in the fertile soup of Georgetown. The brook trout, a wild, reproducing population in the lake, were reaching weights of three to four pounds.

There are hatches on Georgetown that qualify as fly fishing events. In June (exact time depending on the weather) the damselfly nymphs start migrating in mass towards the shallows. The trout don't even have to cruise. They sit in the open lanes in the weeds and capture the nymphs coming towards them. A matching, size-6 or size-8, olive fly has to swim the same direction as the natural, towards the bank, to be completely effective. On a windy day, on the leeward side of the lake, it's also possible to match the freshly emerged adult insects, still internally "soft" and a pewter gray color (it takes an hour or so for them to change to the bright blue body of the adult). The weak, clumsy insects get blown back onto the water by any breeze.

By July the large *Limnephilid* caddisflies start emerging on Georgetown. The adults, size-6 and -8 insects, don't fly off the water after hatching. These "travelers" run over the surface. A trout keys on the wake an adult leaves, swimming up behind the insect and exploding on it. A good dry fly imitation, such as the Devil Bug, has to leave that same V-shaped disturbance when it is brought in with a steady retrieve.

Georgetown gets a spinner fall of Tricos, but not a massive number of insects. The most important mayfly is the *Callibaetis*. The hatches start in August and during the mornings trout cruise the surface hunting for the duns and spinners resting on the surface. The fish move in a pattern and you have to put your fly, such as a size-14 CDC *Callibaetis* Dun or a size-14 Gray Clear Wing Spinner, in a feeding path.

As Wayne Hadley said one day, "Give us the right limits (on possession) and we'll make Georgetown so good you'll be afraid to throw a stick in it for your dog to retrieve."

Goat Mountain Lakes: This half-dozen little waters dotting the side of Goat Mountain are accessible by a poor road and a good trail up the Rock Creek drainage. All of them are full of little cutthroats that love dry flies. A Foam Beetle or a Foam Ant does nicely. This is wonderful country to visit for a few days.

Gold Creek: This pretty stream still hurts from the mining tailings left on its banks decades ago. It is followed by a gravel road off the Gold Creek exit on I-90. There is fishing for rainbows and cutthroats in the meadows, and for cutthroats in the forested reaches up above. Some real nice browns, including a 30-inch fish caught on a Marabou Single Egg in 1990, come up from the Clark Fork in the fall.

Gold Creek Dredge Ponds: There are two of them, one on each side of the Gold Creek road about 7 miles up from I-90. The ponds are, for the most part, very deep, the dredging operations in the first half of this century using large machinery to scoop out tons of gravel. There are brown and cutthroat trout in both waters.

At times you would swear that these ponds are barren, but that's only because the trout go down thirty or more feet and hold on the steep slopes. At other times, rare occasions when a large number of insects fall on the surface, these waters suddenly come alive with rising fish.

Don Kimball has hit the ponds right on occasion, "Being there when fish are working is just pure luck for me. Once, right after ice-out, a huge flight of water boatmen, returning from the springs where they overwintered, splattered the lower pond and I caught eight browns over 15 inches on a Diving Water Boatman in two hours. Then, in the fall, I was on the upper pond when a cloud of flying ants hit the surface, and within seconds the trout were churning the water. That action only lasted a half hour, but I caught an 18-inch cutt and a 22-inch cutt on a Black Flying Ant. I've never hooked anything close to the eighteen-pound brown an ice fisherman took out of the lower pond, but maybe that's why I keep going back there."

Trout hold deep—30 feet or more—in this mining remnant, Gold Creek Dredge Pond.
Photo by Stan Bradshaw

Green Canyon Lake: In the west side of the Copper Creek drainage, this lake is managed for cutthroats, with maybe a few rainbow-cutthroat hybrids remaining from earlier plantings. It is a deep lake and 10- to 16-inch fish cruise close to the edge, along the shallow rim, looking for food.

Green (Pozega No. 3) Lake: This dammed lake suffers from water-level fluctuation in the summer. You can reach it up either the Modesty or Racetrack drainages. Either way involves several miles of hiking. It has rainbows, cutthroats, and hybrids that average over a foot, with some specimens that may hit 20 inches on a full moon.

Hearst Lake: Lying above 8,000 feet in a glacial cirque north of Mount Haggin and southwest of downtown Anaconda, you can hike to Hearst by steep trail. It has a nice population of 12-inch-or-better cutthroats. An unweighted nymph, allowed to sink ever so slowly, brings cruising trout a long way.

Gary Schoen fished this lake in August 1991 and reported, "It's a deep lake, with a rocky bottom. Fishing the middle was a waste. It was more effective casting parallel to the shore and letting the fly settle right to the bottom. My best trick was to jump the fly off the bottom with a sharp tug on the line. I couldn't count how many times a trout took the size-12 Ida May Nymph right after that burst of movement. The best fish of the day was a 16-inch cutthroat."

Hidden Lakes: In the Rock Creek drainage (not THE Rock Creek, but the one that empties into the Clark Fork near Garrison), these five small lakes sit between 8,000 and 9,500 feet, all with hordes of small brookies and cutthroats that make good eating. The fish are overpopulated here. A little thinning would help the remaining stock.

Job Corps (Duck) Ponds: The ponds lie right along I-90 near Warm Springs. To get there take the Warm Springs exit and drive down the gravel road that parallels the interstate. There is a series of ponds, side by side, dug on the flats. They are all shallow (13 feet maximum), weedy, and full of trout. The fish, mostly rainbows but with brooks, browns, and cutts, too, don't run as big as the ones in the close-by Settling Ponds, but there are a lot of trout in the 15- to 20-inch range.

The ponds were built in the 1980s as a training project by the Anaconda Job Corps. The main purpose was to provide waterfowl habitat, not trout habitat, and the fishing season was set accordingly to protect the nesting birds.

The ponds open on August 15th and close on September 30th. By the time they open the *Callibaetis* hatch is going strong and on windless days the fish pock the surface with crossing necklaces of rise forms. None of these trout seem particularly hard to catch, probably because they don't see fishermen for most of the year, and even a general match, a size-14 Adams Parachute, is accepted gratefully. On windy days an imitation of the *Callibaetis* nymph, a size-14 Soft Hackle March Brown, works consistently. A float tube or kick boat helps an angler maneuver, but trees haven't grown up around the ponds yet and it's easy enough to cast from the bank on any of them.

Lower (Little) Barker Lake: Even though this one lies at nearly 8,000 feet, it is reachable by rough road off Montana 10A (the Georgetown Highway). It is good fishing for rainbows and cutthroats, most around 10 inches but with some up to 16 inches.

Little Blackfoot River: Crossed and followed by U.S. 12 and county roads from Garrison (where it enters the Clark Fork) up beyond Elliston, this little stream is quite resilient, despite the best efforts of local ranchers to dewater and channelize sections of it. Prime stretches of the river have been straightened and ruined as trout habitat in unsuccessful attempts at flood control, but in the undisturbed riffle and pool habitat, the water kept cooler than 62 degrees Fahrenheit even during the hottest summer days by numerous small springs, a healthy population of feisty browns holds out for almost the full length of the river. Up above Elliston the brookies and cutthroats finally take over.

Stalking the winter whitefish on the Little Blackfoot
Photo by Stan Bradshaw

The land use along the Little Blackfoot is changing. At least one developer has split a large ranch along the river into 20-acre ranchettes. Sooner or later the buyers with bottom land, most from out of state, are going to build houses next to the river and that is going to be a mistake. The Little Blackfoot, which really roars even during normal runoff (and tore out a 10-foot high railroad bed and a concrete highway bridge one year) is certain to wash away some house and then the poor fools are going to want to run the river down a concrete ditch. (Why not? It works so well in Los Angeles.)

The fishing in the Little Blackfoot can be excellent most of the time except during runoff. The same springs that cool the water in the summer warm it in the winter. On any nice day from November through March nymphing can produce whitefish (great eating when smoked) and trout. A size-16 Olive Tear Drop, which matches the Blue-Winged Olive nymph that will be hatching in March, does well. There is dry fly action on warm winter days during hatches of midges (size-16 to -22 Griffith's Gnat) and Winter Stones (size-18 Snow Stone). By March the Blue-Winged Olives appear (size-16 or -18 Slate/Olive Compara Dun). After this activity the Grannom caddisflies begin emerging in early May in hordes (size-14 or -16 Gray and Bright Green Emergent Sparkle Pupa or Dark Elk Hair Caddis) and provide fast afternoon fishing if runoff doesn't hit early.

After the runoff the river enters a two to three week "golden" period. The stream is still bankfull but clear. Many different species of mayflies, caddisflies, and stone flies are hatching, and the trout are rising joyfully and indiscriminately to the potpourri of surface items. Near the end of this glorious period, in early or mid-July, there is a heavy emergence of Pale Evening Duns, and on this hatch the fish get a bit fussy. A size-14 Light Cahill not only matches this insect but also serves as a good, all-around dry fly for this time frame.

During the summer the Little Blackfoot turns into the perfect grasshopper stream. The water stays cool, especially for browns, and the trout feed actively through the middle of the day. The grass and brush, growing right to the edge of the stream, is full of grasshoppers. You shouldn't just peck around the open water with your flies. Slam them back into and under the deadfalls and brush. The difference may be 10- to 12-inch browns caught in the open water or 14- to 16-inch browns back in the trash (the farther in the better). The best hopper pattern for this fishing is the most aerodynamic one that you can cast accurately with a fast, tight loop. For this reason, a good choice on the Little Blackfoot is the Henry's Fork Hopper. Alternative flies for this bank crashing, useful when a fish refuses a hopper and demands something a bit more subtle, are a size-16 Mohawk for midday, or a size-14 Elk Hair Caddis and a size-14 Brown and Yellow Emergent Sparkle Pupa for the evening.

The same grasshopper tactics work in the fall, but now suddenly the brown trout run bigger. These fish were in the stream all summer, but they were buried so deep in the best cover that nothing would bring them out. In the fall they start to move to spawning areas and they are a little more vulnerable to the good caster (or, at least, the courageous one). Streamers, especially the Little Brown Trout pattern, are exceptionally effective in the fall, right up into November. The lower miles of the Little Blackfoot get a run of browns up from the Clark Fork.

This river, known affectionately to fly fishermen as the Little B, deserves special protection. It is a popular trout fishery for the anglers of a major city, Helena (right over the Continental Divide), local residents, and tourists driving U.S. 12. Concerned individuals, conservation organizations, and the state should work at protecting the riparian habitat and the stream flow. The Little Blackfoot is just small enough to be fragile.

Lost Creek: This stream has two distinct personalities. It comes out of the Flint Creek range, tumbling down a steep canyon and passing through Lost Creek State Park near Anaconda. In these upper reaches it is pure, cold cutthroat and brook trout water, good fishing for anyone skilled with short-line nymph or dry fly tactics.

Lost Creek
Photo by Stan Bradshaw

When Lost Creek hits the limestone floor of the valley, and takes on the characteristics of a spring creek, it changes into a potentially great brown trout stream. The key word is "potentially" because it is trashed by ranches. The dewatering is bad enough; on Lost Creek sheep do an even worse job on the banks than cattle, stomping the streambed into a thirty-feet-wide mud wallow in places. On the last few miles of the creek, below I-90, the riparian habitat is in fair shape and this stretch gets a large, autumn run of spawning brown trout.

In autumn most of the tributaries in this valley get a run of spawning browns from the Clark Fork. From mid-September through November the streams have more water because irrigation demands have dwindled. As far up as the trout can migrate, from the flats to the mountains, the water often is filled with fish (2,000 per mile in Lost Creek). Once an anger finds the spawning trout, any yellow and brown streamer (or any nymph for that matter) drifted in front of them will usually provoke a strike. Territorial behavior is at its peak. But take it easy on these fish. They do have a few things on their diminutive minds.

Lower Willow Creek Reservoir: Take the Drummond exit off I-90 and go to Hall. This reservoir is reached by 9 miles of county road. It's 170 acres, deep (when it is not drawn down to dust for irrigation), with some nice, wild cutthroats that come in from the creek. These fish should be left alone when they are vulnerable in excessively low water.

Meadow Lakes: To get to these six lakes in the Racetrack Creek headwaters, hike 6 miles on the trail from the end of the Racetrack Creek Road. They range in altitude from 7,650 to 8,650 feet and vary in size from 4 to 25 acres. There are fish in the four largest lakes. The two small, mud-bottomed ones are barren. They are all rich in aquatic life, but for some reason only number three grows monsters, up to 30 inches.

When summer storms wail through this barren country you will feel the crack and sizzle of the lightning and smell the ozone when it blasts the gray rock. Originally managed for rainbows, like most alpine waters, they are now getting cutthroat plants on a periodic basis.

Medicine Lake: In the upper Rock Creek drainage, Medicine Lake is managed for westslope cutthroat that do well in the fertile aquatic environment. Even at 7,000 feet damsels are found. Nymphs are the best bet, but splatting an electric-blue dry on the surface, letting the thing sit on the surface, then creating a commotion is interesting. One minute the bug is there. The next minute there is a big hole in the water. The action can be slow, but then you're not in the mountains to punch a clock. You can hike in a couple of miles from the end of Sand Basin Road (south of the West Fork of Rock Creek) or take 4½ miles of jeep road from the junction of Elk Creek and the South Fork of Rock Creek.

Middle Fork Rock Creek: This 25 miles of shallow, easily fished water holds fair numbers of rainbows, cutthroats, and whitefish that might reach 10 inches. Some small bull trout hide under the logs here, too.

Mud Lake: North of Big Racetrack Lake, you can drive to Mud Lake on a four-wheel-drive road. There is some on-again, off-again fishing for 10- to 16-inch cutthroats.

Phyliss Lakes: These two 10-acre lakes in the Anaconda-Pintlar Wilderness are home to cutthroat trout. Upper Phyliss has some 12-inchers. Lower Phyliss receives some plantings on occasion by a devoted fisheries biologist and there are slightly better numbers and sizes in this one. Take the trail about 2 miles southwest of Johnson Lake to get there.

Racetrack Creek: There are over 12 miles of good small-stream fishing through the middle and upper stretches of Racetrack Creek. All the way up to Racetrack Lake it is accessible by county road, Jeep road, and trail. The upper portion above the campground is rough, tumbling water where you move from pool to pool. Below the campground the runs dig through glacial gravel with a good carpet of aquatic weeds. Cutthroats from 8 to 13 inches, along with lesser numbers of brook, brown, rainbow, and bull trout are also in the stream.

As with most mountain streams, on opening day (the third Saturday in May) the stream is normally bank-full and difficult to work. When the stream begins to lower sometime in mid-June through July

Upper Racetrack Creek
Photo by Gary LaFontaine

(depending on the snowpack and weather), the trout go on a feeding spree for a couple of weeks. With ample flows, the fish are spread thoughout the creek. A wet fly, such as a classic Leadwing Coachman or a woven-bodied Sandy Mite, covers a lot of water. A dry fly like a Royal Trude or a Lady Heather drums up the fish. Late in the season, through summer and fall, the trout hold in the deeper pools and slots. The fishing is challenging and you have to study each spot, figuring the angle of approach and the best method of presentation.

The lower alluvial flats of the creek are sucked low for irrigation, not completely destroying, but hurting what could be an excellent brown trout fishery. Somehow, in this puddle-jump water of summer, a population of 15- to 20-inch fish survive (probably because of springs). The stream also plays host to an autumn run of nice browns, but then I've never met a bad brown.

Racetrack Lake: Reached by Jeep road, this dammed, 35-acre, deep lake suffers from irrigation drawdown, but it is still good fishing for 8- to 13-inch cutthroats, rainbows, and hybrids. When in doubt, work the rocky points with small streamers, stripping the fly fast (a method that only works consistently in lakes with eager fish).

Rainbow Lake: In the headwaters of Gold Creek, you can drive to Rainbow Lake by Jeep road above the dismantled ghost town of Pioneer. About 20 acres, it is fertile with good numbers of 16- to 20-inch cutthroats and few big rainbows, up to 30 inches, that are fussy but can be taken with a little stealth and patience.

This lake was poached severely in the 1980s, including by a pair of men using blasting caps to kill hundreds of large rainbows. It is just now coming back to a prime fishery and every trout should be released. The fish have the potential to really grow big here.

One food item Rainbow has in abundance is leeches, and these leeches are the 3- to 4-inch variety. That is what the large, cruising trout are hunting for along the edges. The fish rush towards any puff of silt off the bottom. A fly tied on an upside-down Keel Hook, the Bristle Leech, lays on the bottom without snagging and kicks up a cloud with the first strip of the retrieve. It is a deadly pattern in Rainbow Lake.

Ranch Creek: A tributary of Rock Creek, with Grizzly Campground on the lower end, it is real good small-creek fishing for all the species in the main stream. It's no secret that the mouth of every tributary on Rock Creek gets great in the fall.

The notable catch at the mouth for 1992: Dan Beck used a Buck Bunny (a Bunny streamer with a Muddler head) to take a 24-inch brown and six others over 16 inches on a September afternoon.

Rock Creek (Garrison): Rock Creek drains a bunch of alpine lakes (nearly twenty), and passes through rugged, timbered canyons to Rock Creek Lake. Below the lake it's good fishing for small cutthroats, rainbows, browns, and brookies. The lower portions, before the stream reaches the Clark Fork about 3 miles from Garrison, get dried up during the summer. This is also not THE Rock Creek.

Rock Creek: Don't believe the "creek" part—this is a small river. It is also one of the most famous fly fishing waters in Montana, designated Blue Ribbon by the state. It is hit heavily not only by the people from Missoula (an urban area of 70,000-plus), but also by a good number of tourists. Fortunately, all of these anglers can spread out on 50 miles of prime trout water. Yes, this is THE Rock Creek.

There are two ways to reach Rock Creek. To fish the upper end you can take the Drummond exit off I-90, drive to Philipsburg on Montana 10A, turn right on Montana 38 and go to Gillies Bridge. At that point you hit both the stream and Rock Creek Road.

The Rock Creek Road, finished in 1926 by the Forest Service, is paved only on the bottom 11 miles. For most of its length it is rough gravel (and that's the way local conservationists fight to keep it). You can take the Rock Creek exit and follow the road all the way to the top, but it is quicker and a lot less dusty to reach the upper end by way of Philipsburg. The Rock Creek exit off I-90, 20 miles east of Missoula, is the best way to reach the lower sections of the stream.

Rock Creek starts at the confluence of the East Fork and the West Fork. The stream wanders through a wide valley, a collection of pools, pockets, and riffles, and it is easy fishing for 8- to 12-inch cutthroats, rainbows, and brooks. Any spot deep enough to hold a larger trout usually does, however, and that's the place to throw a bigger streamer, nymph or dry fly.

Rock Creek today looks much the same as it does in this 1927 photograph.
USDA–Forest Service

About a mile above Gillies Bridge the canyon, craggy, orange, and red walls of sedimentary rock, squeezes in and the stream starts to dig better holding spots. Suddenly, this isn't small fish water anymore. There are still plenty of 8- to 12-inch trout here, especially up any side channel, but the fly fisherman who knows how to work rough western water catches 15- to 22-inch rainbows and cutthroats.

Terry Cousens, who fishes this 25-mile stretch from Gillies Bridge to Harry's Flat thirty times a season, writes, "This is consistent water. A good dry fly man averages forty trout a day. The big difference is in the size of the fish, some people getting nothing over 14 inches and others taking plenty of those bigger rainbows and cutthroats.

"The way to catch larger trout on the surface is to use larger flies. That means either matching the biggest insects of the season—Salmon Flies during runoff, Golden Stones after it, grasshoppers or spruce moths during the summer, and the Giant Orange Sedge in the fall—or choosing bigger attractor patterns. Any of the standard attractors are good here, but there are two that seem to do an exceptionally fine job at pulling up decent fish—a Humpy and an Air Head in sizes 6 to 10. Both of these flies present strong, bulky images, and on softer water might not be the entire answer but they're great on Rock Creek all the way down to Harry's Flat."

Nymphs work on this section, but bouncing a weighted fly over the bottom gets you three or four whitefish for every trout. A streamer, on the other hand, doesn't catch as many fish as other types of flies, but it brings out the bigger trout. For real nostalgia you can bounce a Sandy Mite or a Lady Mite, old Potts-style, woven wet flies that are still sold in the area and that are still very effective.

The composition of the fish population in Rock Creek changes from top to bottom. Above Gillies Bridge the predominant trout are cutthroats, cutthroat-rainbow hybrids, and rainbows, with a scattering of brook, brown, and bull trout. The pure rainbows start to dominate below Hogback Creek, making up 60 percent of the population and averaging 12 to 14 inches, but under the strict catch-and-release regulations in effect from the Hogback down to Butte Cabin Creek cutthroats are rebounding in numbers, now amounting to 20 percent of the total. Bull trout are not the main species anywhere in Rock Creek, but the stream has one of the finest populations of this species in the state. Bull trout reach their greatest abundance in the upper and middle reaches.

John Herzer specifically goes after bull trout. "My favorite times are early, in March and April, and then again late, in September and October. But the methods are different for each season. In the spring we fish a Black Woolly Bugger or an Olive Zonker, tied on a size-2 or -4 long shank hook. We don't fish these like streamers. We use a floating line, with an indicator, and dead-drift the flies. The bull trout invariably hold in mid-thigh to chest deep, choppy water, at the heads of pools and long runs. In the fall we still use big flies, unweighted Spuddlers and Kiwi Muddlers, but we work these actively, stripping them erratically just under the surface. The fish, spring and fall, average 16 to 19 inches. A friend of mine caught a 29-incher. The best areas for bull trout on Rock Creek begin 17 miles up from the mouth."

The section around the Dalles is a strange, hard-to-master piece of river. The fish are there, browns becoming more and more prevalent, but the water, flowing around house-size boulders and into huge holes, is so deep that it is hard to catch the decent trout. Some anglers swear that it is impossible. Ordinary tactics only work here when a great hatch of Salmon Flies coincides with clearer and lower than normal runoff. Then the brutes feed along the edges on nymphs and adults.

The other two choices around the Dalles are depth bombing and night fishing. It takes a high-density, sinking line and a weighted fly, either a nymph or a streamer, to get anywhere near the bottom in some of those holes. At night, at least, you can throw an unweighted or lightly weighted fly, even if it is a big one. Either method produces trout over 20 inches for the skilled practitioner.

In the lower section of Rock Creek brown trout take over, making up 80 percent of the population. The water from Ranch Creek (the end of the paved road) down to the mouth is the most heavily hit part of the stream. These cottonwood bottoms are also where many fly fishermen get skunked, probably due to three reasons:

1. Most of the trout are browns, holding in deeper cover and demanding better presentations when they're not feeding, putting them out of reach most of the time.
2. The heavy hatches, combined with better defined pools and flats, let the trout feed selectively.
3. The trout get fished over so much that they get especially wary when they feel the presence of an angler.

Ray Stockton, a visitor from New Zealand, gave up in disgust after spooking a large brown trout, handing back his borrowed tackle, "You Americans are daft. How can you expect to catch the best fish with bright rods, orange lines, and shiny leaders?" It's a good question.

This bottom water receives a great run of spawning browns from the Clark Fork in the fall. These fish move from spot to spot, so preoccupied that they're not nearly as skittish as the resident trout. A good streamer fisherman, pounding out a fly with those brown and yellow colors that bother big browns, takes fish up to five pounds, especially early or late in the day, or on overcast days.

Rock Creek is a very rich river (anyone skating on the algae-slick boulders can attest to that). The big hatch of the year, from the bottom all the way to the top, is the Salmon Fly. The emergence starts in early June, during the high water runoff, creating a trout feeding frenzy and fly fisher madness. The hatch moves upstream 3 to 5 miles a day and many anglers attempt to keep just ahead of the action.

While large dry flies, such as Sofa Pillows, Orange Stimulators, Orange Fluttering Stones, and Elk Hair Salmon Flies, bring up some rainbows, browns, and cutthroats, most anglers ignore the surface fishing and go to nymph imitations. Rock Creek runs high and turbid during normal years, which slows the action on top significantly in the lower sections. If you are willing to work weighted size-2 and -4 nymphs, often with sink-tip lines, quartering upstream and then crawled (not easy in the fast current of spring runoff) towards the bouldery bank, some fine angling awaits you. The retrieve mimics the actions of the stone fly nymphs crawling to shore to dry on the sun-warmed rocks. Seven-weight, 9-foot rods make casting, working the drift, and then picking up the heavy rig much easier. Short leaders, down to 4 feet, with 2X or 3X tippets work well.

Anyone whose heart is set on fishing dry flies during the hatch should find it at the upper end, above the Hog Back. The water still runs high, but it's clear and trout smash the big adults and matching floaters. There are larger trout up here early in the season, too. The 16- to 22-inch rainbows from below, after spawning, stay in the upper section until the water levels start to drop in late June and early July.

Rock Creek is swollen enough during runoff to float (allowed only until June 30th each year). Mark Jones, who guides on the stream, describes the technique, "It's a technical float, with quick maneuvers to get around fallen trees. The upper part of the stream, from Gillies Bridge down to 12 miles above the mouth, is better boat fishing because the trout don't get spooked in the rough water. A special trick here, because the stream isn't big, is to turn the raft sideways and let both anglers cast their flies downstream. That way they both get a good drift with dry flies. If my people are getting a lot of false, splashy rises, I have them down-size the imitation, at least one and sometimes two sizes smaller than the natural."

Once the water returns to normal, steady hatches of caddisflies, mayflies, and stone flies come off well into the fall. Noteworthy hatches include the Great Gray Spotted Sedge, all through June; the Golden Stone, from late June through July; the Spotted Sedge, peaking in early July; the Green Sedge, in July and August; and the Giant Orange Sedge, in early September (the lower 10 miles of Rock Creek have the best hatch of this insect of any river in the western part of the state). There are plenty of small mayflies—Tricos, Pale Morning Duns, and Blue-Winged Olives—but they're more important in the pools of the bottom section than in the rougher currents above Harry's Flat.

Major terrestrials—grasshoppers, ants, and beetles—are important all summer, but the real event is the Spruce Moth flights. When these insects come off the evergreen trees in August and get trapped on the water by the thousands, they push the trout into a slop-feeding frenzy. The trick, since these are local infestations popping up in different places in different years, is finding the heaviest concentration, and that takes a little bit of "road hunting," driving from noon to 4 p.m. looking for moths in the air. They can be anywhere evergreen forests line the stream.

Too many anglers end up discouraged by the August fishing on Rock Creek. Just remember that the bottom section receives by far the most angling pressure. The trout may average 14 inches, with a good mix of sizes, but even the smaller ones are extremely wary by midsummer. The big boys are buried in the gravel, hiding from the thundering herd of neoprene-clad fishermen. They have seen every pattern known to man by now.

So here's a tip for anyone determined to fish the lower, and even the middle, stretches in the summer. There's a myth of gigantic proportions, a silly one, that says that "you don't have to get up early to fish Montana rivers." The truth is that trout everywhere feed heavily at dawn because nymphs and larvae, in the phenomena known as behavioral drift, are washing downstream free in the currents. This usually isn't a great dry fly time, but the fisherman who can present a Prince Nymph, Peeking Caddis, or Montana Stone naturally is going to catch a lot of trout, with an inordinate share of large ones, and probably never see another angler from dawn to 7 a.m.

Ninety percent of the land bordering Rock Creek is owned by the U. S. Forest Service. Access is abundant, at pullouts along the road and in conveniently spaced public campgrounds. With tighter restrictions on kill limits, this popular fishery continues to improve, mainly with larger trout, each season.

There is one last item. In 1991 the Forest Service (God love 'em) tried to sneak through plans to log 70 million board feet (enough lumber to build 12,000 average homes) from the upper sections of Rock Creek. Some people got wind of this jive and blew the whistle, but we all must keep an eye on things or they will try to pull this again. Angry letters and phone calls along with loud voices are the only things the timber industry hears. Reason and conscience are not part of their makeup. Just ask the ghosts of "bull trout past" in the Jim Creek drainage of the Swan Valley.

Ross Fork Rock Creek: Much of this stream is on private and posted land. The open stretches are small pocket water holding small cutthroats, brookies, and some small (for this species) bull trout, and whitefish moving upstream late in the season.

Schwartz Creek: Small, flowing out of timbered mountains near Clinton, it has some decent brookies and cutthroats, and a few spawner rainbows and browns. There's not a lot of casting water, but this is a pretty little stream.

Spring Creek: Filled with rainbows, small brookies, and cutthroats in the upper reaches, the best water flows through the Handley Ranch and permission is required. There are ponds, actually the remains of an old fish hatchery, on the lower end that are good early in the season before weeding up, but the fish are ever so spooky in these shallow waters. The Rock Creek Road crosses the lower reaches several miles up from I-90. Classic, pretty and oh-so-clear water that is small but fertile.

Stewart Lake: Regularly planted with rainbows, this 20-acre lake is reached by road a few miles northeast of Philipsburg. The fish get hit with a good deal of angling pressure, so they never reach any great size.

Storm Lake: In the Anaconda-Pintlar Range, Storm covers 55 acres at nearly 9,000 feet. The water is aquatically fecund, growing fat cutthroats and rainbows to 20 inches or so. The staple food in the lake is scuds. To get to Storm take scenic Highway 10A west of Anaconda, then turn south on the road that parallels Storm Lake Creek.

Thornton Lake: Thirty acres in the headwaters of Racetrack Creek, you can hike to Thornton by an easy, one-mile trail (which makes it a popular destination). It is fair fishing for rainbows that may top out at 12 inches.

Trask Lake: Part of the Hidden Lake group, Trask is the largest of the bunch at an overwhelming 10 acres. It has small (as in stunted) brookies and cutthroats.

Twin Lakes: Go to the Spring Hill Campground, on Highway 10A above Anaconda, and from there drive up the Jeep road for 8 miles and walk up the trail for 1 mile. Neither one is very large or very deep, but both waters support good populations of 12-inch cutthroats. These lakes receive regular plantings.

Wallace Reservoir: Short on aesthetics, especially after drawdown for irrigation, this lake north of I-90 near Clinton still has some fat cutthroat trout, up to 15 inches, that feed on the abundant aquatic insects and some small, dark green frogs that tend to get careless on occasion. Dig out the bass poppers.

Warm Spring Creek (Warm Springs): You can begin working this water inside the city limits of Anaconda. Above town this is a small stream that is both productive and lightly fished, since most people whiz by on their way to Georgetown Lake. The gradient is modest from Washoe Park up to the Job Corps Center, with the channel running behind houses on the left side of Highway 10A. The best fishing in this stretch is in the early season for cutthroats and rainbows.

As you head upstream, the creek passes under the road, changing into a mountain stream. The water is rich with insects and forage fish, and rainbows and cutthroats to over 15 inches feed on them. Eight- to 12-inch trout are the norm here, though. Getting the trout requires small stream tactics, like picking the pockets with an upstream dry, bouncing the bottom with a short-line nymph, and swimming the edges with a downstream wet or streamer. Most of us choose a short rod when working this type of water with a dry fly—7 feet or less. When nymphing, an 8½- foot rod works much better, allowing you to reach out to those prime runs and little pockets where the big trout hide. The typical pattern selection for this type of water would include attractors (Gray Wulff and Royal Trude), general caddis simulations (Elk Hair Caddis and Emergent Sparkle Pupa), and general mayfly simulations (Adams and March Brown). Nymphs such as the Bead Head Hare's Ear and Bright Green Caddis Larva are deadly. A Girdle Bug and a small Woolhead Sculpin are nice swimming flies.

Warm Springs below Anaconda is another story and not a happy one. The stream was dewatered for years for the refining operations. When the smelter shut down in the 1980s, there was suddenly yeararound water. Three years of good flow and the creek blossomed into an incredible brown trout fishery. It became 10 miles of meandering, deep-cut banks holding fish to 18 inches. Because of a greater diversity of insect and fish life, Warm Springs was growing browns faster than the Clark Fork. Then the new owners of the mining operation in Butte started using the water again. What little flow was released found its way onto the hayfields below town. Goodbye brown trout.

Warm Springs Hospital Pond: This little, shallow pond next to the state hospital is planted with rainbows for children thirteen-yearsold and under. Since this spot is fed by springs (like every other depression in the Deer Lodge valley), some trout survive over the winter and grow nicely. Imagine the surprise of a child who hooks a threepound rainbow or an eight-pound brown (the largest documented examples of these species from the pond).

West Fork Rock Creek: This small stream dances and cascades over jumbles of flat, dark rock and between mossy banks. Small logjams add to the habitat that holds small cutthroat, brook, and bull trout, along with some whitefish. This is a wonderful mountain creek that probably will become history if the Forest Service has its clearcutting way.

Other Waters

Altoona Lakes: Cutthroats to 15 inches. It's off the Boulder Creek Road in the Flint Creek drainage. The fact that you can drive to it makes it a nice day trip.

American Gulch: Cutthroats.

Antelope Creek: Poor access.

Basin Creek: Brookies, but not enough.

Basin Creek Reservoirs: Closed to fishing.

Bear Creek: Polluted.

Beaver Creek: Brookies and cutthroats to 9 inches It's a tributary of the North Fork of Rock Creek and yes, there are beaver ponds on this marshy stream.

Beck's Pond: Private. Any place someone digs a hole in the Deer Lodge valley a pond is created. The water table is so high, and the seepage through the limestone so rich, that that new ponds invariably grow fat trout.

Beck's Pond was dug just off the Racetrack Exit on I-90, the gravel used in the construction of an overpass. The pond is private property, but at the moment it is possible to get permission to fish it. It was stocked by the state with brown trout, and specimens to six pounds have been caught.

Beefstraight Creek: Brookies and cutthroats to 7 inches It is one of the prettiest little streams, a series of falls and pools. Go to Gregson Hot Springs, off I-90, to find it.

Big (Upper) Barker Lake: Rainbows.

Big Hogback Creek: Brookies and cutthroats. Bull trout start stacking up at the mouth in August, waiting for the fall rains.

Big Spring Creek: Too small.

Bison Creek Reservoir: Private.

Blacktail Creek: Poor for rainbows. It flows to Butte.

Blum Creek: Too small.

Boulder Creek: Cutthroats.

Bowles Creek: Cutthroats.

Bowman's Lakes: Cutthroats, rainbows, and hybrids.

Brown's Gulch: Poor access.

Bryan Creek: Cutthroats.

Butte Cabin Creek: Too small.

Cable Creek: Too small.

Carp Creek: Bull and cutthroat trout.

Carp Lake: Cutthroats, incredibly stunted ones.

Carpenter Lake: Private.

Cinnabar Creek: Cutthroats.

Clear Creek: Too small.

Conley's Lake: Rainbows. It is on the Prison Farm outside of Deer Lodge.

Copper Creek: Cutthroats and rainbows.

Copper Creek Lakes: Cutthroats and brookies.

Cougar Creek: Brookies and cutthroats.

Cramer Creek: Brookies and cutthroats.

Crevice Creek: Too small.

Deep Creek: Too small.

East Fork Brewster Creek: Bull and cutthroat trout.

Edelman Creek: Too small.

Edith Lake: Rainbows to 15 inches The 6-mile trail goes off the Middle Fork of Rock Creek Road.

Eight Mile Creek: Brookies, cutthroats, and rainbows.

Elbow Lake: Rainbows.

Elk Creek: Cutthroats.

Elk's Tin Cup Creek Pond: Brookies in a 5-acre pond on the Prison Ranch. I'd pass on this one.

Emerine Lake: Cutthroats.

Falls Fork Creek: Cutthroat and bull trout.

Fisher Lake: Cutthroats to 10 inches, but they're not skinny. You can get there by really rough Jeep ruts off the Racetrack Creek Road. Save the vehicle and hike the last mile.

Foster Creek: Brookies and cutthroats.

Fred Burr Creek: Access limited.

German Gulch: Cutthroats.

Gilbert (Finlen) Creek: Good fishing for small trout. Poor access off the Rock Creek Road.

Gold Bar Lakes: Brookies and rainbows.

Gold Creek Lakes: Up the Gold Creek drainage. It always seems like any water named gold creek (except for the Dredge Ponds) is lousy fishing in Montana. These lakes are no exception, offering marginal action for rainbows.

Grizzly Creek: Too small.

Haggin Lake: Rainbows to 15 inches It is perched below Mt. Haggin above Anaconda.

Hail Columbia Creek: Too small.

Harvey Creek: Brookies and cutthroats.

Hogback Creek: Brookies and cutthroats.

Hoover Creek: Poor fishing.

Hope Creek: Too small.

Hope Lake: Cutthroats and hybrids.

Hunter's Lake: Poor fishing.

Ivanhoe Lake: Rainbows.

Jacobus Ponds: Private.

Johnson Lake: Cutthroats.

Jones Pond: Private, but it's possible to get permission from the caretaker. It is just off Lost Creek, fed by a small spring. It's a small, ugly pond, but it's crammed with scuds and it grows browns to fourteen pounds.

Kaiser Lake: Cutthroat, rainbow, and bull trout. It is up the Middle Fork of Rock Creek Road, and then up a 1- mile Jeep road. Swing a streamer through the inlet cove for a chance at a nice bull trout in the fall.

Lake Abundance: Cutthroats.

Lake Ellen (YMCA): Private

Lake of the Isles: Cutthroats.

Little Blackfoot Spring Creek: A tributary that empties into the Little Blackfoot near Elliston. This is a true spring flow, running at 6 to 10 cfs, with water temperatures typically below 60 degrees Fahrenheit. There are clumps of watercress on the gravel substrate. The population of browns, brookies, and cutts is depressed because the channel has been severely degraded by cattle grazing. The beaver dams at the lower end offer the best fishing.

Little Fish Lake: Little fish.

Little Hogback Creek: Too small.

Little Pozega Lake: Rainbows.

Little Racetrack Lake: Cutthroats, rainbows, and hybrids. Less than a mile from Racetrack Lake. Hit it right after ice-out. Some of those rainbows go up to 18 inches.

Little Thorton Lake: Rainbows.

Lower Carp Lake: Cutthroats.

Lower Elliot Lake: Cutthroats.

Lower Willow Creek: Brookies, browns, and cutthroats.

Mallard Creek: Too small.

Marshall Creek: Brookies, browns, and cutthroats.

Martin Lake: Cutthroats to 10 inches. Martin is above Deer Lodge, at 9,000 feet, and a wicked 5-mile climb. There have to be better reasons for going to the top of the world than small cutthroat trout, and the view up here might be one of them.

Meadow Creek (Rock Creek): Cutthroats.

Meadow Creek (Mullan Pass): Brookies and cutthroats.

Meadow Lakes (Rock Creek): Cutthroats, rainbows, and hybrids.

Mike Renig Gulch: Brookies and cutthroats.

Mill Creek: Brookies, cutthroats, and rainbows.

Miller (Mill Creek) Lake: Cutthroats.

Minnesota Gulch: Too small.

Modesty Creek: A visitor to this drainage would have difficulty locating the stream, let alone the tiny trout. What water there is gets split up into irrigation channels around Galen.

Monarch Creek: Too small.

Moose Creek: Cutthroats.

Moose Lake: Cutthroats.

Mosquito Lake: Cutthroats.

Mountain Ben Lake: Cutthroats and hybrids.

Mud Lake (Deer Lodge): Brookies.

Mud Lake (Skalkaho): Cutthroats.

North Fork Flint Creek: Brookies and cutthroats.

North Fork Gold Creek: Too small.

North Fork Lower Willow Creek: Brookies and cutthroats.

North Fork Rock Creek: Cutthroats.

Ontario Creek: Brookies and cutthroats.

Ophir Creek: Too small.

Perkin's Reservoir: Brookies.

Peterson Creek: Brook, brown, cutthroat, and rainbow trout in the parts that aren't dewatered. It flows right into Deer Lodge.

Pfister Pond: Private.

Powell Lake: Browns.

Poorman Creek: Too small.

Rock Creek Lake: Private.

Ryan Lake: Brookies.

Sallyann Creek: Too small.

Sand Basin Creek: Cutthroats.

Sauer Lake: Cutthroats.

Sawmill Creek: Brookies and cutthroats.

Senate Creek: Too small.

Senecal Ponds: Private.

Sidney Lake: Cutthroats and hybrids.

Silver Bow Creek: Polluted (see Clark Fork entry).

Silver Lake: Kokanee salmon, rainbow

trout, and lake trout. It is right along Scenic Highway 10A, downstream from Georgetown Lake (which draws all the pressure). It is worth a visit early in the season.

Smart Creek: Cutthroats.

Snowshoe Creek: Take a short rod. This is fishing in a tunnel of trees on the lower end for cutthroats, rainbows, and some surprisingly large browns up from the Little Blackfoot.

Snowshoe Lakes: Private.

South Boulder Creek: Brookies, cutthroats, and rainbows.

South Fork of Mill Creek: Too small.

South Fork Ross Fork Rock Creek: Cutthroats.

Spotted Dog Creek: Brookies, cutthroats, and rainbows. This tributary of the Little Blackfoot is being rehabilitated by the current owner to correct past agricultural problems.

Stony Creek: Cutthroats.

Storm Lake Creek: Cutthroats.

Stuart Mill Creek: A tributary of Georgetown and closed to protect spawning fish, but it's fun to go there in late May and watch the rainbows pack into the stream.

Sydney Lake: Cutthroats and hybrids.

Tamarack Lake: In the Anaconda-Pintlar Wilderness. It is full of the most garishly colored, 12- to 14-inch cutthroats that you've ever seen.

Telegraph Creek: Brookies, browns, and cutthroats in this Little Blackfoot tributary.

Three Mile Creek: A little spring creek that flows to the Little Blackfoot near Avon. It has browns and cutthroats up to 12 inches Try crawling on your belly and dapping this stream.

Tin Cup Joe Creek: Cutthroats and rainbows.

Trout Creek (Flint Creek): Brookies and cutthroats.

Trout Creek (Little Blackfoot): Brookies, cutthroats, and browns.

Twin Lakes Creek: Brookies and cutthroats.

Tyler Creek: No access.

Upper Elliot Lake: Cutthroats.

Upper Willow Creek: Poor access.

Wahlquist Creek: Too small.

Wallace Creek: Too small. Polluted.

Warm Springs Creek (Garrison): Brookies, browns, and cutthroats. Don't tell anyone about this one. Those browns in the lower end average 12 to 14 inches and there are good numbers of them. It's a strange little stream, aptly named (the water temperature even in October is in the high sixties). Six miles upstream there's a 150-foot waterfall, and it is worth the drive to see it.

Welcome Creek: A tributary of Rock Creek. It has mostly cutthroats above, and a fine population of brookies in the lower mile.

West Fork Cramer Creek: Cutthroats.

West Fork Lower Willow Creek: Too small.

West Fork Willow Creek: Too small.

Willow Creek (Garrison): Brookies and cutthroats.

Willow Creek (Opportunity): Brookies and cuttthroats. This is a small, cold spring-fed fishery. There is a tangled maze of beaver ponds between Opportunity and I-90 with plenty of brookies (most small, but a few to 16 inches). Plan an all day trip—take survival gear and leave a map for the rescue team.

Wyman Creek: Brookies and cutthroats.

Wyman Gulch: Too small.

■ *Special thanks to Ron Beck, Jeff Bird, Terry Cousens, Bill Dudley, Dennis Fross, Wayne Hadley, John Herzer, James Hess, Mark Jones, Don Kimball, Paul Koller, John Lamoureux, Dennis Osada, Gary Schoen, Ray Stockton, and Powell Swanser for their help on the Upper Clark Fork drainage.*

Two avid fishermen share a day on the Thompson River.
Photo by Don Roberts

The Yellowstone, the Missouri, and the Kootenai come to mind when thinking of the big waters of Montana. These are large streams, but they are all considerably smaller than the lower Clark Fork River. Before the Clark Fork enters Idaho, on its way to joining the Columbia, it receives the waters of the Blackfoot, Bitterroot, Thompson, and St. Regis rivers, along with the entire Flathead drainage, and it grows into the largest flow in the state. Even at St. Regis, before the Flathead enters, the gauging station records stream flows of 25,000 cfs on the Clark Fork during the peak May runoff.

A river of this dimension can intimidate even the most experienced fly fishermen. Where does one start? How do you bring the trout up to the surface or drop the fly down to the fish? What is the most productive water?

Mouth of the Blackfoot River to Kelly Island—The Blackfoot, clear and pure compared to the highly enriched Clark Fork, is actually the bigger of the two rivers, doubling the flow at Milltown Dam. The stretch from the dam to Missoula is known as the "urban float." You can put a boat in below the dam (far below the churning water of the spillway) and reach the city limits in a few hours. The trout species in this section, in order of abundance, are browns, rainbows, and cutthroats.

Below Milltown Dam in high water, 1908—it was tough to get a nymph down in these flows.
Photo courtesy of Mansfield Library, University of Montana

To Troy
N Fork
Lowell Lake
CABINET MOUNTAINS
To Libby
Bull River
Moran Basin Lakes
Little McGregor Lake
56
E Fork
St Paul Lake
Rock Lake
2
Thompson Lakes
McGregor Lake
To Sandpoint
E Fork
Bull River
Wanless Lake
Cabinet Gorge Dam
Heron
Rock Cr
Cirque Lakes
Noxon
Dam
Swamp Cr
Sims Cr
Elk Lake
Fishtrap Creek
Pilgrim Cr
Noxon Reservoir
Falls
Thompson River
Vermilion R
Cataract Creek
Stony Lake
Terrace Lakes
W Fork
E Fork Trout Cr
Trout Creek
Beaver
Graves Cr
Cabin Lake
West Fork
Lower
Lawn Lake
COEUR
Big Beaver
Arrowhead Lake
Big Spruce Cr
Little Beaver
Duck-head Lake
Deer Lake
D'ALENE
IDAHO
Thompson Falls
Dam
Clark Fork
200
Prospect Creek
MOUNTAINS
Tuffys Lake
Dry Cr
Eddy Cr
W Fork Swamp
Acorn Lake
East Fork
To Spokane
Saltese
90
Twelvemile Cr
St. Regis
Silver
W Fork
St. Regis River
Silver Lake
E Fork
Big Cr
Hazel Lake
Ward Cr
Two Mile Cr
S Fork Little Joe Cr
Moore Lake
Torino Cr
Cliff Lake
Lost Lake
Bonanza Lakes
LEGEND
Paved Road
Unpaved Road
Campsite
Fishing Access Site
Rapid

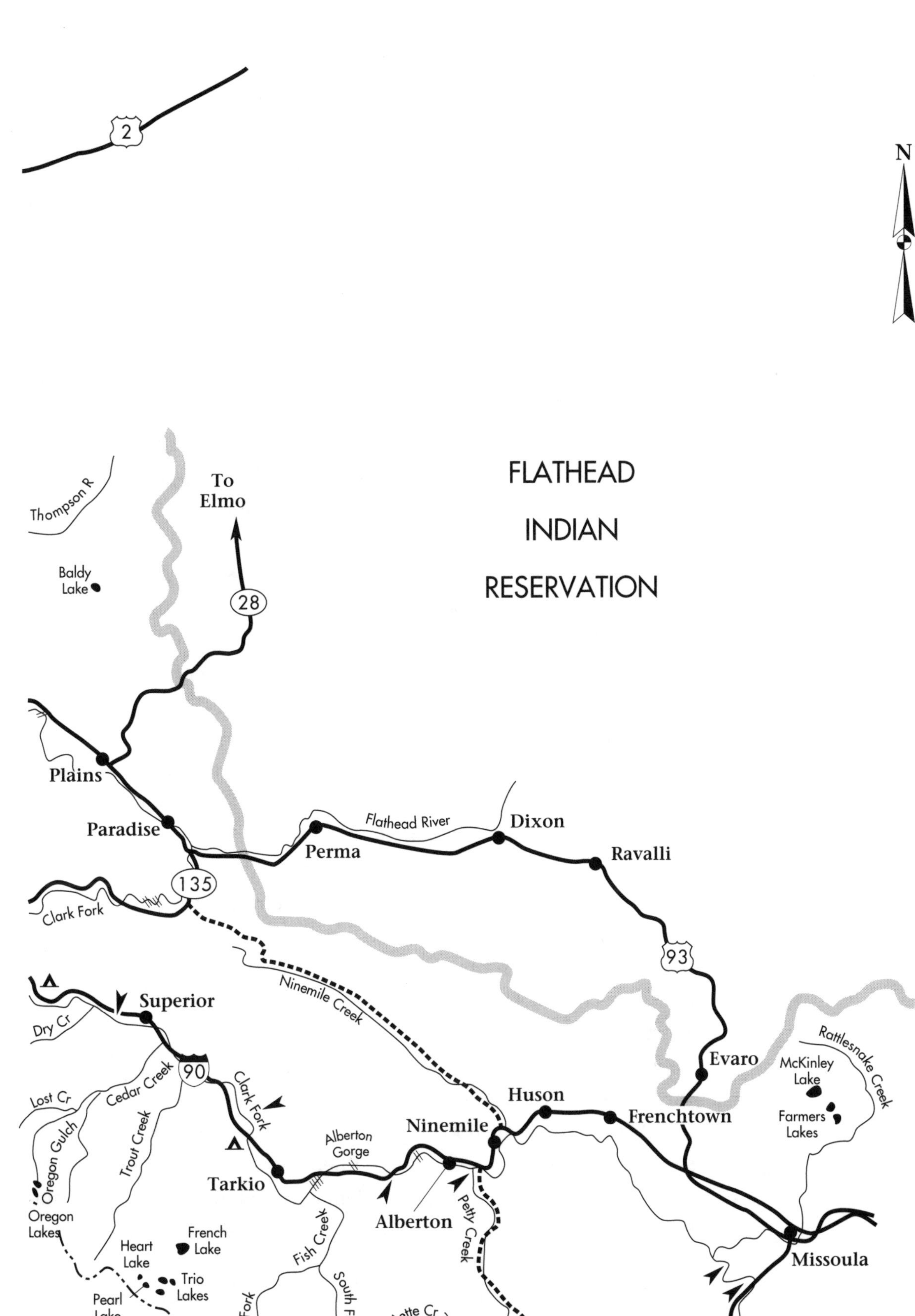
2
N
FLATHEAD
INDIAN
RESERVATION
To
Elmo
Thompson R
Baldy
Lake
28
Plains
Paradise
Perma
Flathead River
Dixon
Ravalli
135
Clark Fork
93
Superior
Dry Cr
Ninemile Creek
90
Clark Fork
Lost Cr
Cedar Creek
Oregon Gulch
Trout Creek
Oregon
Lakes
Tarkio
Alberton
Gorge
Ninemile
Huson
Frenchtown
Evaro
Rattlesnake Creek
McKinley
Lake
Farmers
Lakes
Alberton
Petty Creek
Fish Creek
French
Lake
Heart
Lake
Trio
Lakes
Pearl
Lake
Siamese
Lakes
West Fork
South Fork
Burdette Cr
Cedar Log Cr.
Cache Cr
Cedar Log
Lakes
Missoula
Bitterroot River
93
To
Hamilton

The river is a mix of short riffles with long, smooth runs and flats. Hit the banks with a big fly, maybe a greased Muddler on top, or a Woolly Bugger under the surface, and try to pull the browns out of the brush. At the flats, if fish are rising, you can wade and stalk individual trout, but if there are no insects on the water these areas are usually dead. In the deep, swift runs you either have to pull trout up with a big attractor, maybe a size 6 or 4 Outlaw Hopper, or find fish below with a large nymph, maybe a size 8 or 6 Casual Dress.

Kelly Island (the mouth of the Bitteroot) to Petty Creek—This section below Missoula is a mystery even to the Fish and Game biologists. It is big, rich water, but there are only about five hundred trout per mile in this part of the Clark Fork. No one really knows the reason for the low populations. Lack of spawning areas (with little recruitment from dewatered tributaries)? Not enough holding structure? Residual pollution? Too much competition from rough fish? One thing is for certain, the problems have nothing to do with the food supply. The insect hatches are predictable and spectacular and there is a great forage base of crawfish and minnows.

Five hundred trout per mile in a large river sounds dismal, but actually there are plenty of fish to cast to on a normal day. The rainbows and cutthroats, the predominant species down here, gather into pods. Pockets of feeding activity are scattered throughout the river. Thirty fish gulping here. Three hundred yards of lifeless water there. Then forty fat, 12- to 18-inch rainbows dimpling the surface below that gravel bar over along the far bank. And so on.

Many productive-looking pieces of water are poor fishing, while similar areas just downstream are filled with trout. Finding working fish is as much a part of the challenge as making quality presentations with effective flies. Many local anglers cruise the roads looking for rising fish before rigging up.

It helps immensely to know the hatches on this water. Often there'll be two or three major insects present at the same time and the fish will get real fussy. Typically the important species in this part of the river will also be important above Kelly Island and below Petty Creek.

There are midge hatches all winter and on nice days the pods gather on the slower flats and sip drifting pupae or adults. It takes small flies and fine tippets to consistently fool trout. The most practical approach is a "two-fly" method. Try a big, visible dry fly, like a Royal Wulff, combined with a size 18 or smaller matching pattern, a Griffith Gnat or a Halo Midge Pupa, on 18 inches of leader tied directly to the eye of the bigger fly. This is a lot more fun than going blind trying to pick out a tiny pattern in the flat, gray light so common in Montana winters.

Mid-March brings two fine stone fly hatches. The Skwala, better known on the Bitteroot River, is present in good numbers on the Clark Fork, also. There is an even more abundant hatch, the *Nemoura* stone. The emergence of this grayish-brown-bodied stone fly moves upstream four or five miles each day and the fishing is best in areas of peak abundance. The fickle spring weather can rain, snow, or blow out the fishing anytime, but local anglers wait for those warm but overcast days ideal for dry fly fishing.

Some early mayflies and caddisflies also trigger good rises of trout in the pre-runoff period. One abundant hatch is the early Red Quill mayfly, matched with a size 14 Red Quill or a Red Quill Parachute, the activity stretching out over parts of April and May. By mid-May the Blue-Wing Olive mayfly and the Grannom caddis bust out in great numbers and if the river doesn't rise and muddy with runoff the surface activity is wonderful.

The runoff period is generally poor fishing on the lower river. The diehard can flog away wth a Sparkle Bugger (tied with Krystal chenille) or a Zonker and find the occasional nice trout, but local fly fisherman usually wait until late June or early July for clear water and heavy hatches.

Paul Koller notes some of the important insects over the season:

Light Cahill (3 species) (includes *Heptagenia)*	July	Light Cahills in a variety of sizes
Spotted Sedge	most of the summer	Size 14 Brown and Yellow Diving Caddis and Emergent Sparkle Pupa
Pale Morning Dun	most of the summer	Size 18 Comparadun
Little Sister Sedge	most of the summer	Size 16 Elk Hair Caddis and Ginger Emergent Sparkle Pupa

Gray Drake	starts in July	Sizes 10–12 Adams
Trico	through August and September	Size 16 Double Spinner (two size 20 flies on a size 16 hook) and a size 18 Black Clear Wing Spinner
Callibaetis	late August and September	Sizes 14–16 Adams
Slate Wing	September	Size 14 Mahogany Thorax
Blue Wing Olive	late September through October	size 16 or size 18 Olive Comparadun or No-Hackle

There are a lot of little quirks on this tough river that are worth knowing. Streamer fishing? From late June through July the redside shiners spawn, the males of this minnow developing a bright band of red, and a red streamer outfishes any other color during this period. Best searching dry fly? The streamside willows on the Clark Fork get infested with small black beetles, the insects turning the leaves into lacework, and enough of these terrestrials fall into the river to make the trout responsive to a beetle imitation, a size-18 or size-20 Crowe Beetle or Black Mohawk.

Justin Baker, between guiding and fishing it, probably spends as much time as anyone on the Kelly Island to Petty Creek stretch. One morning, fishing in a party with Rich Anderson and Dave Inks, he caught eight rainbows and cutthroats over 16 inches—the best a 26-inch cutt on a Red Bunny streamer—all before the afternoon hatches started. He says about the summer months, "By August the middle of the day is not the best time to be on the water. One of the secrets is just staying out late, and fishing the last hour of light right into pitch black. The trout line up in current creases, the pods holding in the smooth water just under the surface and sipping insects. The fly has to be right

A Special Fly for the Lower Clark Fork

The Outlaw Hopper is the result of a lot of fishing. The creator, Powell Swanser, lives just below Turah next to the Clark Fork. Any attempt at imitation with this pattern is general, depending more on silhouette than colors to mimic downwing forms such as stone flies, caddisflies, and grasshoppers. It is a large, visible, and buoyant pattern, good characteristics for a big-fish surface fly anywhere.

OUTLAW HOPPER

Hook: 2X long dry fly

Extended Body: gray yarn (twisted)

Palmered Hackle: furnace (a low-quality, soft saddle hackle)

Body: high-density gray foam

Head and Collar: white deer hair

The lower river is big and powerful, swinging from side to side in a deep, dominating channel. For the most part, the shallow margins of the main river don't hold decent trout during the day unless there is a heavy hatch. The big fish, full-bodied cutthroats, rainbows, and browns from 13 to 26 inches, stay in the deeper slots.

What does it take to bring those fish up? Not any ordinary sized fly. The Outlaw Hopper is tied on a long shank hook. On the boiling, sucking undertows of the Clark Fork, the foam body keeps the fly bobbing like a cork. It looks like a substantial chunk of food. On many summer evenings it has racked up numbers of 15-inch-plus trout for Powell and his wife, Tazun, while other fishermen with smaller flies catch the little fish.

Float fishing is an effective way to cover the water on the lower Clark Fork.
Photo by Don Roberts

on the nose of a fish, in time with his feeding rhythm, and completely drag free. Even then it usually takes a number of perfect drifts to catch any particular trout."

All of this water is easy floating. There are no dangerous stretches before the Petty Creek access. A stiff upstream wind can make a long day of floating, stopping a boat dead on the slow-moving flats. That's when you have to row downstream.

Petty Creek to Forest Grove (Alberton Gorge)—From Alberton to Tarkio the quiet Clark Fork changes as it churns through Cyr Canyon for roughly twelve miles. This is a truly dangerous stretch for all but the most talented white-water rafters. There are standing waves and powerful whirlpools. There are five major rapids—Rest Stop, Shelf, Tumbleweed, Boat Eater, and Fang. Just looking at the river here is a bit frightening.

It is difficult to hike down into the canyon and once there it is impossible to walk far up or down the river. The only way to effectively fish the gorge is by floating it. Why bother? The gorge has incredible habitat. Fish, Wildlife, and Parks Department biologists say that this is the only section of the lower river with high numbers of trout per mile. Many of those trout, with prime holding spots, abundant food supply, and virtually no fishing pressure, are trophy specimens.

Fly fishing outfitter Mark Jones describes fishing the gorge: "We don't start floating it until late July. There's a lot more fishable water then. Also, everyone in the boat is going to get drenched by the waves, so we only go down in warm weather. This is legitimate Class IV white water. We use at least thirteen-foot rafts.

"We stop and fish, concentrating on the tail end of the rapids. Techniques vary from slinging big, weighted nymphs, a Kaufmann Stone, or a Sioux Falls Stonefly, to laying out small, matching dry flies, especially when the Tricos start coming off in late July."

One of the best ways to catch a trophy fish here is to throw streamers with a sinking line. Woolly Buggers, Hornbergs, and Matukas are good, but the best fly, imitating a major food item, is a crayfish imitation. The largest trout jump a pattern such as a Bugskin Crawfish.

The water at the bottom of the gorge is a short transition zone between fast and slow sections. The walking angler can find some fine hatches here, including a great Skwala flight (and, according to Dean Ludwig, there is no one down here in March).

Forest Grove to Paradise—The fish populations get spotty again once the river leaves Alberton Gorge. And this section is even wider and flatter, with more space for the trout to spread out in, than other parts. The bonus is that the fish—rainbow, brown, and cutthroat trout—run a bit larger here.

Salmon flies show in late May and last through June, but this is often a period of high water. Dark Woolly Buggers retrieved slowly or drifted near the shoreline imitate the behavior of migrating nymphs and often take trout in turbid conditions. By midsummer, and clear water, the best flies for the flats are the exacting imitations, but on the riffles Wulffs or Trudes, approximating the shape, size, and color of the naturals, are good plays. They are easy to see for both the angler and the trout. Summer is also a great time to blast hoppers noisily to the banks.

Paradise to Thompson Falls—From Paradise to the mouth of the Thompson River is warmer and still larger water due to the entrance of the Flathead River. There is some difficult, pounding water west of Plains known as the Plains Rapids, but most of the river is long, deep runs and large pools. Browns and rainbows grow well here, feeding on sculpins and other forage fish, but imitating these species by working streamers with sinking lines is hard, often unproductive work. Popular patterns include Matukas, Spruce Flies, Buggers, and Marabou Muddlers in sizes from 1/0 to 4.

Northern pike over twenty pounds are found in this area. Red and white, 2/0 streamers draw the northerns and also some of the best trout. Ten-foot sink-tip lines and seven-weight rods (at least) are required. Even largemouth bass are taken, usually unintentionally, by anglers swimming large patterns.

Thompson Falls to Idaho—From Thompson Falls into Idaho the river is a series of impoundments. In the running water between the lakes there are, aside from largemouth bass, smallmouth bass, crappie, northern pike, and yellow perch, some brown, rainbow, and bull trout. The browns provide some elusive but highly fascinating fishing as they move up into their spawning tributaries each autumn. Finding these big fish is, if anything, more hunting than fishing, and often the fall rains turn the streams muddy and unfishable.

Some of the state fishing access sites along the Clark Fork working downstream include Erskine, Petty Creek, Forest Grove, and Flat Iron Ridge. Forest Service camping areas are Quartz Flats, Trout Creek, Sloway, and Cascade.

One of the pleasures of fly fishing is taking trout from peculiar and difficult water. For most of us the Clark Fork qualifies on both counts. But by either floating on your own or with a guide, or by just wading and casting to working fish, there is a definite possibility of a good day's action for some of the healthiest, hardest fighting trout anywhere.

POPULAR FLIES

Adams
Black Mohawk
Bugskin Crawfish
Casual Dress
Clear Wing Spinner
Comparadun
Crowe Beetle
Diving Caddis
Double Spinner
Elk Hair Caddis
Emergent Sparkle Pupa
Hornberg
Kaufmann Stone
Light Cahill
Mahogany Thorax
Marabou Muddler
Matuka
Outlaw Hopper
Red Quill
Red Quill Parachute
Spruce Fly
Trude
Woolly Bugger
Wulff

Fishing Waters in the Lower Clark Fork Drainage

Acorn Lake: Not bad fishing, but you have to be willing to go through some tough country up from the Eddy Creek Road. The trout are not very big, so handle the 10-inch cutthroats with care if they are going to be released.

Arrowhead Lake: In the Thompson River drainage at the head of Big Spruce Creek, Arrowhead is only 12 acres, but it's fairly deep and has holdover cutthroats. The population is augmented with helicopter plantings every few years, and the number of trout can vary widely over the seasons. This is a lake where it's smart to call the Fish, Wildlife, and Parks Department and check the current status of the fishery before hiking into it.

Baldy Lake: Surprisingly, this 15-acre lake is not far from Mt. Baldy, about 7 miles west of Hot Springs, and 2 miles by trail from the McGinnis Creek Road. It also receives periodic plantings of cutthroats, which grow to maybe 12 inches, and it also has its up-years and down-years.

Beaver Creek: Beaver Creek begins when Big Beaver Creek and Little Beaver Creek join and runs for 8 miles before dumping into Noxon Reservoir. It has small rainbows, cutthroats, and brookies, in roughly that order as fulltime residents, and some big browns move up into this creek in the autumn.

When searching for eager cutthroats, always look to the upper, colder, and cleaner reaches of a stream. Cutts are delightful fish worthy of respect and capable of creating wonder in an angler when observed in their native, wild alpine waters.

As streams warm and silt up the environment becomes despoiled so much that cutthroats are unable to survive. Nothing but the best for this fragile species. And there are not enough pure waters left for them.

Big Beaver Creek: Followed by roads, this creek is popular with area anglers for cutthroats (see Beaver Creek diatribe) in the upper reaches, brookies in some beaver ponds, and rainbows in the bottom runs. Access, with a gravel road following the stream, is good from the flat land all the way up to the canyon headwaters.

Bonanza Lakes: Two lakes lie a stone's throw apart in the Bitterroot Range west of Superior. One lake is 10 acres; the other lake is just short of 20 acres. They are both filled with small brookies willing to jump on almost any fly.

Bull River: There are more than 20 miles of this locally popular stream. Anglers like it for the easy access off a good road and for consistent catches of 10- to 14-inch rainbow, cutthroat, brook, and bull trout. There are also whitefish and, at certain times of the year, brown trout in the river.

The Bull River empties into the Clark Fork at Noxon Reservoir and this makes the water interesting from late October into November. A couple of hundred large browns run up out of the lake to spawn. These are big, wary fish, with all the fickleness of moving fish in an unfamiliar environment, and the problems are finding them and catching them.

Chris Hess reports, "Everything depends on the fall rains. The watershed has been clearcut so much that any steady precipitation turns the river into a muddy torrent. Still, there has to be some rain before the fish will come up out of the lake.

"I'll go out two or three days after a rain, when the water has cleared, and drive the road. I'll stop at various spots, especially the pools just above any long riffle, and look for fish and even make a few casts.

"These are brown trout and they're not going to be sitting out in the open in the bright sun. The best times to fish for them are early in the morning, late in the evening, or on overcast days. My favorite fly is a weighted Egg-Sucking Leech, or something similarly nasty, but there's no need for sinking lines in a small river like the Bull. I use a weight-forward, floating, 8-weight line, with a 3-foot leader with no smaller than 1X for the tippet. Even with that, I still get broken off.

"This is chancy fishing. I've probably been skunked as many days as not, even though I know the good spots and the fishing techniques. The good part is that once I find the trout, there will be a bunch of them and they'll all be big, averaging four pounds and running well over ten pounds My best spurt was four fish—six pounds, three ounces; six pounds,twelve ounces; nine pounds, four ounces; ten pounds, one ounce—caught and released in less than two hours."

For the angler unwilling to hunt those elusive autumn trout, there is more consistent fishing in May, before the runoff. Some people even float the river during this period. There always seem to be nice browns, not the biggest ones, but fish up to 20 inches, that stay in the river after spawning. After a winter there they are acclimated to the environment and feed and act like residents. They don't leave for the lake until early summer.

Burdette Creek: Cutthroats to 10 inches. Burdette, up in the Fish Creek drainage, is a fine little stream for beaver pond lovers.

Cabin Lake: An easy hike, 1 mile from the West Fork of Thompson River road, makes this a popular spot. It's a beautiful little lake, about 20 acres at 7,000 feet, and good fishing for 8- to 12-inch cutthroats. The trout used to average a little larger, but the angling pressure has cropped the numbers of nicer fish.

Cabinet Gorge Reservoir: Twelve miles long and extending into Idaho, Cabinet Gorge is a wide, dammed spot on the Clark Fork that has brown, rainbow, and bull trout, plus large and smallmouth bass, kokanee salmon, yellow perch, crappie, northern pike, and trash fish. This place is a real zoo used by water-sports enthusiasts of all kinds during the summer months, but there are some big fish here. The head of the reservoir is the best bet for the browns, except in late summer when these fish begin heading towards the creek mouths preparatory to spawn.

Cache Creek: The fun part of this stream in the Fish Creek drainage is that the angler can drive the South Fork Fish Creek road to the mouth and then hike up it by good trail for 9 miles. Anyone with a bit of ambition is going to have a lot of water all to himself after a few miles.

Hobie Roberts scouted this one, writing, "There are plenty of rainbows and cutthroats, 8 to 11 inches. My best fish was a 13-inch cutthroat. I worked upstream, getting bigger trout whenever I found deeper, slower water. I mostly used a size-14 Mosquito, but the fish were looking to the surface for anything edible."

Cataract Creek: Fast fishing for small cutthroats, 6 to 9 inches, for the angler tough enough to reach them. Cataract tumbles down from Seven Point Mountain, entering a gorge in its last 5 miles. There are, of course, plenty of deep pools within this crashing water.

Cedar Log Lakes: In hard-to-reach country, these lakes are snugged up against the Idaho border, up in the headwaters of the Fish Creek country (use a good topo map to follow the USFS trail). East Cedar is 44 acres and West Cedar is 14 acres. Both are good fishing for cutthroats that run up to 14 inches. The trout in both lakes, when they aren't rising to surface food, relish olive scud imitations retrieved steadily along the drop-offs.

Cirque (Upper Wanless) Lakes: North of Noxon Reservoir in glaciated country, these four lakes are reached by a 6-mile trail. They all have good populations of cutthroats up to 14 inches. Cirque Lakes number one and number two are planted every now and then with supplementary stockings of small cutts.

Cliff Lake: Cutthroats, including some nice ones. Just the sight of the aquatic vegetation at the outlet tells the angler that this is a fertile (and therefore not always easy) lake. It's in the Dry Creek drainage, which enters the Clark Fork a few miles northwest of Superior.

Duckhead Lake: In the backcountry of the West Fork Thompson River country (3½ miles by trail up Honeymoon Creek), Duckhead is good fishing for cutthroats that average 12 inches. There are larger trout, too, but they hang along the drop-offs of this deep, more than a quarter-mile-long lake.

Bruce Moore consistently catches 16- to 22-inch cutthroats. He uses a sinking, 20-foot shooting head, and two streamer patterns on a 6-foot leader. He ties the 2 feet of extra monofiliment right to the eye of the primary streamer's hook, eliminating any tangles, and trails the second streamer right behind the first.

Bruce positions his float tube parallel to the drop-off. He believes that imitation is important with streamers in not only Duckhead but other high mountain lakes. "My favorite fly is a Baby Cutt streamer, sizes 2 to 10, exact right down to the parr marks," he said. "A small cutthroat, coming out of the shallows, has to look like a fool to any larger fish holding in deep water. Two of them, in a chase, have to look even more vulnerable. A basic rule in nature is that anything foolish doesn't live long."

East Fork Bull River: Not all that big, and tough to fish. There's so much brush crowding the banks that unless you have a good, tight roll cast, you're not going to be able to effectively present a fly. There are tiny cutthroats (10 inches is a monster), some bull trout, and a very few large brown trout up from Noxon Reservoir to spawn. A Yellow Marabou Muddler fished in the deeper holes and darker crannies always seems to produce a few surprising moments here.

East Fork Rock Creek: Perhaps 4 miles of fishable water from where it comes out of Rock Lake, it has a fine population of 6- to 10-inch cutthroats that are fools for a dry fly of almost any type and size. The special parts of this stream are the deep and beautiful pools in the lower 2½ miles.

Elk (or Sims) Lake: In this fertile lake the regularly planted cutthroats grow to a pound or more without much trouble. This 7-acre pond lies 2 miles north of the Vermilion River Road off the Sims Creek jeep trail. Because of the abundance of food, these fish are often selective (for cutthroats, that is).

This is one of those waters that separates the real still water anglers from the floggers. It's probably best to use those imitations designed specifically for lakes, matching the items that dominate the food base.

The basic fact is that Elk Lake trout are never desperately hungry. They browse instead of hunt. During one of the major hatches, such as the *Callibaetis* mayfly of summer and early fall, these fish pick off flies that look and act like the nymph, and a Cates Turkey or Timberline Emerger (proven flies here) in proper size and color is going to catch a lot more fish than a randomly retrieved Woolly Worm.

Farmer's Lakes: There are two of them, well up the Rattlesnake Creek drainage above Missoula. Located below Stuart Peak, both of these lakes have some cutthroats in them. You won't be alone here. Politically correct yupsters from town roam here flinging frisbees and lifestyle dogma in the mountain air. The Rattlesnake area is extremely popular with Missoula backpackers, mountain bikers, and other travelers.

Fish Creek: Think of this stream as a slightly smaller version of Rock Creek. It is a rugged and beautiful watershed, one of the best places to glimpse wildlife. You might surprise a moose, mountain lion, or black bear (animals seen on one trip in the summer of 1993).

Fish Creek flows into the Clark Fork near Tarkio, entering the Alberton Gorge section of the river. The lower 8 miles run mostly through a steep canyon, accesible only by foot trail. This is rough water, but large pools hold the trout. In late May, right after the season opens, there are still big rainbows here, to five pounds, that come up from the river to spawn in the canyon stretch. Large, weighted flies, such as the Bitch Creek, or Montana Stone nymphs or Marabou Muddler or Dark Spruce streamers, take these fish.

The upper 7 miles are followed by a good

Fish Creek
Photo by Don Roberts

logging road. This is popular water, but good fishing in spite of the pressure for mainly rainbows, cutthroats, and brookies. The insect hatches are so diverse, with different kinds of stone flies, mayflies, and caddisflies on the water all the time, that the trout rarely get selective. They will generally take an upwing Wulff or a downwing Stimulator, or a Bead Head Peacock or a Cased Caddis Larva nymph, as well as anything. Most of the fish (except for some large bull trout) measure under 16 inches, but they are willing feeders in this bouncing stream. It splits into North and South Forks above Clearwater crossing.

Fishtrap Creek: This pretty, pine forest stream, tributary to the Thompson, is followed by a logging road for its entire length into the Cabinet Mountains. The cutts, brookies, and rainbows do not grow big here (although a few nice rainbows move up in the spring before the general season opens just to drive you nuts).

Fishtrap Lake: Mostly cutthroats, up to 14 inches. Skip the real deep water at the lower end. The bulk of the food (and the trout) are at the shallow, upper end of this 35-acre lake. Take the Thompson River Road past the Bend Ranger Station then about 11 miles up the Lazier Creek road.

French Lake: Fourteen acres in cirque country, French Lake nestles well back in the Fish Creek drainage. The cutthroat are small, with a few foot-and-a-half exceptions. This lake is good all-purpose Olive Nymph or Hare's Ear Nymph turf. Cast these flies far out on a floating line. Let them sink slowly and then begin a very slow, halting retrieve. The trout will find this hard to resist. If they do, lob large Olive Woolly Worms at them. If this fails, light a cigar and drink a beer.

Graves Creek: A Clark Fork tributary, Graves is small and heavily fished by Thompson Falls anglers for rainbows and a smattering of everything else. Most of the trout are in the 8- to 12-inch range.

Heart Lake: Heart Lake is in the headwaters of the South Fork of Trout Creek (Superior). You reach it by 3 miles of trail from the South

Fork Road. There are 60 acres of water full of brook trout, mostly 8 to 10 inches, with the occasional big one. Classic eastern wet flies, bright patterns such as the Trout Fin, are specifically effective here (And why not? They have been proven brookie killers for over a hundred years). Fish them two or three at a time on a dropper rig.

Lawn Lake: In the Graves Creek drainage, and not famous for its fishing, Lawn nonetheless receives sporadic helicopter plants of cutthroat trout that offer fair sport.

Little McGregor Lake: Just north of U.S. 2 with public access, Little McGregor is less than 100 acres with good numbers of brookies, some rainbows, yellow perch, and largemouth bass. The brook trout reach weights of a pound or two.

Little Thompson River: From timbered mountains in the east, this stream rolls through grazing country in its midsection and down a steep gorge in its bottom part, then flows into the Thompson River. It sees a good deal of action for small cutthroats, rainbows (the big ones are gone by opening day), brookies, mountain whitefish, and modest-sized bull trout.

Lost Lake: We found it. This is one of several brook trout waters in the land cooked by the great fires of 1910. The brookies are somewhat stunted but willing takers of dry flies, wet flies, nymphs and small streamers.

Tim Forbes, who fishes this water frequently, says, "I use a size 8 Mickey Finn strictly to keep the smaller fish off the hook."

Lowell Lake: Deep and fairly large for a cirque in the Cabinet Mountain country, Llowell is periodically planted with westslope cutthroats by helicopter. The fish do well. Lowell is reached from the end of the North Fork Bull River trail in steep, rugged, and uncrowded country.

Lower Thompson Lake: Just to the south of U.S. 2 between Kalispell and Libby, Lower Thompson covers 240 acres and is more than 140 feet deep. It is managed extensively for kokanee salmon and rainbows. Also, brown trout are planted here and, since there is plenty to eat, they grow quite large. The fly fisherman who tries big, perch-colored streamers along the shore and near the inlets in the fall might be surprised by the quality of the brown trout angling.

The attraction for the fanatic bass fisherman is the fine summer fly fishing. There really is no slump once the water warms enough—from late June until early fall this is a great top-water lake. The best area is at the inlet, with its long shallows and wide bays, or along the shorelines. The 12- to 15-inch largemouths hit the surface well in the clear water.

Favorite flies? A Sneaky Pete, a cork bug with rubber legs and a bullet front, fished with hard strips to make the fly dive in a shallow swim. The bass hit it on the pauses between the strips. Or a weighted Dahlberg Diver, a deeper running fly with a deer hair lip, worked with a sink-tip to make this pattern wobble over the bottom.

McGregor Lake: Over two square miles in surface area, McGregor lies right next to U.S. 2 midway between Libby and Kalispell. There are summer homes and resorts, plus plenty of boat traffic on this lake. Some large Mackinaw (lake trout) are caught with streamers in the spring and fall. There are also lots of rainbows and some cutthroat and brook trout. After ice-out this is not all that bad a place to cast a streamer, especially around the inlets. Also, in the early season, focus on Mackinaw Point. A bar runs across the lake here, concentrating the gamefish in reasonably shallow water.

Middle Thompson Lake: Almost a square mile in area and right by U.S. 2, Middle Thompson has plenty of summer homes. This lake is planted regularly with rainbow and brown trout that do well. There are also kokanee salmon, cutthroats, and maybe a big lake trout or two, and populations of yellow perch, northern pike, and largemouth bass.

A number of small creeks run into the lake and they are prime locations for rainbows early in the year and for browns (especially around Davis Creek and Tallulah Creek) in the fall. Streamers that look like small perch may pick off any of the predators from a bass to a marauding northern.

Mike Ashley writes, "The bass run as large as six pounds, but the average size is one to three pounds. Middle Thompson has the best boat access of the Thompson chain of lakes, and as a result is the most popular. It starts fishing well in June, when largemouths are staging to spawn. By July and August the surface bugging is at its peak. The best places are on the ends, both shallower than the middle."

Moore Lake: A 13-acre mountain lake, you get to Moore by logging road up the South Fork of Little Joe Creek west of St. Regis. This lake is fairly fertile, with deep water in the middle and aquatic weeds around the edges. An excellent population of brook trout, including a few in the 15-inch range, cruise the shoreline, hunting the vegetation.

These aren't dumb, hungry brookies. Good matching flies, especially a Green Damsel Nymph or a Flashback Scud, take the best fish when nothing is on the surface. The damsel hatch, lasting through June and July some years, is highlight time on this water.

Moran Basin Lakes: The lower water is barren, but the upper, 14-acre lake, in the East Fork Bull River drainage, has lots of westslope cutthroats that are usually hungry.

Ninemile Creek: About 25 miles west of Missoula, this stream used to be excellent fishing for cutthroats, along with big rainbow and bull trout up from the main river. The lower 3 miles of Ninemile, which should be prime spawning habitat, is hammered by sedimentation from flood irrigation return flows. The Soil Conservation Service is working on a project to recover this stretch.

By the early seventies you could tell the fishing was going to hell—an inverse correlation between the number of homes and the number of trout. Now a movie actress has purchased a large ranch towards the head of the valley, so the country must be really shot. The tiny feeder creeks also used to be great fishing, especially for spring spawners (after the opening of the general season, of course). Most of the access is gone to private landowners. There were elk and black bear here, too, with big elk in the high timber and lots of ducks on the beaver ponds. Some wolves tried to establish a home, but they were shot. Get the picture? Sometimes if you look at things too hard, you get a damn, hollow feeling in your gut. Say hi to the "starlet" for me if you wander up that way.

Noxon Reservoir: Lying behind Noxon Rapids Dam, the reservoir is about 38 miles long by a half mile wide, U.S. 10A follows it on one side and county roads flank the other side. This lake needs to be fished from a boat unless you are of the "heavily-weighted-dough-ball" school of fishing made famous on the Rock River in Beloit, Wisconsin Everything has been planted here from burbot to brown trout to kokanee

John Chisholm cradles a Noxon Reservoir brown trout.
Photo by John Chisholm

salmon to smallmouth bass to rainbow trout to largemouth bass. There are also northern pike and yellow perch. If you must fish this water, try the upper end or near the mouths of the many creeks pouring into the reservoir. Try fall for the browns and spring for the rainbows. The smallmouth fishing sounds as good as anything.

Oregon Lakes: These three brook trout lakes are in the headwaters of Cedar Creek near the Idaho State Line west of Superior. The lakes range in size from 3 to 27 acres and the fish run around 8 inches.

Pearl Lake: Fourteen acres in the Trout Creek (Superior) drainage,

Pearl lies at 5,000 feet. It was stocked regularly with cutthroats in the past and it is still decent fishing for 10- to 12-inch fish.

Petty Creek: This used to be a pleasant little mountain and meadow stream to fish for small brookies and cutthroats, but subdividers have ruined the country and access is marginal at best. The lower end goes underground for the last quarter mile during low water years. A few large trout sneak up the creek a little ways in spring and fall, but that's about all the action for the remainder of my lifetime.

Pilgrim Creek: One of the tributaries to Noxon Reservoir, Pilgrim Creek has a small run of large brown trout. If you chase these and are lucky enough to connect, enjoy the fight, let the trout go and leave the rest in peace. Greed on a trout stream is obscene. There are also resident brook, cutthroat, and rainbow trout in this meadowland stream. Access is limited.

Poacher (Tuffy) Lake: Located west of Tarkio, Poacher is periodically planted from the air with cutthroats that provide nice fishing for average trout.

Prospect Creek: Across the river from Thompson Falls, it flows over 20 miles of water offering rainbow, bull, and brook trout in the lower reaches and cutthroats above. Once in a while a good brown cruises upstream. Fish streamers for the brown and bull trout and attractor dry flies for everything else.

Rattlesnake Creek
Photo courtesy of USDA–Forest Service

Rattlesnake Creek: A Clark Fork tributary entering the river right in Missoula, Rattlesnake provides much of the city's water supply. From the mouth of the stream up to the Mountain Water Company Dam, roughly 6 miles, the creek is very good for rainbows and cutthroats up to 14 inches. This is fun water to cover with a Royal Wulff or a Renegade. The 7 miles from the dam up to Beeskove Creek, along with all of the tributaries in this section, are permanently closed to angling. Above Beeskove fishing is catch-

and-release only with artificial lures.

The upper water, above Beeskove, offers prime fly fishing. Fish, Wildlife, and Parks Department personnel, snorkeling the stream, found many 16- to 17-inch trout, and one 26-inch, brood cutthroat female. Sculpin minnows are an important food source, and even though it may feel odd fishing a large streamer in such a small creek, this approach is effective up here. In this pure, cold water there are abundant populations of stone fly nymphs, and a Bitch Creek or a Natural Drift Stonefly Nymph always makes a good searching fly. Bright dry flies during the middle of the day, and hatch-matching dry flies in the evening, catch more but smaller fish. This entire upper watershed is some of the best bear and elk country in Montana.

Rock Creek: Followed by logging road from its mouth north of the Noxon Dam, Rock Creek is fished a lot by locals for 6- to 10-inch cutthroats and lesser numbers of other species.

Rock Creek Lake (or simply Rock Lake): Cutthroats—some of them very large (over 20 inches) and difficult to catch cutthroats. This mystery lake, just below Rock Peak and 3 miles off the East Fork

A gentle release on Rock Creek
Photo by Don Roberts

of Rock Creek road, is on my "must see" list for some future summer.

St. Paul Lake: A high, above-timberline cirque lake reached by trail from the end of the East Fork Bull River road. It is planted now and then with cutthroats and they grow to better than 12 inches. Like most of these small, deep lakes the trout concentrate around the lake edges and are easy to find.

St. Regis River: A nice little stream from a scenic perspective. the St. Regis runs along I-90 from the headwaters near the Idaho border at Lookout Pass down to the Clark Fork. The fishing isn't much, with the catch consisting of modest numbers of cutthroats and brookies. There are some bigger fish up from the main river in the lower stretch. Mining, logging, and highway construction, to name a few problems, destroyed much of the riparian habitat of the St. Regis, though this is slowly recovering. Give the stream fifty years or so and it may be a top-notch piece of water.

Siamese Lakes: Both are about 30 acres and deep. They are reached by 13 miles of trail up the West Fork of Fish Creek. The fishing is good enough for 9- to 11-inch rainbows and cutthroats for the lakes to receive a lot of pressure from July until the snow flies.

The way to avoid the crowds here is to, in Trip Payne's words, "Get up there early. Sometimes that means hiking through lingering snow drifts in June, but the closer to ice-out the better the fishing, especially on Lower Siamese. On Lower Siamese the biggest concentrations of trout are along the cliffs during most of the summer, but in spring and fall they are on the shallow shoreline, and more accessible to a fly fisherman."

Silver Lake: Reached by jeep road, Silver Lake lies near the Idaho border a few miles south of Saltese. It is deep enough to avoid winterkill, so there is a stable population of 8- to 10-inch brook trout. They are free-rising little buggers, working the shallows at the lower end, and they take dry flies well every evening.

Stony Lake: In the Fishtrap drainage, Stony is not very deep, but a few springs save the cutthroats during the winter. It is reached by poor road, so it gets hit by locals and visitors with nearly equal intensity. Fortunately, it is planted once in awhile.

Swamp Creek: Not bad action early in the season for rainbows up from the Clark Fork. Browns move up in the fall and cutthroats hang out all year. Timing is important for finding the good fish here. This stream is a few miles west of Plains, easily accessible all the way by road.

Terrace Lake: These lakes, like many mountain lake, has a naturally reproducing population. But even on these backcountry waters rough winters and excessive angler pressure often decimate trout populations, so stocking is needed to maintain the alpine fishery. Terrace is planted every couple of years with cutthroats and they average about a foot with a few bigger. You'll find it about a mile from the end of the road on the West Fork of Fishtrap Creek.

Bruce Moore, a real backpacker who stalks the highcountry most of the summer, hunts the larger trout around the tangles of drowned logs in the bays. He writes, "This is sight fishing for me. I'm letting a nymph, usually a Muskrat or a Kelso in a size 10, sink just above the wood, and then I'm retrieving with a slow hand twist, keeping the fly at that level. The cutts come out of the shadows to grab the nymph."

Thompson River: The Thompson flows from Lower Thompson Lake for over 50 miles to the Clark Fork above Thompson Falls. Followed on both sides by the most confusing, braided network of logging roads found in the Northwest. The river is excellent, though according to Hugh Spencer of Spencer's Hackles in Plains, the increased levels of sediment from logging are having a deleterious effect on the numbers of large rainbows. From December to the general season opener in May the water is catch and release only.

Up above the stream is characterized by riffles and pools, but as you move downstream there are deep runs, large pools, small cascades, and rapids cutting through igneous rock shelves. With some planning and caution, wading is not difficult, although chest waders are advised.

The middle section, roughly 20 miles long, starts holding larger trout. Rainbows up to three pounds will rise freely during the best hatches. This rich little river has a fine emergence of Green Drakes and Brown Drakes, for example, and anglers ready with flies such as the Paradrake or the Mess take the best and fussiest trout.

In early May the Grannom caddis appears in good numbers. A good population of salmon flies hatches from mid-May through June, bringing the hefty rainbows to life. During the summer months cad-

Western Montana largemouth bass
Photo by John Chisholm

dis imitations, especially brown wing and rusty yellow body variations in sizes 14 and 16, to match the Spotted Sedge, consistently produce. Some Gray Drakes show up in August and last into fall, along with Tricos and Baetis.

Among terrestrial insects, there are usually grasshoppers around, but in some years the major news is the Spruce Moth. This chunky, size-10 or -12 bug lands on the water, gets trapped and struggles feebly. Even a few of them attract attention, but when the population cycle is high and moths are landing on the stream by the thousands, the trout focus on nothing else. A good imitation, such as a Spruce Moth, is critical.

Stone fly nymphs are consistently effective searchers, but you'll need weight and a sink-tip line to reach the fish in the deepest, heaviest waters. Those fish will include a good number of eager mountain whitefish to maybe two pounds. They love to roll and twist up your tippet, but they mean well.

There are also brookies and cutthroats in smaller numbers and size. Beginning in August, big browns and bulls (to several pounds) up from the Clark Fork can provide excitement on streamers. Almost any pattern works if stripped and wriggled through the current seams and between the rocks, but I prefer an Olive Woolly Bugger, size 2, weighted at the head, fished with a floating line, a 6-foot leader tapered to 2X, and attached with a Duncan Loop for better swimming action. Buggers always work anywhere trout swim and I've developed a strong (unhealthy?) attachment to the pattern.

Triangle Pond: This borrow pit 3 miles southwest of Noxon is planted with 7- to 9-inch cutthroats, which grow nicely, along with some big brood stock. This is a good place to fish early in the season, right after opening day, when the streams and rivers are high and muddy with runoff. At times Triangle is reminiscent of the fee ponds in the Midwest, with all the anglers of various persuasions, only this one is free.

Trio Lakes: You can reach the trail head from the end of South Fork Trout Creek road. Then there's several miles of tough hiking up to three lakes that offer brookies, rainbows, and ever-increasing numbers of cutthroats and rainbow-cutthroat hybrids that may reach 15 inches or so. Not many people come here, or could find the place even if they wanted to. This topo-map country for sure.

Trout Creek: This is a very popular stream near Superior for spunky cutthroats and some rainbows. Logging is beginning to hurt the drainage. Mining already has damaged the stream in the lower reaches, although this is ever so slowly flushing itself out and on down to the river. Caddis patterns are popular here (the Elk Hair and Goddard rank one and two), mainly because there always seem to be fine evening hatches. In the lower water, near the Clark Fork, some good bull trout and fair numbers of whitefish show up.

Trout Creek (Noxon Reservoir): This small, brushy stream bounces through a canyon. Local anglers work it over for rainbows, brookies, and cutthroats. A few fat browns sneak up here in the fall, but not in sufficient numbers to warrant a concerted angling effort.

Twelvemile Creek: Obviously there's twelve miles of it, followed by logging road west of St. Regis and crossed at the mouth by I-90. It is average fishing for cutthroats and rainbows, with a small helping of browns and some whitefish tossed in for variety.

Upper Thompson Lake: Another one of the numerous large lakes lying right next to U.S. 2 between Libby and Kalispell (and the shallowest in the Thompson chain). It doesn't get hit hard because boating access is poor, but this just makes it a great float tubing spot. There are largemouth bass, yellow perch, and nothern pike in this 230-acre lake, along with cutthroats and a few other trout.

This is not the best of the trout lakes in this area, but it's full of willing warmwater fish. There are extensive shallows between two deeper basins, and this middle band of Upper Thompson gives up bass all summer long (including eight largemouths between two and four pounds on a Purple Leech one July evening).

Vermilion River: Followed by road for its 25 miles through a couple of deep gorges and timbered hills. Mining and some logging have speeded up the rate of water delivery during runoff and rainstorms raise havoc with the streambed. Insects and habitat are regularly washed away. Cutthroat, rainbow, brook, and bull trout provide marginal action. The scrubbing of the stream gravels has attracted the attention of the Noxon Reservoir browns. Maybe a hundred or so of the big boys swagger upstream to reproduce each fall. Finding them, as always, is tough.

Wanless Lake: Deep and big water, Wanless Lake covers120 acres at the end of a spectacular glacial cirque up Swamp Creek from Noxon

Reservoir. It was originally planted with Yellowstone cutthroats, years ago, but it is being turned into a westslope water now. It produces a lot of trout up to 16 inches. It's on the same trail as the Cirque Lakes, sitting about 1 mile below them. Wanless is proof that anglers use and love (maybe too much) our high country.

West Fork Thompson River: Not a lot of water to work here, but it's still heavily fished for small brookies and cutthroats (plus some bull trout on the spawning move in late summer and fall). A good road running alongside it makes it easy to hit anywhere.

West Fork Trout Creek (Noxon Reservoir): If you don't mind walking from the end of the Trout Creek Road, this is a pretty stream to try for cutthroats and brookies up to 14 inches. This is nice country that is dying an ugly death from the bite of the chainsaw. Hike the stream, use the campsites, and release the fish.

Other Waters

Albert Creek: Cutthroats. This stream still hasn't fully recovered, more than thirty years later, from heavy logging in the drainage.

Ashley Creek: Too small.

Beatrice Creek: Bull trout and cutthroats.

Beeskove Creek: Too small.

Big Creek: Brookies and cutthroats. This is a tributary of the St. Regis, entering the river a couple miles from DeBorgia. It's 3 miles of brush-beating fun for 6- to 9-inch trout for the type of anglers who enjoy small waters.

Big Lake: Malnourished rainbows in this Rattlesnake system lake.

Big Rock Creek: Brookies and cutthroats.

Blossom Lakes: Brookies.

Blue Creek: No access.

Boiling Spring Creek: Brookies.

Buck Lake: Cutthroats.

Butler Creek: Cutthroats and rainbows.

Canyon Creek: Too small.

Carters Lake: Poor fishing for rainbows.

Cedar Creek: Enters the Clark Fork near Superior. There's a full house of trout species—cutthroat, rainbow, brown, brook, and bull—in this small stream, especially in the canyon section above the mouth.

Cedar Log Creek: Cutthroats.

Cement Gulch: Too small.

Cherry Creek: Brookies and cutthroats.

Chippewa Creek: Very small, but the last mile, before it enters the South Fork Bull River, has enough 6- to 10-inch cutthroats to make an interesting few hours.

Chippy Creek: Too small.

Clear Creek: Brookies and cutthroats. There are some nice holes in this tributary of Prospect Creek.

Clear Lake: Brookies.

Combpest Creek: Too small.

Cooper Gulch: Cutthroats.

Copper (Silvex) Lake: Cutthroats in a 6-acre, muddy lake near Lookout Pass.

Corona Lake: Receives periodic plants of Arlee rainbows and Rogers Lake grayling progeny.

Crater Lake: Cutthroats.

Crystal Lake: Brookies.

Dalton Lake: Cutthroats.

Deep Creek: Too small.

Deer Creek: Brookies, cutthroats, and rainbows.

Deer Lake: Small, in the West Thompson drainage, Deer Lake is reached by trail for foot-long cutthroats that have their numbers enhanced every other year with a couple of thousand battling two-inchers.

Denna Mora Creek: Too small.

Devil Gap Creek: Too small.

Diamond Lake: Fast fishing for small brookies. Hit it on the way in to Cliff. It's only a short hike up from the end of the Dry Creek Road.

Dry Creek: Pretty water, if you don't look too hard at the encroaching clearcuts. It is not all that great for fishing, unless you are challenged by down-sized cutthroats and brookies.

Dominion Creek: Too small.

Eagle Peak Lake: Cutthroats.

East Fork Big Creek: Brook, bull, and cutthroat trout.

East Fork Blue Creek: Cutthroats.

East Fork Dry Creek: Too small.

East Fork Elk Creek: Cutthroats.

East Fork Petty Creek: Cutthroats.

East Fork Twelve Mile Creek: Too small.

Eddy Creek (Superior): Cutthroats.

Eddy Creek (Weeksville): Too small.

Elk Creek: Brook, bull, and cutthroat trout. Dumps into the Clark Fork near Heron; popular because a road follows it.

First Creek: Too small.

Flat Creek: Too small.

Flat Rock Creek: Brookies, cutthroats, and rainbows.

Four Lakes Creek: Too small.

Frenchtown Pond: You can see this public swimming hole on the north from I-90 west of Missoula. It's not worth making a special trip to fish it, but if you're there anyway you might cast a streamer. A few years ago it gave up an eighteen-pound pike, and there are bass and perch in Frenchtown Pond.

Frog Lake: Barren.

Glacier Lake: Cutthroats.

Gold Lake: Rainbows.

Grant Creek: Cutthroats.

Grass Lake: Barren.

Hazel Lake: Cutthroats. It's a rich, 7-acre lake at the head of Ward Creek in the St. Regis drainage; popular with horse packers.

Heart (Big Creek) Lake: Cutthroats and rainbows.

Henderson Creek: Too small.

Henry Creek: Too small.

High Falls Creek: Too small.

Honeymoon Creek: Too small.

Hoodoo Creek: Too small.

Hoodoo Lake: Small brookies.

Hub Lake: Cutthroats.

Illinois Creek: 6- to 10-inch rainbows, mainly in the beaver ponds on the Cedar Creek tributary.

Imagine Lake: Barren.

Irish Creek: Cutthroats.

Johnson Creek: Too small.

Jungle Creek: Cutthroats.

Knowles Lake: Barren.

Kreises Pond: Poor access.

Lake Creek: Closed to angling because

it's in the Rattlesnake water supply system for Missoula.

Lang Creek: Too small.

Lazier Creek: Too small.

Lenore Creek: Cutthroats.

Little Beaver Creek: Poor access.

Little Joe Creek: Cutthroats and rainbows, mostly 7 to 10 inches, in this St. Regis tributary. This creek is big enough to fish easily, wading upstream, popping a dry fly on pools and runs.

Little Lake: Skinny cutthroats.

Little Rock Creek: Bull and rainbow trout.

Little Trout Creek: Poor access.

Loder Pond: Private.

Lost Creek: Cutthroats and rainbows.

Lynch Creek: Too small.

Martin Creek: Brookies, cutthroats, and rainbows.

Marshall Lake: Cutthroats.

McCormick Creek: Cutthroats.

McGinnis Creek: Too small.

McGregor Creek: Brook, cutthroat, and rainbow trout. This is the outlet of McGregor Lake, and is overshadowed by the fishing in the lake, but it's worth poking around here for trout up to 16 inches.

McKinley Lake: Cutthroats and rainbows. There are fat, 14- to 16-inch fish in this drawdown lake, but the anglers who hit it all say that they are "tough to catch."

Middle Fork Big Creek: Bull, brook, and cutthroat trout.

Middle Fork Bull River: 6- to 10-inch brookies and cutthroats in a tangled, rough canyon.

Middle Fork Indian Creek: Cutthroats.

Mill Creek: Mostly cutthroats, but there is a smattering of other species. This stream has been been ruined by development.

Missoula Gulch: Cutthroats.

Montana Creek: Cutthroats.

Mosquito Creek: Brookies.

Murr Creek: Cutthroats.

Nemote Creek: Too small most of the season, but it's a pastureland stream and there are fish in the deeper holes right after runoff. Nemote runs into the Clark Fork just below Tarkio.

North Cache Lake: Cutthroats.

North Fork Bull River: Brown, cutthroat, and bull trout. Some of those bull trout are sizable.

North Fork East Fork Bull River: Too small.

North Fork Fish Creek: Cutthroats and rainbows.

North Fork Little Joe Creek: Cutthroats.

North Fork Little Thompson River: Brookies and rainbows.

North Fork Second Creek: Too small.

North Fork Trout Creek: Cutthroats.

Oregon Gulch: Small cutthroats and a few rainbows in this tributary of Lost Creek in the Cedar Creek drainage. Oregon Gulch doesn't have enough room for an angler to spray out casts and get drifts with a dry fly, but Brian Priest likes to dangle a Black Gnat wet fly for fast catches on this stream.

Outlaw Lake: Cutthroats.

Packer Creek: Too small.

Pilcher Creek: Too small.

Quartz Creek: Small resident rainbows. This Clark Fork tributary gets some spawners from April through May.

Rainy Creek: Too small.

Randolph Creek: Too small.

Rattlesnake Lakes: The name given to a group of lakes—Big, Carter, Glacier, McKinley, and Sheridan (all listed separately in this section).

Rock Creek: Enters the Clark Fork across from Tarkio. Too small, even in the upper sections (where it doesn't go dry), but there are some cutthroats here.

Rock Meadow Ponds: 6- to 10-inch cutthroats in a series of five ponds near Rock Creek Lake.

Rudie Lake: Brookies.

St. Louis Creek: Too small.

St. Regis Lakes: Poor fishing.

Savenac Creek: Too small for most anglers, but Gil Crutchfield lives on this tributary of the St. Regis and his boy Rob goes out a few times every week during the summer and brings back a breakfast mess of 8- to 12-inch brook trout.

Savenac Nursery Pond: Water for the kids.

Schley Lake: Cutthroats.

Second Creek: Too small.

Semen Creek: Too small.

Sheridan Lake: Stunted rainbows.

Shroder Creek: Cutthroats.

Silver Creek: Closed to fishing. This is the water supply for Saltese.

Six Mile Creek: Too small.

Sleman Reservoir: Poor fishing.

Slimmer Creek: Brookies and cutthroats.

South Branch Big Beaver Creek: Too small.

South Branch West Trout Creek: Too small.

South Fork Bull River: Cutthroats, a good population of 6- to 10-inchers, but this is a real overgrown little stream.

South Fork Fish Creek: Brook, bull, cutthroat, and rainbow trout.

South Fork Little Joe Creek: Bull and cutthroat trout.

South Martin Creek: Too small.

South Nemote Creek: Too small.

South Fork Trout Creek: Cutthroats.

Square Lake: Cutthroats.

Squaw Creek: Too small.

Stahl Pond: Private.

Straight Creek: Brook, cutthroat, and rainbow trout in this tributary of the North Fork of Fish Creek. It's an enjoyable, easy to fish stream.

Straight Peak Lake: Cutthroats.

Surveyor Creek: Rainbows.

Sylvan Lake: Brookies and cutthroats.

Tadpole Lake: Cutthroats.

Tamarack Creek: Cutthroats.

Thompson Creek: Too small.

Torino Creek: Too small.

Trail Lake: Brook trout.

Tuscor Creek: Too small.

Twenty-four Mile Creek: Too small.

Twin Lakes: Cutthroats.

Two Mile Creek: 6 miles of good fishing for 8- to 10-inch brook, bull and cutthroat trout. These streams in the St. Regis area, less than 3,000 feet in elevation in the bottom reaches, get their runoff earlier than the Missoula waters. They are usually fishable sometime in June.

Ward Creek: Brook, bull, and cutthroat trout.

Weeksville Creek: Too small.

West Fork Big Creek: Brookies and cutthroats.

West Fork Blue Creek: Cutthroats.

West Fork Dry Creek: Too small.

West Fork Fish Creek: Bull and cutthroat trout.

West Fork Fishtrap Creek: Too small.

West Fork Swamp Creek: Too small.

White Creek: Too small.

White Pine Creek: Poor access.

Willow Creek: Numerous 6- to 10-inch cutthroats in this Vermillion River tributary, especially in the beaver working on the upper end.

Wrangle Creek: A Rattlesnake Creek tributary (and closed to fishing as part of the Missoula water supply system).

■ *Special thanks to Mike Ashley, Gil Crutchfield, Tim Forbes, Chris Hess, Mark Jones, Dean Ludwig, Bruce Moore, Trip Payne, Brian Priest, Hobie Roberts, and Hugh Spencer for their help on the Lower Clark Fork drainage.*

Flathead Lake
Photo courtesy of Mansfield Library, University of Montana

FLATHEAD LAKE ▪ Dragging balsa wood logs for lures and doorknobs for sinkers through 200 feet of water in hopes of hooking a lake trout is not fly fishing. But trolling big stuff on down riggers is what Flathead Lake is famous for as a fishery.

Still, there are some intriguing prospects for fly fishers such as the almost unfathomable amount of large Lake Superior whitefish, some approaching ten pounds, that will take nymphs. And there is an abundance of three- to eight-pound lake trout. With the collapse of the kokanee salmon population for a variety of reasons, including competition from the introduced mysis shrimp, lake trout and lake whitefish make up 80 percent of the biomass in Flathead Lake. There are also fair numbers of cutthroat and bull trout.

To say that Flathead is huge is an understatement of considerable proportion. It is the largest natural body of fresh water west of the Mississippi, running 28 miles long by an average of around 6 miles wide. The lake covers more than 200 square miles and is the repository of the Flathead, Swan, Whitefish, and Stillwater river drainages, an area that includes Glacier National Park, much of both the Bob Marshall and Mission Mountain wildernesses, and the Whitefish Mountains. The Missions rise over a mile straight up along the eastern shore, and gentle hills of native grasses and pines roll off in the west. Good highways surround the lake and connect towns like Polson, Elmo, Somers, and Bigfork. Numerous state and tribal parks provide camping and access to the lake.

The south end of Flathead Lake is Flathead Indian Reservation—get tribal permits.

The lake is so big it creates its own microclimate. Huge storms come up out of nowhere, killing unwary anglers with some regularity. Waterspouts have been sighted here.

Early fall is one of the best times to chase whitefish in the shallow-water areas of bays like Woods and Yellow. The species congregate in these areas and if you are lucky they will be holding in 20 feet of water or less.

Using a sinking line and a leader of about 6 feet tapered to 3X and a Hare's Ear Nymph, you probe the water from boats (which are easier and safer to fish from than float tubes or canoes on Flathead) until the whitefish are located. This is not all that difficult. Many people fish for them, and you'll often see several boats working a productive spot.

Catch and release is appropriate in almost all salmonid angling in the state, but according to Region One fisheries manager Jim Vashro, the whitefish population needs to be kept in check (along with the lake trout in the "smaller" three- to eight-pound class) and may someday need to be reduced to protect the other native species. So if you want to keep a few for a decent fish dinner, go ahead. You will actually be helping to restore the natural order of things in Flathead, at least to some minor extent.

Whitefish will not provide the excitement or challenge of browns or rainbows, but for easy, steady action, they're a worthy quarry.

The cutts and bulls have provided good action in the past, but at the moment, this intriguing, quality fishery is being threatened (as are many waters in the West) by the introduction of unwanted creatures. It is a serious situation.

Walleyes have their place in the world, but not in Flathead Lake. There has been a distorted suggestion by a northwest Montana angling group (obviously not Trout Unlimited) to introduce these overgrown perch into Flathead Lake. To its credit, the Montana Department of Fish, Wildlife, and Parks has opposed the introduction of walleyes into cold water fisheries.

Add to this the "introduction" by uneducated or selfish fishermen of northern pike, largemouth bass, yellow perch, and others, and the threat to Montana's native trout becomes obvious.

These "exotics" thrive on salmonid eggs, fry and, in the case of northerns, trout exceeding 12 inches. The number of trout a twenty-pound pike eats in a year or the number of eggs and fry a five-pound walleye ingests in a season is significant.

Anyone interested in cropping the pike population is invited to Flathead. The spring fishing with large streamers in the sloughs (especially Church, Egan, and Fennon Sloughs) can be productive. The pike are in the shallows to spawn.

Why do people want these fish in trout waters? Many anglers have moved to the state (and to places like Idaho and Wyoming—locations experiencing similar problems) from regions (notably the Midwest) that offered excellent walleye, perch, sunfish, and northern pike fishing. So, these souls decided to bring a little bit of home along west with them. And bait fishers have accidentally introduced such

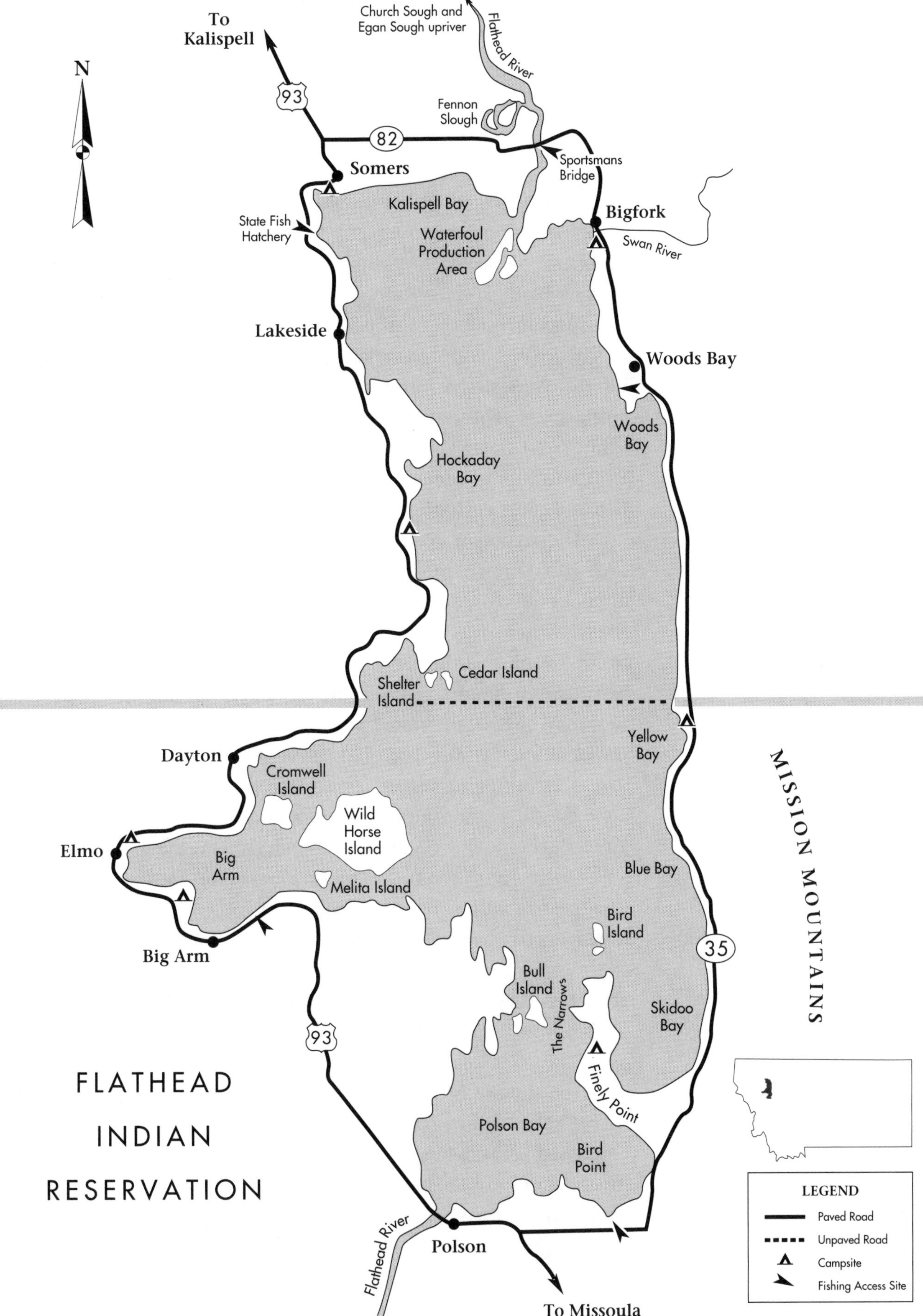
To Kalispell
N
93
82
Church Sough and Egan Sough upriver
Flathead River
Fennon Slough
Somers
Sportsmans Bridge
Kalispell Bay
State Fish Hatchery
Bigfork
Waterfoul Production Area
Swan River
Lakeside
Woods Bay
Woods Bay
Hockaday Bay
Cedar Island
Shelter Island
Dayton
Yellow Bay
Cromwell Island
Wild Horse Island
Elmo
Big Arm
Melita Island
Blue Bay
MISSION MOUNTAINS
Bird Island
Big Arm
35
Bull Island
The Narrows
Skidoo Bay
93
Finely Point
FLATHEAD INDIAN RESERVATION
Polson Bay
Bird Point
Flathead River
Polson
To Missoula
LEGEND
Paved Road
Unpaved Road
Campsite
Fishing Access Site

species as carp and redside shiners.

"This is not becoming a serious problem. It already *is* a serious problem," according to Vashro. "The illegal or accidental introduction of exotic species really impacts the existing fisheries, and we have documented that throughout the state."

Once the exotics are in lakes, they often quickly spread throughout the rivers, streams, and creeks, devastating a drainage with frightening speed. Those that want their favorite exotic introduced into prime trout water are extremely vocal about their desires. Walleyes Unlimited, for example, has been known to make life miserable for fish and game personnel throughout Montana.

The argument against stocking walleyes often is countered by saying that brown, brook, golden, and, in many cases, rainbow trout are not native to Montana. To some extent there is some validity to this viewpoint, but for the most part these salmonids have either so firmly established themselves in rivers like the Madison or Missouri or in barren mountain lakes and streams, that any initial damage that may have been done, has long since been compensated for by the creation of world-class or at the very least, quality fisheries.

Also, for the most part, species like walleye, perch, and northern are successful in outcompeting trout for both food sources and habitat. You really cannot have walleyes and trout hanging out in the same river.

Obviously this is not a minor problem. Trout populations can disappear rapidly with the introduction of a "few buckets full" of northerns or walleyes or perch or bait fish.

"I don't think most anglers realize the effect they have on a fishery when they empty their bait buckets into a lake at the end of a day's fishing," said Vashro. "We have to educate people as much and as quickly as possible."

The state of Montana is publicizing a three-pronged program that it hopes will curb the spread of exotic species and this includes emphasizing to anglers that they should not move live fish or aquatic invertebrates from one body of water to another for any reason, nor should they release aquarium fish into natural waters. Finally and most importantly in Vashro's eyes is that anglers should report any illegal plantings they witness to the Department of Fish, Wildlife, and Parks.

"The potential for disaster from illegally introducing exotics is truly terrifying," concludes Vashro.

As mentioned earlier, bull trout and cutthroats live in the lake, but many of them spend a large portion of their lives moving out of the lake and upstream beginning prior to spring runoff to reach spawning tributaries pouring into the Middle, North, and South Forks of the Flathead River. Following spawning some of these fish drop back down the tributaries and rivers to rest up in the lake for the winter. There are times when the cutts rise to mayflies from late spring into early summer near shore, providing interesting fishing on drys with Green Drake overtones. Even the aloof bull trout will succumb to these insects on occasion—a rare sight and treat to take this trout on a dry fly.

Western Green Drake
Photo by Bob Scammell

The most interesting action on Flathead Lake occurs in the fall when the big lake trout—to over twenty pounds—are spotted cruising near shore. This is streamer fishing for what amounts to very big brook trout.

You need a 14- to 16-foot (at least) flatbottom boat both for stability in the often choppy water and for use as a casting platform. Depending on shoreline structure, fish will be swimming in ten feet or maybe a bit more water. Using a seven-weight, ten-foot sink-tip and a large streamer—size 2 and larger—imitating another fish (trout, cisco, perch), the idea is to spot a lake trout, anticipate its movement and then cast far enough ahead of its perceived course to allow the fly to sink to the bottom. Then when the trout closes in, a few tantalizing strips will do the trick most of the time. The fish are aggressive at this stage in their life cycle, and they attack a streamer with an obvious display of territorial imperative.

So, the best bets are to work the bays and other shallow-water areas from late summer into autumn for whitefish and lake trout. Spring and early summer in the same spots are good for cutthroats and maybe a bull trout or two. Flathead Lake is very big water with a lot of good-sized fish.

FLATHEAD RIVER ▪ The Flathead River is large by any measure. Water from an immense wilderness drainage pours in from three main forks—Middle, North, South—and the Swan River plus lesser waters including the Stillwater and Whitefish rivers.

Big trout swim here, even in the section running between the head of Flathead Lake and the South Fork's confluence. Below the lake and Kerr Dam not only are there a few big trout, there are also large northern pike and some largemouth bass. With so much wilderness and national forest water available, few anglers bother or even know about the opportunities in the main Flathead, but there is some quality action here.

Dusk on the Flathead
Photo courtesy of Hungry Horse News

You can reach the upper river both from the highway and by state fishing access sites. Fishing from shore or wading is not only difficult in most situations, but dangerous as well during high flows and below Kerr Dam when power generation is taking place.

Anglers with rafts or boats will find good summertime action for cutthroats and rainbows reaching a few pounds on the river between Columbia Falls and Kalispell. Toward evening larger caddis imitations cast next to the banks or run through the graveled riffles will produce. During the day, drys will work, but large nymphs—stone fly patterns, Prince Nymphs, Montana Nymphs, and the like—or big streamers turn the trouts' heads. This time of year bull trout move upstream to spawning grounds in isolated creeks. They will hit big streamers if drifted in front of them down along the streambed. Sink-tips, weighted patterns, lead weights, and plenty of slack are needed to drop down into the deeper holes and runs of this river.

Autumn and winter are catch-and-release seasons for trout, including a burgeoning population of lake trout that are moving into the river from Flathead Lake. Large—to ten pounds—Lake Superior

Whitefish are present in astounding numbers in the upper river, especially from the Old Steel Bridge in Kalispell up through Pressentine Bar north of town. Sink-tip lines with large nymphs take both species and streamers stripped along the bottom trigger the lake trout. Essentially the Flathead Lake system is out of balance with the introduction of mysis shrimp and the collapse of the kokanee salmon population. Lake trout and whitefish (mainly whitefish) make up over 80 percent of the lake's biomass. This is one place where you would be doing the trout a favor if you kept your limit of lake trout (averaging around three or four pounds) and whitefish (averaging around four pounds with a one hundred-fish limit). These species are threatening the native bull trout and cutthroat trout and their numbers need to be substantially reduced to improve the odds.

You can reach the upper Flathead at Blankenship Bridge, near the mouth of the South Fork, at Teakettle, Kokanee Bend, and at the mouth of the Stillwater.

The Flathead is not difficult to float but this is big water and there are strong eddies and currents that can suck a swimmer or anyone else under with ease. Wear your life vest.

The secret to fishing this river is cutting the water down to size. Look for smaller current seams, braided channels, cover along the banks or midstream obstructions. Any place offering shelter for the trout. While caddisflies are ever-present, any large—size 10 to 12—high-floating dry fly will take fish if presented properly in prime locations.

Many Flathead waters are on the Flathead Indian Reservation—get tribal permits.

While the upper river is a straightforward angling proposition, the lower Flathead below Kerr Dam is a complicated management mess—a situation that is currently harming a potentially top-notch tailwater environment.

The main questions involved are: Should Kerr be managed for power or fish or for both equally? How good can the fishery become—another Bighorn or just another average east-of-the-Mississippi trout stream? With the kind of power-generation money at stake—hundreds of millions—does the fishery really have a chance?

Montana Power Company (MPC) is required to design a mitigation plan for its Kerr Dam operation as part of the federal relicensing procedure begun in 1985 and not completed yet. The plan calls for

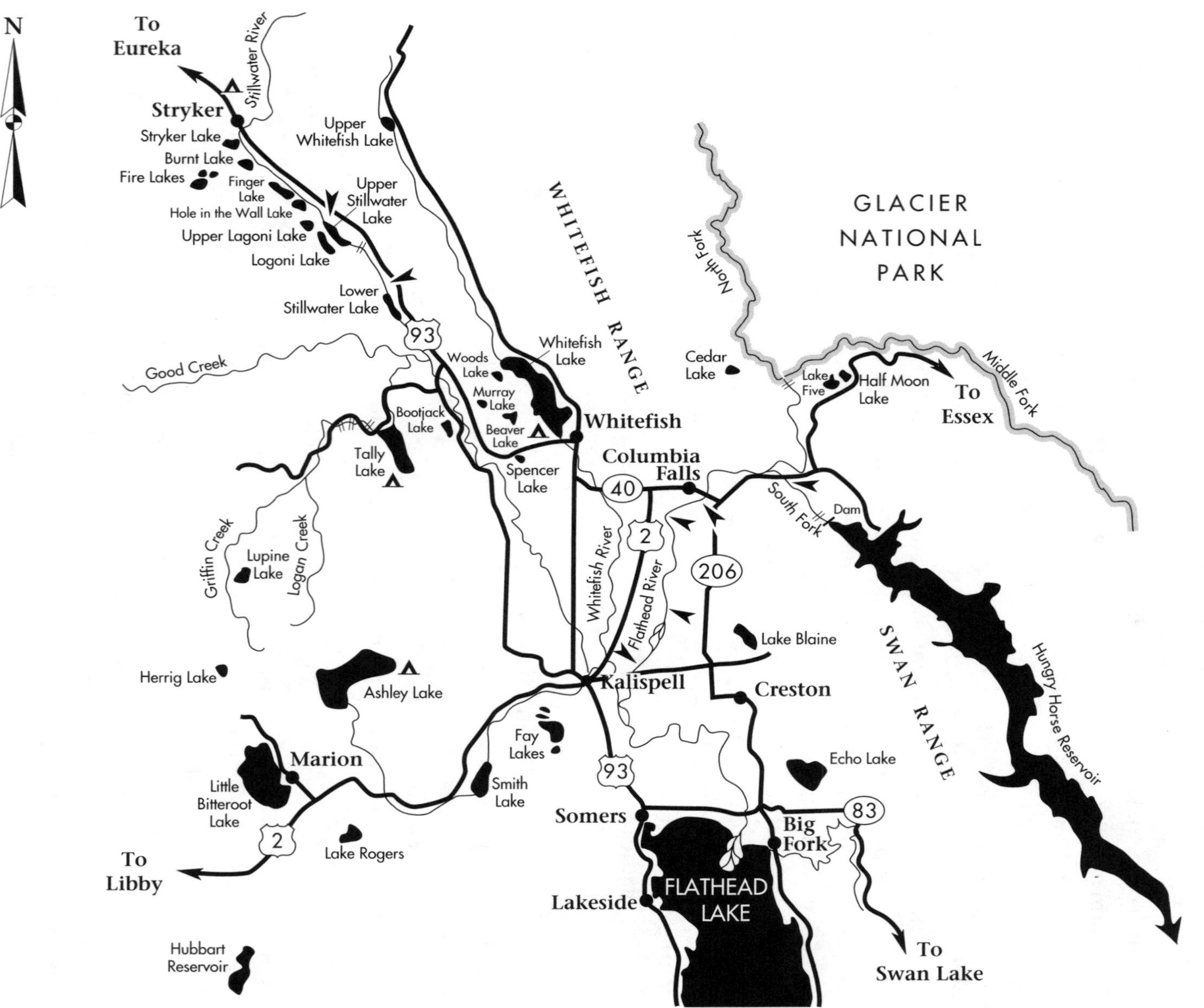
N
To Eureka
Stillwater River
Stryker
Stryker Lake
Burnt Lake
Fire Lakes
Finger Lake
Hole in the Wall Lake
Upper Lagoni Lake
Logoni Lake
Upper Whitefish Lake
Upper Stillwater Lake
Lower Stillwater Lake
93
WHITEFISH RANGE
GLACIER NATIONAL PARK
North Fork
Middle Fork
Good Creek
Woods Lake
Murray Lake
Whitefish Lake
Bootjack Lake
Beaver Lake
Whitefish
Cedar Lake
Lake Five
Half Moon Lake
To Essex
Tally Lake
Spencer Lake
Columbia Falls
40
South Fork
Dam
2
206
Griffin Creek
Lupine Lake
Logan Creek
Whitefish River
Flathead River
Lake Blaine
SWAN RANGE
Hungry Horse Reservoir
Herrig Lake
Ashley Lake
Kalispell
Creston
Fay Lakes
Marion
Echo Lake
Smith Lake
Little Bitteroot Lake
93
Somers
83
Big Fork
2
Lake Rogers
To Libby
FLATHEAD LAKE
Lakeside
To Swan Lake
Hubbart Reservoir

FLATHEAD RIVER

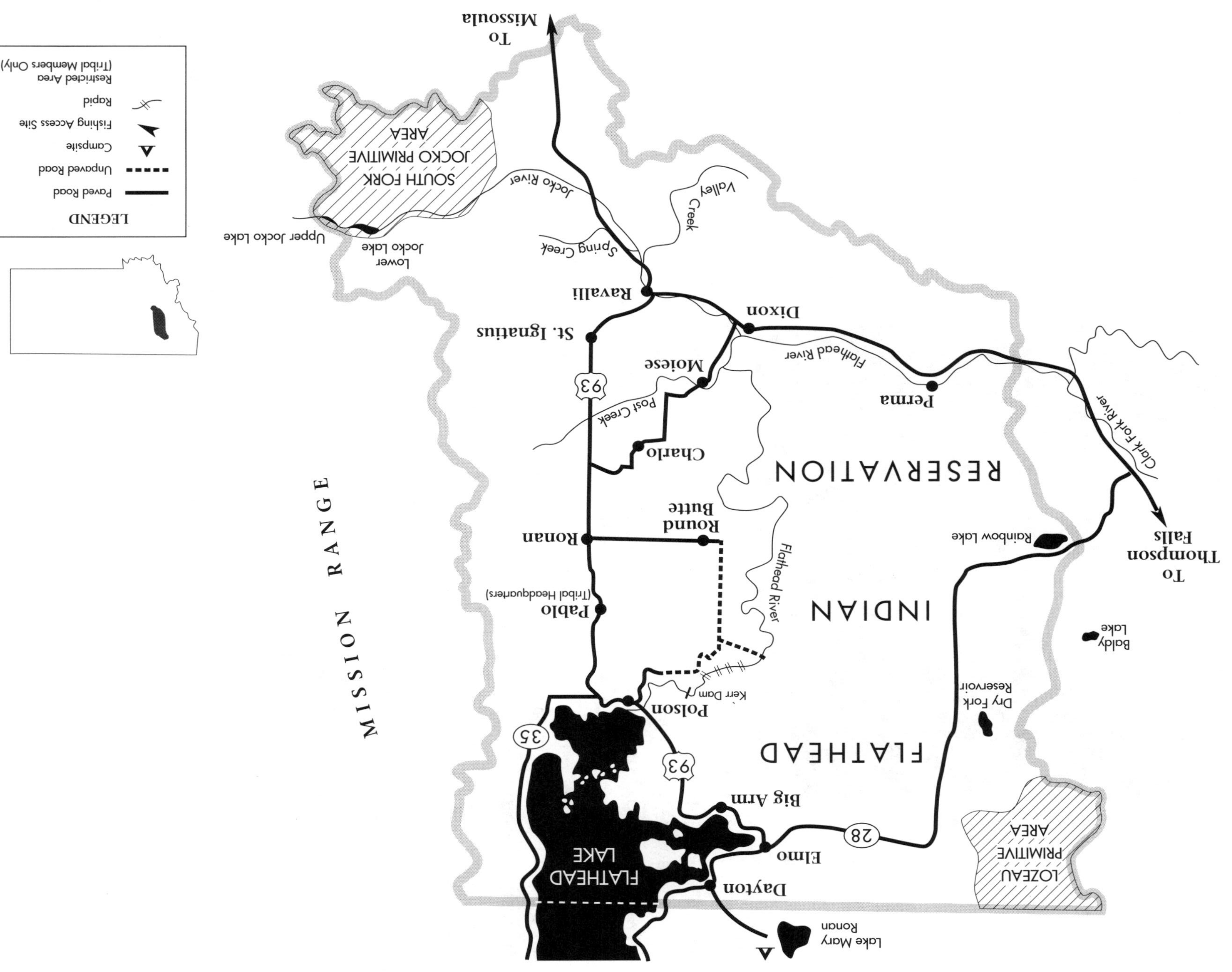

rate payers to finance an initial $15.4 million for fish and wildlife enhancement, erosion protection, and fish hatchery construction and improvement. Millions more will be needed for monitoring and management until the year 2015 when the Salish and Kootenai tribes take over operation of the dam from MPC as part of a previous agreement.

The river below the dam flows through a steep-walled narrow canyon for a brief distance before opening up to drift through a valley bordered by gentle (for Montana) hills of native grasses, scattered pines, and rattlesnakes. This is drier, more open country than the river's glacier-carved mountain headwaters to the north. Scattered in among the few trout are some northern pike that the area's fisheries biologists say provide little if any serious competition for trout. Each lives in its own world, so to speak.

According to anglers who remember such things, prior to the 1930s the Flathead River below Kerr Dam was an excellent fishery for native species of salmonids. Large westslope cutthroat trout and bull trout were relatively common catches here. Since the late 1930s operation of Kerr Dam by Montana Power for generation of electricity

Bull trout—a vanishing species
Photo by John Holt

has caused wildly fluctuating water releases that have unseasonably flooded or dried up shoreline and shallow-water habitat (varial zone) critical to many insects that are important food sources for trout.

Dr. Jack Stanford of the nearby Flathead Lake Biological Station describes this as the "yo-yo" effect.

"It's still good for those who know how to fish it," said Joe DosSantos, Salish and Kootenai tribal fisheries manager. "It's not bad for cutthroats in the canyon stretch below the dam and now for browns farther down." DosSantos adds that while water temperatures vary from around 70 degrees Fahrenheit in the summer to near freezing in the winter, a measurable population of insects including baetis, ephemerella, midges, and "lots of caddis" thrive in the permanently wet areas of the stream course. Drys in the evening along with big stuff on sink-tips worked down deep are the tactics of choice in this water.

"We can gain a 72-mile fishery if certain changes are made," said Trout Unlimited Westslope chapter member Ric Smith. He adds that erratic water fluctuations from the dam's production of power on demand have made the lower Flathead River the "sacrifice area" for fisheries. "Montana Power never allowed a more natural flow regime to be put on the table during plan negotiations."

A number of lakes and tributaries of the Flathead River are located in or along the Mission Mountain Range on the Flathead Indian Reservation. These waters are discussed in detail in the section about the reservation. Some waters that are discussed here are also on tribal land and are so designated.

Basically, Montana Power operates Kerr Dam from the standpoint of base-load and peak-load operation. Kerr Dam is just one of many power generation facilities in the Columbia Basin grid, each operated by private entities such as Montana Power for substantial profit. During peak load the water stored in Flathead Lake is released from the dam at volumes as high as 55,000 cubic feet per second (cfs). During base load this level drops as low as 3,200 cfs. Complicating things further is the fact that Kerr's releases are tied to other dam releases in the Columbia River system.

This is Dr. Stanford's yo-yo. Insects and trout lay their eggs in areas that may be under water at one time and high and dry at another.

"Streams and lake level regulation for hydropower remains the greatest threat to the integrity of the Flathead River–Lake ecosystem," said Stanford in a paper on mitigating the impacts of this type of management in the Flathead River Basin.

Said MDFWP's John Fraley, "We feel, based on evidence, that there is no question that if natural flows returned the fisheries would improve, but because of substrate and other considerations, the Flat-

A Special Fly for the Flathead

For taking large northern pike out of the weed beds along the lower Flathead (or anywhere else, for that matter), this cobbled pattern works wonders. A quick, but varied, retrieve is best and also provokes responses from large trout.

THE PIKE FLY

Hook: Mustad #3191, size 2/0 or 3/0

Thread: red pre-waxed Kevlar

Tail: white marabou

Body: weighted, yellow polypro yarn

Ribbing: copper wire

Wings: long dyed white bucktail three times longer than the hook; pearl Crystal Hair two times longer than the hook; and red marabou the same length as the hook

Head: red thread

head would not improve to anywhere near the levels of an eastern [Montana] river."

Fraley is referring to the relatively sterile nature of rivers west of the continental divide in Montana. These rivers rely heavily on snowmelt that is low in nutrients when compared to rivers on the other side of the mountains like the Bighorn or Missouri.

"The river below Kerr Dam has unrealized potential, but at the moment we are not in charge of the dam's operation," said DosSantos, who also sides with Fraley concerning the fecundity of the system. It is incorrect to compare the Missouri to the Flathead. Flathead Lake is a nutrient sink and always has been, but in 2015, after we return the dam to base-load operation, a substantial fishery will exist.

The situation will not be resolved in the near future. We will probably have to wait until the tribes take over control of the dam for true quality angling to return. Until then we must content ourselves with the large trout that do swim in the few miles of cold water below the dam, and with the trophy northern pike fishing that exists near Dixon. All of this water is on the Flathead Indian Reservation, requiring a tribal permit, and there is limited roadside access. Highway 200 parallels the river from Ravalli to Paradise and there is some access at Dixon.

Once on the water, fish the extensive weed beds and sand and gravel bars along the edges of the strong current. The big pike—over twenty pounds—hide here waiting for smaller forage fish and even trout to swim past. Shock tippets and at least seven-weight rods are needed. Any large streamer of 1/0 and up, especially in red and white, will take the pike. Cast in and along the bars and weed beds, then strip the pattern swiftly and erratically.

Bass are fewer in number and normally taken in the sloughs and slower water on leeches and poppers in the evening. Just be dead sure you are not trespassing on tribal members' land. This is not worth the trouble (nor for that matter is it a good practice anywhere in the state—respecting private property is the basic axiom for preserving public access to prime waters).

So, for now at least, the future of the trout fishery below Kerr Dam is in doubt, but the fishing is still adequate for cutthroats, browns, and a few rainbows. Action for pike is very good, and, for bass, average. On the upper river the fishing is varied and good throughout the season after spring runoff.

The Flathead River offers fly fishers cutthroat, rainbow, brown, lake, and bull trout to at least a couple of pounds and northerns to over twenty. Not bad for a no-name river.

Fishing Waters in the Flathead River Drainage

Ashley Creek: This is a pretty little stream with some good water between the outlet of Smith Lake near Kila and the water treatment plant in Kalispell. Fish for rainbows up to 15 inches and a few brookies and cutthroats. Access is not easy but the stream is crossed and paralleled by county roads here and there and you can see some of the best runs from U.S. 2. Below the treatment plant, which has cleaned up its act in recent years, the fishing is still good but somewhat short on aesthetic values. Above Smith Lake the stream flows through, in descending order, Ashley Lake, Lone Lake, and Lake Monroe (Lower Ashley). This is good hopper water in July and August.

Sitting out a storm on Ashley Lake
Photo by Stan Bradshaw

Ashley Lake: It's about nine square miles and over 200 feet deep in spots, with summer homes all over the place and clearcuts scarring the hillsides. The world record rainbow-cutthroat hybrid came out of here and meat-and-trophy hunters poach the spawning streams with gay abandon. Some good cutthroat and large—over five pounds—rainbows cruise the shallows especially near inlets and outlets. But during spawning season give the trout a break.

Beaver Lake: Beaver, 5 miles west of Whitefish, is stocked yearly with rainbows that do well in this 106-acre, deep-blue water, but they get hammered by the local bait-flinging contingent. There are some white-mud sandbars, points, and beaches along the southern end that fish well with leech patterns around dusk.

Lake Blaine: This is a summer-resort, madhouse lake—the kind they had in mind when they made Bill Murray's summer-camp movie. Lake Blaine received the first known plant in Montana of largemouth in early 1900s. Lots of homes, speed boats, northern pike, largemouth bass, squaw fish, and some terrorized rainbow, cutthroat and kokanee salmon. This one's shot for the fly fisher.

Bootjack Lake: If you care about yourself or your car you will pay a local fly fisher to take you here. The 65-acre lake is good fishing for some decent cutthroats and rainbows, especially from a float tube. It's on private land with some public access about 8 miles west of Whitefish. The fish are cruisers and it takes two anglers to set each other up as the trout work back and forth.

Burnt Lake: An up-to-date Flathead National Forest travel-plan map will get you started on the diminishing lane into this water near Stryker. Managed for cutthroat and not too bad if you find it.

Dry Fork (Lone Pine) Reservoir: Yellow perch, northern pike, and a very few cutthroats. The fly fishing attraction is the pike. There is a good population of them, and there are some big ones. You'll find this one off of Highway 28 near Lonepine on the Flathead Reservation.

Finger Lake (Wall or Lower Wall): There is a trail near the end of a logging road on the west side (farthest from the highway) of Duck Lake. A few minutes walk and you are on fishing water and there are some big brook trout here that will occasionally hit a flashy streamer in the Zonker style.

Foy Lakes: The lower two are barren or almost so. The upper lake is large, filled with ski boats and partying teenagers in the summer, surrounded by homes, and has some nice but frightened rainbows that kill time dodging whirling propellers and baited hooks.

Good Creek: This tributary to the Stillwater used to be decent fishing for brook trout, but access is limited in the best stretches and there are a lot of people living up here with guns and signs on their access roads indicating they know how to use guns. Despite the logging, this is pretty country but full of strange people. Have you ever seen *Deliverance*?

Griffin Creek: This used to be a beautiful, fun little stream to fish for cutthroats with an Adams and an 6½ foot rod. Now the whole area is logged to hell. The Talley Lake Ranger District is a disaster. A national sacrifice area that looks like it was bombed, scalped, and burned.

Herrig Lake: On the southern side of Pleasant Mountain, it is managed for cutthroats. It's not far from Little Bitterroot Lake west of Kalispell. Herrig Creek is closed all year.

Hole-in-the-Wall: See Finger Lake above and then stagger southeastward up and over some rock ridges for a quarter-mile to the water. There are good brookies here, too.

Hubbart Reservoir: Hubbart is drawn down a bit in the summer but it's good float-tube fishing for rainbow trout (and there are some kokanee here also). West and south of Kalispell. Over 400 acres with weed beds. Leeches, damsel nymphs, and the like produce.

Many of these waters are on the Flathead Indian Reservation—get tribal permits.

Jocko River: The Jocko flows for about 20 miles from its junction with the Middle and South Forks of the Jocko past Arlee on the Flathead Indian Reservation. It joins the Flathead River at Dixon. The water is visible and crossed by U.S. 93. Good dry fly water for brown trout with some rainbows, brooks, cutthroats, bull trout, and a lot of whitefish that love nymphs (catch and release for all except lake and brook trout). You can reach it by road most of the way, but keep an eye out for rattlesnakes dozing in the hot summer sun.

Lagoni Lake: This one is managed for rainbow and cutthroat with a few hold-over brook trout from earlier days. Hard to find, but there really are 20 acres of deep water just west of Upper Stillwater Lake in timber-and-rock-cliff country. There are plenty of northern pike here that gorge on small trout. Lug in a float tube. Big streamers in spring and early summer are effective for the slashing pike.

Lake Mary Ronan: Four-hundred thousand kokanee are dumped into this 1,506-acre lake 8 miles northwest of Dayton off U.S. 93 every year along with 50,000 cutthroat. Rainbows and some nice largemouth also cruise the shorelines here. Opening day here (unlike most still waters that are open all year, Lake Mary Ronan is closed from March 15 through the third Saturday in May) looks like Woodstock with boats. By early June things settle down a bit and float tubers have a fighting chance if they are interested.

North end of Little Bitterroot Lake
Photo by Stan Bradshaw

Little Bitterroot Lake: There are summer homes, resorts and lots of boats on this 3 by 1½ mile lake 25 miles west of Kalispell. Fishing is for stocked rainbow and kokanee and some cutthroats. It's easy to find and it has a state park on the north end. A few large trout here.

Logan Creek: This is a scenic, little free-stone stream that heads in the logged-over Star Meadows area, where there are brook trout in brushy-shored beaver ponds. The fast-water reaches hold 6- to 10-inch cutthroats that love attractor patterns popped into the pocket water before the creek enters Tally Lake. Stream cleats help when the water is high early in the season. There are some rainbow and whitefish in the lower reaches.

Lower Stillwater Lake: It's scenic, 248 acres with shallow drop-offs. The fishing for rainbows is mediocre, but in the spring, fishing is excellent in the shallows for northern pike up to maybe ten pounds. Early in the day and toward evening a streamer cast to shore and stripped in will take a lot of pike that really tear up the water and your leader—shock tippet helps.

Lupine Lake: Lupine is 13 acres, reached by marked trail from Griffin Creek road. It's about 2 miles in and there are still some trees left here despite the best efforts of the Forest Service on the Tally Lake District. There used to be Yellowstone cutthroats here; now it's managed for westslope cutts.

Murray Lake: There are lots of lure and bait fishers at this 45-acre lake a few miles north of Whitefish off U.S. 93. Murray is managed for rainbow and a few nice ones work the shoreline near evening sipping caddis, mayflies, and flying ants.

Post Creek: This fine, little stream was a favorite of the late Harmon Henkin, who first schooled me in the ways of bamboo and mayflies. The outlet of McDonald Lake, it flows to the Flathead River a few miles above Dixon on the Flathead Reservation. It's posted in spots, but good for rainbows, cutthroats, hybrids, and sometimes a brown in the lower reaches. This one has been beaten up pretty hard in recent times, but a few years of tribal management should help this stream come back to its former pleasant self.

Rainbow Lake: Out in semi-arid farmland north of Plains on the Flathead Indian Reservation, Rainbow is primarily a northern pike and yellow perch fishery with an occasional stocking of brood stock rainbows. Off the beaten path but offers good action on the surface.

Rogers Lake: This was once an excellent grayling lake until some subnormal introduced "exotic" species that wiped out the sail-finned natives. Fish, Wildlife, and Parks would like to restock the grayling but cost of rehabilitating it and the fear of another episode of illegal planting delay the process.

Smith Lake: It looks interesting from the road, but this wetland, 300-acre lake is better known for its winter perch fishing than for the few rainbows taken each year. There is an access site ten minutes west of Kalispell if you are interested in the perch.

Spencer Lake: Spencer is limited to artificial lures and you can keep one rainbow over 22 inches. It's just out of Whitefish on the south side of U.S. 93. Early and late in the season it's an entertaining lake to float tube. Nymphs cast into the weed beds on the east shore work well at times. Sunfish sneak in from nearby Skyles Lake.

Spring Creek: This beautiful, little creek meets the Jocko River just south of Ravalli on the Flathead Indian Reservation. Fished a lot, it is still good dry fly water for brown, brook, and rainbow trout. It runs along U.S. 93.

Stillwater River: The lower reaches from the town of Stryker down to the Whitefish River near Kalispell wander through farm and ranch land and some timber. The water is mostly slow but there are some rainbows and lesser numbers of cutthroat and brook trout. The lower water is locally famous for the huge—over thirty pounds—northern pike that are infrequently taken each spring on large streamers. The water above Stryker flows out of the Whitefish Range and offers limited fast-water angling for small cutthroat and some bull trout and other salmonids. This is pretty country but the fish are small. Ten inches is a trophy.

Strawberry Lake: Up near the Swan Crest west of Bigfork, this small lake used to have some trout but is no longer on the stocking program, so the action may be a bit slim. So what? This is a nice, steep hike for a couple of miles in pretty country. Take a chance.

Stryker Lake: This used to be an excellent brook trout water with fish to a few pounds and loons swimming here and there with their broods in the spring, but meat fishers hammered the water and there are not many fish left. It's about forty minutes north of Whitefish below Stryker Ridge.

Tally Lake: Large (1,326 acres) and almost 500 feet deep (deepest in the state) but it is lousy fishing. Whatever was planted here never really took. There are still some remnant cutthroat, rainbow, kokanee, whitefish, and brook trout. About thirty minutes west of Whitefish with a large campground. More a party lake anymore.

Upper Lagoni Lake: This is another hard-to-find, wall-lake-country piece of water about 8 acres with good fishing for foot-long cutthroats.

Upper Stillwater Lake: About one square mile and shallow, it's average fishing for several species of trout, trash fish, perch, and northern pike (especially early in the year). Twenty-five miles north of Whitefish west of U.S. 93.

Upper Whitefish Lake: You can reach this one by gravel road from Olney east off U.S. 93. It's pretty but only mediocre for small cutthroats to maybe 10 inches or a touch larger. The campground is always crowded in good weather and there have been weddings, beer busts, and human sacrifices here in the past. It's somewhat of a zoo for this far back in the woods.

Upper Whitefish Lake
Photo by Stan Bradshaw

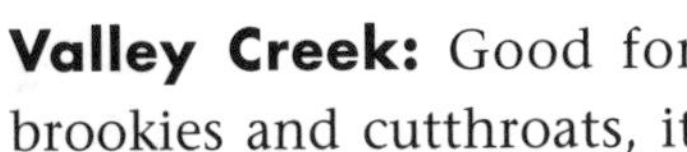

Valley Creek: Good for brookies and cutthroats, it empties into the Jocko near Ravalli on the Flathead Indian Reservation. Like most of these winding, meadow streams, the biggest trout hold under the brush at the deep bends. Try slapping a hopper pattern as far back into the sticks as possible, and the average size of the fish in Valley might surprise you.

Whitefish Lake: A resort lake surrounded by summer homes, it's one of the best lakes in the country for lake trout up to thirty pounds. Trolling is the preferred method, but you can turn up fish by slowly working a Hi-D line down deep with big streamers in the swirling water at the inlet of Swift Creek, especially in the fall. You'll need to put a boat in at the south end and head up lake 6 miles to this water. Cutthroat take mayflies in late spring and early summer near evening along the west shore in the bays. Some also cruise the points and shallow-water areas. Lots of kokanee (How exciting!) are also planted here each year.

Whitefish River: A slow-moving stream for most of its length from the lake down to the Stillwater River just east of Kalispell it's best known for big northern pike taken in the spring. There are also some good rainbow in the weed beds growing below the sewage treatment plant outside of Whitefish and in the water near the Stillwater (but there is no easy access here).

Woods Lake: This used to be an excellent for rainbow trout of several pounds that would hit damsel fly nymphs worked from a float tube, or flying ant imitations in the evening during summer. Management decided to dump some very large hatchery brood fish in here and then publicize the event. The regs say you can keep only one trout over 22 inches, but the meat fishers here nailed Woods and there was no enforcement, so the fishing dropped off a notch or two to say the least. Three damn catch-and-release lakes in the entire Flathead Valley and they can't leave them alone.

Float tubing on Woods Lake
Photo by Stan Bradshaw

Other Waters

Abbot Creek: Too small for "serious" fly fishermen, but it's the stream where children can learn the rudiments of fly fishing while catching 6- to 8-inch brook trout. It enters the Flathead at Martin City.

Alder Creek: Too small.

Allentown Pond: No trout.

Banana Lake: Rainbows.

Basham Lake: No trout.

Bead Pond: Put-and-take rainbows planted regularly.

Big Knife Lake: Closed to non-tribal members

Big Lost Creek: Marginal fishing for brookies and cutthroats not far from Ashley Lake.

Billings Pond: Rainbows.

Blanchard Lake: No trout in this 147-acre lake, but there are sunfish, yellow perch, and largemouth bass here.

Blast Lake: This one's a few acres and maybe 20 feet deep, managed for rainbow, not too far from Tally Lake west of Whitefish.

Blue Lake: No trout.

Blue Lake (near Stryker): Small brook trout.

Bock Lake: Private.

Boyle Lake: No trout.

Brenneman Slough: Kokanees and cutthroats.

Bull Lake: Limited access.

Burgess Lake (Flathead Indian Reservation): Rainbows. This shallow lake, off U.S. 93 near Perma, fishes best in the spring and, if the planted rainbows survive the warm water of the summer months, in the fall.

Cabin Lake: Private.

Canyon Lake: Rainbow and brook trout.

Carter's Pond: Private.

Cedar Creek: Closed.

Cedar Lake: Small fish in this boggy pond a few miles north of Columbia Falls. It's impossible to fish from shore, but it's a fun place to putter around in a boat or a float tube.

Chinook Lake: Few, if any, fish, but the rumor is that there is a remnant population of very large trout. Cutthroats. Anyone willing to hike up and check out this lake, about 2½ miles from the Tally Lake Ranger Station, for me?

Circle Lake: Private.

Clark Lake: Private.

Cliff Lake (Flathead Indian Reservation): Cutthroats. Closed from July 1 to October 1.

Corduroy Creek: Too small.

Creek Lake: Private.

Creston (Jessup Mill Pond) Lake: Brook trout.

Crow Creek (Flathead Indian Reservation): Small brookies.

Crystal Creek: Small fish.

Crystal Lake: Private.

Dog Creek: Small fish.

Dog Lake: Few trout.

Dollar Lake: Rainbows.

Donaldson Creek: Closed.

Double Lake: Private.

Dry Lake: No trout here but there are fine yellow perch. They strike best at small streamers. Find one and you've located a school, so work a hot area fast. Dry Lake is north of Bif Fork off the Creston Road on private land.

Ducharme Creek (Flathead Indian Reservation): Small fish.

Duck Lake: North of Whitefish and above Upper Stillwater, there are a few good trout here and some small cutthroats, brookies, and so on. Not worth the bother.

Dunsire Creek: Small fish.

East Bass Lake: Private.

Echo Lake: This is a popular lake for warm-water species (see Bass section).

Emmet Slough or Horseshoe Bend: Largemouth bass.

Estes Lake: Rainbows.

Evers Creek: Small brookies throughout, with some 10-inch "monsters" in the beaver ponds.

Fire Lakes: Brook trout. These three lakes west of Finger Lakes can be reached by a rough, cross-country hike from the Sunday Creek Road. For someone who loves nice-sized brookies, they are worth the trek.

Fitzsimmons Creek: Too small.

Freeland Creek: Closed.

Garlick Lake: Private.

Gilbertson Lake: Private.

Grayling Lakes: Private.

Griffin Creek: Few fish.

Half Moon Lake: Smallmouth bass in this 80-acre lake 4½ miles from Coram (and smallmouths are such a rarity in the state that they alone make it worth a visit).

Hand Creek: Small fish.

Hanson Lake: Private.

Harbin Lake: Rainbows.

Haskill Creek: Closed.

Hewolf Creek (Flathead Indian Reservation): Too small.

Horseshoe Lake: Smallmouth bass were stocked here in 1914, the first known plant in the state of this fish.

Jette Lake: Private.

Johnson Lakes: Private.

Lake Five: It has largemouth bass but this is such a big lake, at over 200 acres, that it is hard to find them sometime. Fly fishermen who know it do well here, though.

Lake Monroe or Lower Ashley: Private.

Lake of the Woods: Private.

Lazy Creek: Small brook trout.

LeBeau Creek: A small stream with small brookies, but there are lots of them. You'll find it west of the Stillwater Ranger Station.

Leech Lake: Cutthroats.

Lone or Middle Ashley Lake: Poor access.

Loon Lake: Northern pike and bass.

Lore Lake: Poor access.

Lost Creek (Flathead Indian Reservation): Small brookies.

Lost Lake: Brook trout.

Lost Lake (Flathead Indian Reservation): Cutthroats.

Lost Sheep Lake (Flathead Indian Reservation): Cutthroats.

Lower Crow Reservoir (Flathead Indian Reservation): Mediocre fishing.

Lower Sunday Lake: Rainbows.

Magpie Creek (Flathead Indian Reservation): Too small.

Martin Lakes: Brookies.

Martha Lake: Rainbow-cutthroat hybrids. This is one of those "masochist's delights" for hard-core backpackers. It's up Birch Creek in high alpine country.

McCaffery or Long Lake: Limited access.

McGilbray Lake: No access.

McWinegar Slough: Largemouth bass and yellow perch.

Meadow Lake: Closed to non-tribal members.

Middle Fork Jocko River: Closed to non-tribal members.

Mission Creek (Flathead Indian Reservation): Rainbow and brook trout.

Morning Slough: Largemouth bass.

Mud Creek (Flathead Indian Reservation): Too small.

Mud Lake (Flathead Indian Reservation): Poor fishing.

Mystery Lake: Cutthroats.

No Tellum Reservoir: Rainbows.

North Fork Jocko River (Flathead Indian Reservation): Catch and release for trout (except you can keep brookies).

Olive Lake: No trout here, but it is an oddity. A hike-in lake for largemouths. Go out of Bigfork by the Creston Highway.

Pablo Lake (Flathead Indian Reservation): Bass, perch, and limited trout.

Parker Lakes: Private.

Petersen Lake: Largemouth bass.

Plummer's Lake: Private.

Pratt Lake: Private.

Rainbow Lake (near Whitefish): Winter kills.

Redmond Creek: Too small.

Revais Creek (Flathead Indian Reservation): Small brookies.

Russell or Fenan or Moon Slough: A fine place for largemouth bass, especially early in the season. It's 4 miles west of Bigfork.

Sabine Creek (Flathead Indian Reservation): Few fish.

St. Mary Lake (Flathead Indian Reservation): Rainbows and planted cutthroats.

Sheppard Creek: Cutthroat and brook trout.

Skaggs Lake: No access.

Smith Lake (near Whitefish): Brook trout.

Skyles Lake: Largemouth bass. There's a state fishing access site here.

Smokey Lake: Rainbow and brook trout.

South Fork Jocko River: Closed to non-tribal members.

Spill Lake: Private.

Spring Creek (Kalispell): Brook and rainbow trout.

Spring Creek (Flathead Indian Reservation): Small fish.

Spring Creek (drains Morning Slough): Brook trout.

Squaw Lake: Cutthroats.

Stoner Creek: Small brook trout.

Sunrise Lake: Private.

Sunday Creek: Brook trout.

Swartz Lake (Flathead Indian Reservation): Brook trout.

Swimming Lake: Private.

Tamarack Creek: Too small

Thornburg Lake: Brook trout.

West Fork Swift Creek: Cutthroats.

White Clay Creek: Small brookies.

White Horse Lake (Flathead Indian Reservation): Closed to non-tribal members.

■ *Special thanks to Joe DosSantos, John Fraley, Tom McDonald, Dr. Jack Stanford, and Jim Vashro for their help on the Flathead River drainage.*

MIDDLE FORK OF THE FLATHEAD RIVER ▪ Flowing for ninety miles from its formation at the confluence of Strawberry and Bowl Creeks in the heart of the Bob Marshall Wilderness (the Bob); the Middle Fork of the Flathead River is a remarkable stream.

Even running alongside U.S. 2, it looks wild and free. Creeks wind northward into the jagged peaks of Glacier National Park. Standing waves and severe rapids pound through towering, narrow canyons. Acres and acres of charred trees stand as testimony to lightning-inspired wild fires. Dark green pine forest cloaks the mountains to timberline where rock and ice then hold sway. The northern east-west line of Burlington Northern clings to the mountain sides. Piles of graying snags, some several feet in diameter, lie in huge piles on midstream gravel bars, reminders of the tremendous power of the Middle Fork during its swollen, ferocious spring runoff.

Elk, eagles, grizzlies, deer, mountain goats—all are sighted along the river.

The wind blasts through here in the winter and U.S. 2 is no place at all to be during a snowstorm. This is rough country masquerading as scenic splendor.

One sight you will not see with any regularity is that of a fly

Casting for that earthly reward
Photo courtesy of Hungry Horse News

FLATHEAD RIVER—MIDDLE FORK

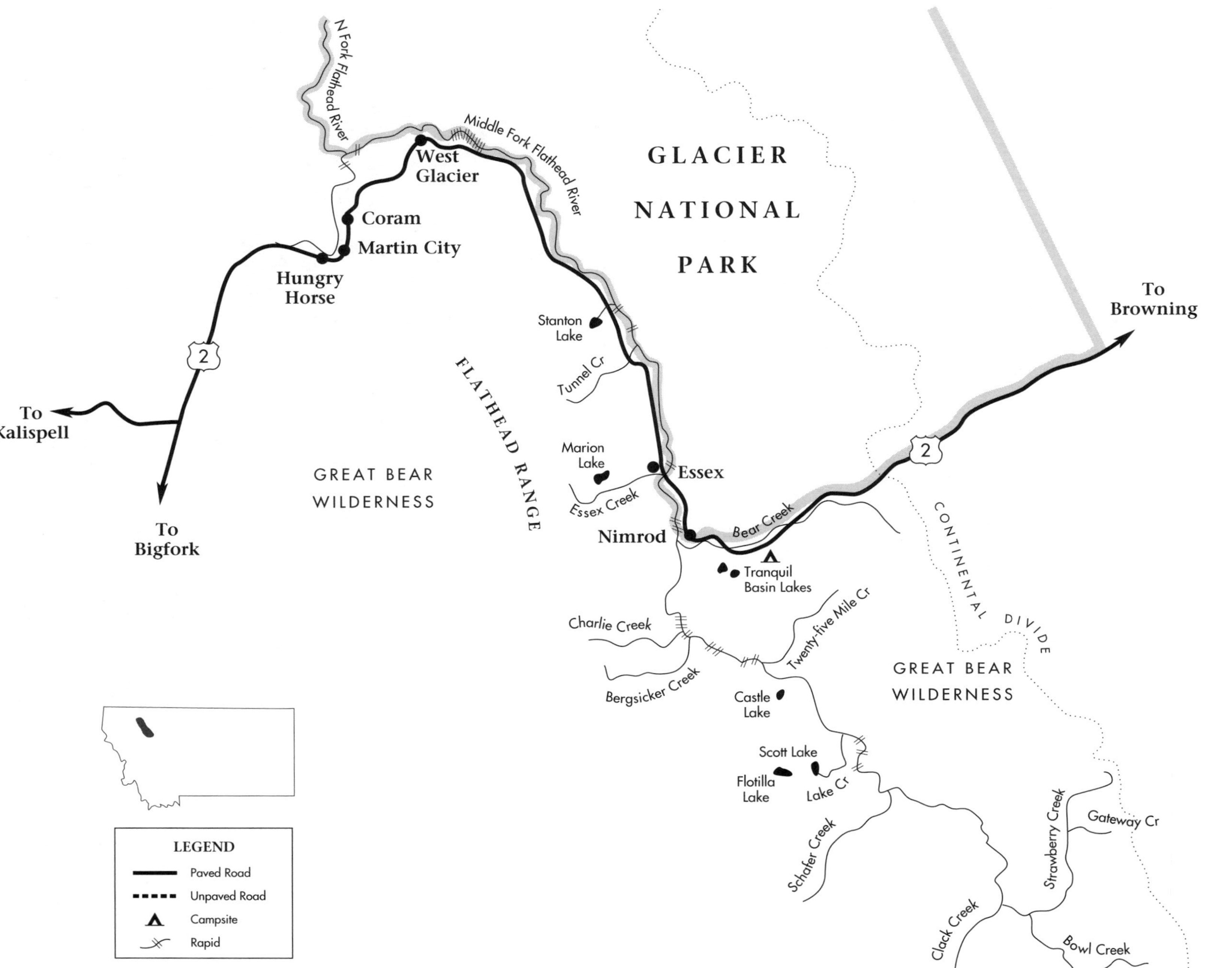

fisher wading and casting into the deep, emerald runs and pools or drifting a Sofa Pillow next to a logjam. The Middle Fork has a terrible reputation as far as fishing goes where it drifts and bends outside of the Bob Marshall Wilderness complex. Some of this is deserved, some is a result of rumor taking on the trappings of reality.

Yet, in the wilderness, fishing is considered good for westslope cutthroat trout that hit dry flies with little selectivity from the end of runoff through October if the weather holds. Fish to 16 inches are not uncommon.

The first dozen or so miles from the headwaters down to Schafer Meadows is an easy float through unspoiled country. Below Schafer for 32 miles to U.S. 2, the river rips through a steep-walled canyon. In June and July this is an exciting float for experienced rafters. Others should hire a guide.

Fishing here is best from July into early fall, but low water levels make floating difficult. Large bull trout of over 30 inches are moving through the system and will hit large streamers drifted down deep. The bigger the pattern the better and 1/0 and 2/0 northern pike patterns work just fine. You cannot intimidate a large bull trout. If a fly comes into view, no matter how large, it will attack. Whitefish and cutthroats make up a large portion of its diet. On rare occasions the bull trout will take drys like Royal Wulffs and big Elk Hair Caddis.

Many floaters hire an airplane and fly into the strip at Schaefer Meadows to make a float of a couple of days. Others reach the interior on horseback or on foot along trails that parallel the river or the various tributaries that join it. Flying in takes less than an hour. A horse takes a day and hiking has its own rewards. The Bob is larger than some eastern states, and much of the finest dry fly fishing for cutthroat trout is found here. Floating provides best access, but even on foot, wading opportunities are bountiful, and a 60-foot cast will cover a lot of prime water.

Stone fly nymphs and drys, even well after the hatches, will take fish, as will flashy streamers like Spruce Flies and Black-Nosed Dace.

Where Bear Creek enters the Middle Fork at a large gravel parking area on the south side of U.S. 2 is a nice place to stop and work your way upriver casting for cutthroat and bull trout. In winter this is one of the best runs for mountain whitefish found anywhere. A Gold Ribbed Hare's ear nymph bounced along the bottom may take a lot of fish.

A good trail up Bear Creek strikes off into the Great Bear Wilderness (part of the Bob Marshall Wilderness Complex) and after five miles or so the fishing picks up. Some of the paths that break off and drop down to the river are less than a foot wide and cling to loose rock and dirt on the sides of cliffs. The trip to the river frequently rivals the fishing in terms of excitement. Sink-tip lines help reach the trout during the heat and bright light of summer.

From Bear Creek to its meeting with the North Fork just above Blankenship Bridge, the Middle Fork keeps company with U.S. 2 for 44 miles. This water is considered borderline sterile by most fly fishers and there is some truth to this.

The Middle Fork, along with both the North and South forks, is not nutrient rich, receiving most of its water from snow and ice melt—a pretty sterile system. Caddisflies, closely followed by mayflies and dipterans, head the dietary list for cutthroats here and in the other

Treat 'em gently when you release 'em.
Photo courtesy of Hungry Horse News

A Special Fly for the Middle Fork of the Flathead River

The cutthroats in the Middle Fork are seldom so filled with insects or bait fish that they will stop feeding. In this pure (read, "unproductive if not downright sterile") water the fish are always looking for an easy meal. This means that the angler can have a lot of fun bouncing a juicy looking, terrestrial dry fly over the riffles and pools.

MCMURRAY ANT

Hook: standard dry fly

Body: balsa wood sections connected with monofilament (lacquered black or red)

Hackle: black or ginger (wrapped at the waist)

This is the perfect terrestrial for rough, western rivers like the Middle Fork. It is buoyant, never needing a lot of false casting, and in larger sizes it is easy to see on the water. The favorite for this river is a size 12, and it pays to carry both black and red versions. On different days different colors work better.

The McMurray Ant (and a number of other McMurray balsa variations) are widely available commercially, but they are also easy and quick to make from preformed parts. The same stores that sell the finished flies sell the parts. This is an eastern pattern, but it is such a practical searching fly, especially on streams like the Middle Fork where terrestrials form the bulk of the summer food, that it is catching on throughout the West.

two forks. Stone flies, bees, wasps, beetles, and ants are about equal on the next rung. Emphemerellidae and Baetidae lead the mayfly parade, but in numbers rank far, far below that associated with waters like the Missouri. Fish top the bull trout preference list followed by mayflies and small dogs.

Bull trout of size use this stretch as a corridor to reach isolated spawning grounds far back in the forest. Finding these fish is difficult. And most of the cutthroats are small (a 12-incher is above average), but fairly numerous. They will hit small drys drifted near shore and around midstream boulders.

The fishing below West Glacier is similar except that in some of the narrow canyon runs some good-sized rainbows will occasionally hit streamers or even hoppers, Sofa Pillows, and the like. When these fish are on, usually near evening in late July and August, the action is quite good. Unfortunately, no one has been able to predict this outbreak of rainbow enthusiasm with any consistency. If you've got several weeks and wish to float from West Glacier to Blankenship every afternoon and early evening, a number of local fly fishers, including myself, would probably buy you a drink or two in exchange for a glance at your angling log.

One technique that seems to produce results, though infrequently, is to use a super-fast-sinking 15-foot sink tip and something like a Flashabou Woolly Bugger. Dropping this down through the eddies and then pulsing it near bottom sometimes triggers a response, which often includes a rainbow arcing above the water, pulling 20 feet of slack fly line and leader. Such is life.

The main company you will have on the Middle Fork are large tour-operated rafts filled with giggling floaters soaking up cold water, hot sun, and cold beverages (quite original). Most of this action takes place above West Glacier on the rougher water. The Middle Fork below town consists of boulder runs, riffles, deep holes, and some relatively tame white water. Not the stuff of thrilling rafting memories. There are plenty of small cutthroats and some bull trout here and the float is a dandy way to kill an afternoon.

All in all, the Middle Fork of the Flathead River will never be confused with the Madison for its angling quality, but it is one of the least-spoiled wild rivers remaining in the lower forty-eight states.

May it always be so.

Streams and lakes that are part of the Middle Fork drainage but are also located in Glacier National Park are discussed in the section on the park.

As is mentioned in the chapter on the North Fork, cutthroats are not sophisticated when it comes to chasing flies. They will hit almost anything that reasonably approximates the size, shape, and color of the naturals. They are also delicate members of the trout clan and need special care when being played and released.

Fishing Waters in the Middle Fork Drainage

Bear Creek: One of the larger tributaries of the river, Bear Creek parallels U.S. 2 for 13 miles before making a break for freedom turning south into the wilderness. Large bull trout move up here to spawn, which is a marvel considering how small the stream is as it vanishes from roadside view. Some wild cutthroats also swim here.

Bergsicker Creek: Heading below Prospector Mountain, Bergsicker is not much to fish above, but down by the Middle Fork it offers some runs and holes for cutthroats and spawning bull trout. By trail, it's 8 miles above Nimrod.

Bowl Creek: Way back in the wilderness, this true mountain stream meets the Middle Fork 20 miles above Schafer Meadows. The fishing diminishes the farther upstream you travel, but there are fair numbers of 6- to 9-inch cutthroats. Lots of people on horseback or foot hit this water. Hike in from the Middle Fork of the Flathead or the West Fork of the Teton River.

Castle Lake: A steep hike of a mile or so a bit above Twentyfive Mile Creek, there are nice cutthroats here in good country.

Charlie Creek: This one, 6 miles above Nimrod, is followed by trail and is of interest to bull trout fanatics who might find the occasional 20-incher intriguing.

Essex Creek: Here, just off U.S. Highway 2, you'll find a few small cutthroats that receive more attention than they deserve.

Yellow fritillaries welcome the early spring in meadows along Montana's rivers and streams.
Photo by Stan Bradshaw

Flotilla Lake: Lots of people stagger in here on a good trail north of Miner Creek and it is big—146 acres—with plenty of cutthroats to 17 inches. They're spooky but the cruisers will hit a nymph twitched in front of their epicurean snouts. Even with the people, you feel like you are in wild country.

Gateway Creek: Flowing mostly in spectacular canyon country near the headwaters, Gateway Creek's lower timbered reaches have some nice wilderness cutthroats.

Lake Creek: Small, pretty, not far from Scott Lake, Lake Creek has some cutthroat and bull trout.

Marion Lake: Another roadside attraction that gets some back country pressure mainly because it has lots of cutt-rainbow hybrids up to 15 inches. Pack snowshoes and time ice-out perfectly on the 80-acre, 145-foot deep lake and the action is sporting. It's 4 trail miles from Walton Ranger Station on U.S. 2.

Schafer Creek: In late summer and early autumn this is a stream to hit if you've never caught (and released) a bull trout of more than five pounds. Most people do not care or know how to fish for the species, nor do they come all the way back here to do so. Big streamers turn the trick. It enters the Middle Fork from the south at Shafer Meadows.

Scott Lake: You'll find good fishing on this lake on Miner Creek, but it's swampy and oh so buggy with wild animals, especially surly moose. Springs keep the shallow water from freezing and there are good numbers of 12-inch cutthroats and a few larger.

Stanton Lake: Only twenty minutes from U.S. 2, Stanton gets hammered constantly, but sometimes yields a rainbow or cutthroat of some size. A lazy man's wilderness day hike.

Strawberry Creek: In headwaters territory near the Continental Divide, Strawberry Creek has half-foot cutthroats and some decent bull trout on the spawning move. Muddlers around size 6 can work on bull trout if you are cramped for space.

Tranquil Basin Lakes: These small lakes of 10 and 8 acres are about a half an hour south of Nimrod. Some big fish, for cutthroat anyway, are here. This is glacial cirque country.

Tunnel Creek: Small, flowing through the forest, Tunnel Creek is fun to fish on your knees with a short rod for small cutthroats. You can get to it from U.S 2 about a mile or so west of Pinnacle.

Other Waters

Almeda Lake: Planted cutthroats.

Basin Creek: Small fish.

Beaver Lake: Barren

Bersicker Lake: Barren

Bradley Lake: Barren—not enough water.

Calbick Creek: Small trout.

Challenge Creek: Closed for spawning.

Clack Creek: Some cutthroat and bull trout. The reason these small tributaries aren't bothered much is that they are hard to reach just for the fishing, but if you're there anyway they are worth dabbling a fly on for 8- to 10-inch trout.

Coal Creek: Few fish.

Cox Creek: Some cutthroats.

Cup Lake: Barren

Cy Creek: Too small.

Deerlick Creek: Too small.

Devil Creek: Too small.

Dickey Creek: Too small.

Dirtyface Creek: You hear something about this water every now and then.

It is only 3 miles up from the highway at Bear Creek, but unless you find 3-inch trout a challenge forget this water.

Geifer Creek: Too small.

Granite Creek: Closed for spawning.

Lodgepole Creek: Closed for spawning.

Logan Creek: Too small.

Long Creek: Closed for spawning.

Miner Creek: Few small cutthroats.

Moose Creek: Freezes out.

Morrison Creek: Closed for spawning.

Paola Creek: Too small.

Stanton Creek: Some small cutthroats.

Trail Creek: Poor for cutthroats; some bull trout.

Tunnel Creek Lake: Cutthroats.

Twentyfive Mile Creek: Some cutthroats.

Winter Creek: Too small.

NORTH FORK OF THE FLATHEAD RIVER ▪ Wild, unspoiled, pure, and, at best, a modest trout fishery pretty much sums up the North Fork of the Flathead River, which has its feral beginnings in the McDonald Mountains of British Columbia, the Whitefish Range to the west, and the Livingston Range to the east in Glacier National Park.

North Fork of the Flathead River
Photo by John Holt

Grizzly bears, black bears, gray wolves, bald eagles, lynx, ptarmigan, porcupines, possible caribou, bull trout, and westslope cutthroat trout thrive in the drainage's heavily timbered acres. Many of these species are on threatened or endangered lists.

Three of Montana's native salmonids are found in the river—westslope cutthroat trout, bull trout, and mountain whitefish (which you will catch on occasion without trying). The cutthroats are found hiding behind rocks and boulders and beneath logjams all year long while the bull trout migrate up from Flathead Lake fifty miles to the south.

From spring through early September the river is filled with countless silvery cutthroats that run small—8 to 12 inches—with maybe a

FLATHEAD RIVER—NORTH FORK

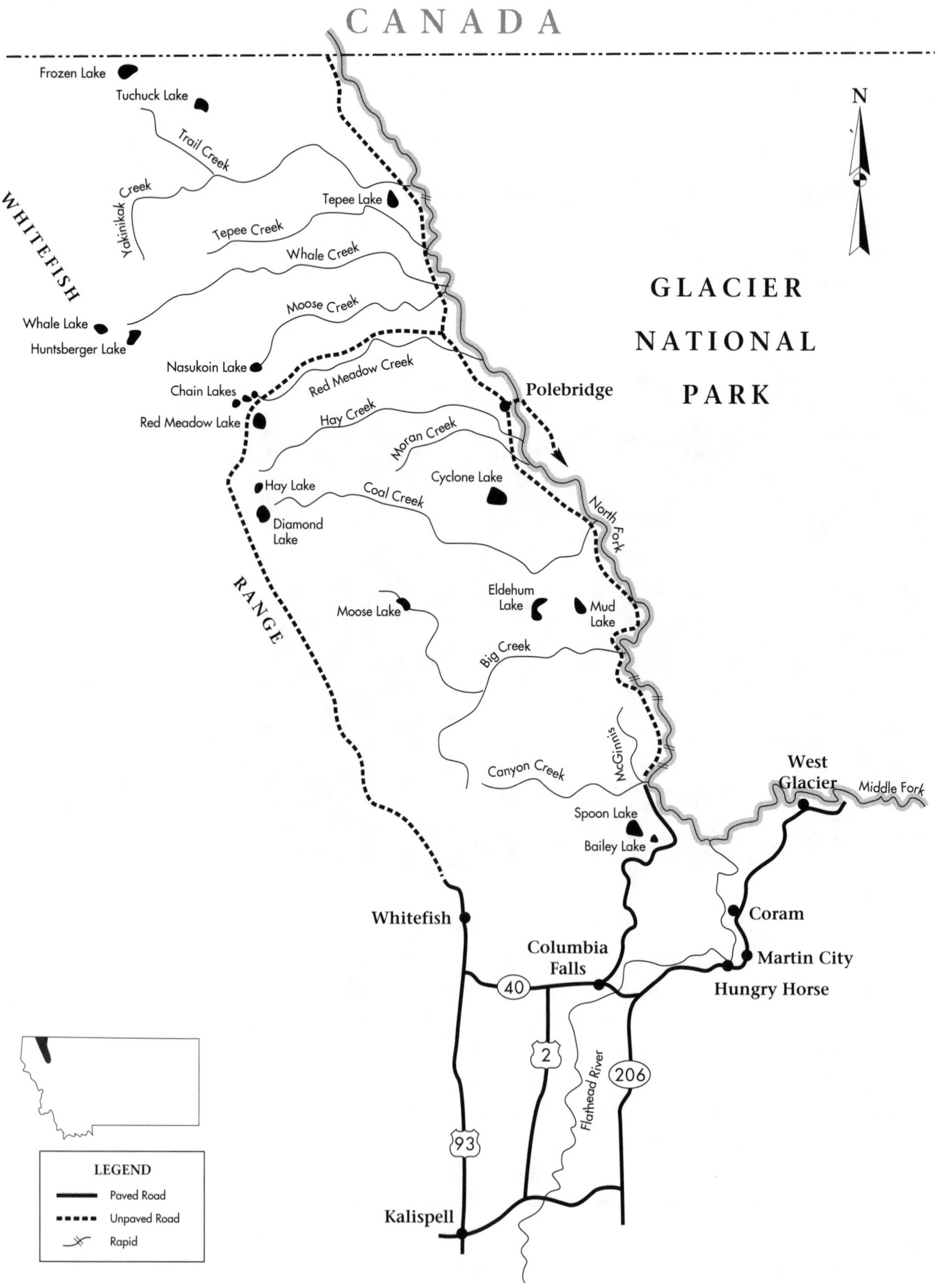

CANADA

GLACIER NATIONAL PARK

N

WHITEFISH RANGE

Frozen Lake
Tuchuck Lake
Trail Creek
Yakinikak Creek
Tepee Lake
Tepee Creek
Whale Creek
Whale Lake
Huntsberger Lake
Moose Creek
Nasukoin Lake
Chain Lakes
Red Meadow Creek
Red Meadow Lake
Polebridge
Hay Creek
Moran Creek
Hay Lake
Coal Creek
Cyclone Lake
Diamond Lake
North Fork
Eldehum Lake
Mud Lake
Moose Lake
Big Creek
McGinnis
Canyon Creek
West Glacier
Middle Fork
Spoon Lake
Bailey Lake
Whitefish
Coram
Columbia Falls
Martin City
Hungry Horse
40
2
206
Flathead River
93
Kalispell

LEGEND
Paved Road
Unpaved Road
Rapid

few up to 19 inches. They are easy pickings for dry flies such as the Royal Humpy, Elk Hair Caddis, and hoppers, and wet flies such as Hare's Ear and Black Gnat. Whether you wade near shore (be careful, this river is much faster and deeper than it first appears) or fish from a raft, cast the fly near shore towards any submerged or partially submerged rocks and boulders. Pay particular attention to seams or channels through underwater rocks. You may take larger fish in these mini-runs. Sometimes a Woolly Bugger worked like a snake will move the larger fish.

Both the gravel and dirt North Fork Road and the dirt inside road (in Glacier Park) provide ready access to the river. Both roads are tough to negotiate in wet weather due to mudslides, gumbo, etc. Access is also abundant for the floater, and one of the easier floats is from the Big Creek Access down to Glacier Rim—an easy four hours of fishing runs, glides, flats, riffles, pools, and banks. Taking a few dozen cutts is possible. Ford Creek Ranger work station down to Polebridge is a longer float, taking all day.

Unlike many rivers that are noted for having certain species in specific stretches of water, the North Fork is egalitarian in this respect. Any of the three species may be found more or less equally in any part of the river, though numbers decline somewhat as you move upstream.

The river near its confluence with the Middle Fork and at Moose City where it enters this country is turquoise clear, swiftly flowing, and has rock and boulder substrate. As a result, both of these floats are prime bull trout cruises, also. The Ford Creek float, beginning near the Canadian border, is best from mid-July into August and the float below Polebridge works as soon as the runoff ends. Never hit this river at peak flow. You will probably die. House-sized boulders and 100-foot deadfalls are propelled downstream like toys at runoff. Near the end of high water as the North Fork lowers and begins to clear, this compression can trigger some fairly good action and the cutts will run a bit larger. Even without the trout, the scenery is worth the float.

As for *Salvelinus confluentus,* bull trout feed extensively on other fish that hang out in the benthic currents well below the surface. I've caught fish that have disgorged a half dozen whitefish during release attempts. They'll eat other trout, perch, sculpins—anything. They seem to come out of nowhere and strike with a sudden swiftness and power that is impressive to feel. Large streamers, red-and-white 1/0 and 2/0 Deceivers, produce down deep with sink tips along rough, bouldery runs, and in and under any logs or logjams. Large stonefly nymphs also produce. Size 0X or 1X tippets on 4- or 5-foot leaders, seven-weight, nine-foot rods and some luck will handle these fish. Large stonefly nymphs also produce.

In August bull trout begin to color up like very big brook trout. Find the fish, run a streamer past their noses, and you will catch one (when the season opens again). Locating these migratory creatures is the trick. Most of the prime spawning tributaries are closed to fishing to protect the species.

Bull trout are closely related to the anadromous Dolly Varden, being differentiated by such things as mandibular pores and gill raker morphology. They tend to run larger than Dolly Varden and are strictly a freshwater species.

Bull trout inhabit clear, cold lakes and streams in Montana, Idaho, Utah, British Columbia, Alberta, and the Northwest Territories. In the lower forty-eight states, Montana has the most and the best habitat and most of that lies in the northwest corner of the state. The Flathead River drainage extending into Canada, the western edge of Glacier National Park, and the Bob Marshall Wilderness complex is considered nearly perfect habitat.

The fish is a long-distance spawner by freshwater standards, often covering over 150 miles from Flathead Lake up into the tiny tributaries in British Columbia. Movement begins in late April and lasts through early summer with much of the mileage covered during spring runoff in very high, turbid conditions. Spawning takes place from September through November on gravel redds constructed in areas of good flow. Spotting a twenty-pound fish lying in ten inches of water in a stream less than 15 feet wide is a hell of a sight. The fish rarely spawn before they are four or five years old and deposit, on average, 1,000 eggs per pound of body weight. No one has been able to pin down a consistent spawning pattern for the fish.

"Bull trout are an anomaly in the trout world," said state fisheries biologist Pat Clancy. "Some fish spawn each year, some every other year, and some less frequently than that. And some of the fish don't move back downstream until late winter or early spring of the next year. The same is true of juvenile fish. Some stay in the stream for a couple of years. Others move after just one year. No one really knows for sure what triggers the movement."

To the west, larch, lodgepole, and fir cover the slopes to the distant horizon. The sides of Huckleberry Mountain in Glacier National Park on the east are still recovering from the brutal fires of 1910 and 1927. Add to this the fact that the Forest Service is allowing extensive clearcuts on the western side of the river, some in dwindling old growth forest along major bull trout spawning streams, and it is easy to see why anglers and fisheries biologists are concerned about the future of this under-appreciated gamefish.

Because the North Fork is a low productivity system, it cannot stand much fishing pressure (like that found on even the Upper Clark Fork). Any significant deterioration in the water quality could be devastating. Timber harvest and the cumulative effects of canopy removal

Landing one on the North Fork
Photo courtesy of Hungry Horse News

could cause a rapid melting of the snowpack, increasing sedimentation and bank erosion. Sedimentation chokes bull trout eggs and they die. Add to this possible threats from proposed coal mines in Canada, oil drilling near the river, and housing development, and it is easy to understand how tenuous the bull trout's hold on life is here.

But for now this is still one of the finest wild rivers in the world, as its Wild and Scenic River designation indicates. The cutthroat and bull trout are doing pretty well and the fishing is active enough to hold an angler's attention for a few hours.

Fishing Waters in the North Fork Drainage

The following lakes and streams are found only on the western side of the drainage. North Fork country is filled with running water. Every trickle seems to have a name, even the ones that dry up by July 15. These are not mentioned and are so small you would not be likely to notice them as you drove or walked over them. All others are located in Glacier National Park and are discussed in that section.

Pattern selection is not sophisticated for cutthroats. The fish are wild and not selective. Drys such as an Adams, Royal or Green Humpy (this one is superb in fast water), Goddard Caddis, Hare's Ear nymph, size-8 Brown stone, Prince nymph, and olive Woolly Worm will cover the action. Simple but fun. The challenge on mountain lakes is anticipating the trout's feeding route and then making the appropriate cast. On streams, hitting pocket water is the game.

Bailey Lake: This lake (7½ miles north of Columbia Falls) looks like a potential candidate for a housing development pond, but it has some foot-long cutts.

Canyon Creek: A pretty stream, Canyon Creek flows beneath the North Fork Road and has average fishing for small cutthroats for a few miles. Goddard and Elk Hair Caddis country.

Chain Lakes: You can get to these four pretty lakes in the Whitefish

Mountains on a rough road just over the crest from Red Meadow Lake. Three of the lakes, averaging about 15 acres each, used to be excellent fishing for large, fat cutthroats. Wilderness advocates, in an attempt to publicize the location's attributes so that they would be included in a wilderness bill, turned northwest Montana onto the spot and now the place is overrun with hikers and anglers. You always hurt the ones you love. Still, on occasion, especially from late September on, when the weather turns cool and often ugly and the yupster masses have turned their attentions to the impending cross-country skiing, lycra-fashion explosion, the fishing can be fun like it should be with small drys, including caddis and Adams or a nymph slowly stripped near the surface.

Coal Creek: It's closed to protect spawning bull trout, but if I ever find out I only have weeks to live, I'll fish this one. One of the best-looking pieces of water in the region—deep runs and clear pools highlighted by weathered gray logjams.

Cyclone Lake: It's not bad in late May and early June before the thundering herd hits this out-of-the-way 120-acre water. Nymphs worked around the shoreline produce cutthroats to perhaps 13 inches. A canoe or float tube are needed and dragging the former in from where you park your rig is not easy, especially in the swampy parts. It is hard to find off the Coal Creek Road.

Diamond Lake: This small lake could freeze out, but has some nice 12-inch cutthroats. Take a twenty-minute stroll from the end of the Coal Creek road to get there.

Elelehum Lake: It used to be just a mile walk from the end of the Elelehum Creek Road, which is now closed (to protect wildlife), so you hike through some thick forest, uphill, with bear vibes everywhere in the air. There are cutthroats here, but they are not trophies.

Frozen Lake: This lake is located in some weird country along the U.S.-Canada border. After turning off U.S. Highway 93 at Grave Creek and driving to and then along Weasel Creek Road through massive

A Special Fly for the North Fork of the Flathead River

Some of the oldest patterns are still the best. The classic, downwing wet fly is perfect for the North Fork. Fished with a swing across the riffles and flats, a wet fly covers a lot of water. And, with the spunky cutthroats of the North Fork, that is often the key to finding the larger specimens.

BLACK GNAT

Hook: heavier, wet fly hook

Body: black chenille

Wing: slate mallard quill

Hackle: black hen

It's not a bad idea to carry a selection of classic wet flies, including the Black Gnat, Blue Quill, Hare's Ear, Leadwing Coachman, Light Cahill, McGinty, and Queen of the Waters, for all western waters. The Black Gnat is a particular favorite because of that bulky body. Fished dead drift, like a nymph, it works on the toughest rivers; and fished with a swing, cutting across the current in a steady arc, it brings trout out for the chase.

clearcuts following the signs to Frozen Lake, you come to land that is so intensively logged over, it looks as though the two countries had a tag-team clearcutting contest. The place looks like an asteroid having a bad day. A walk of about a half mile down an old skid trail takes you to a timbered shoreline where you can cast from a float tube streamers like Matukas, Buggers, and Zonkers to cutthroats up to four pounds and a few nice bull trout. On the Canadian side there is a boat launch and you'll share the water with smoking motors and bobbing beer cans. This could be a hell of a fishery, but the aesthetics are shot.

Hay Lake: This lake lies in clearcut, swampy country at the end of the Hay Creek drainage. In the fall the road is often closed 4 miles from the lake to protect wildlife. All the same, there are some pretty cutthroats of maybe 10 to 11 inches here that hit any dry fly thrown their way.

Holt Creek: You'll find marginal fishing for cutthroats and a very few bull trout in this pretty drainage that is too brushy to fish properly.

Huntsberger Lake: Huntsberger is a nice fishery for colorful, wild cutthroats that are fat and maybe 12 inches on a generous day. Take the Whale Creek Road. Very good bear country.

McGinnis Creek: This tributary to Canyon Creek has a few cutthroats and, rarely, a decent bull trout.

Moran Creek: A tributary of Hay Creek, Moran grows a few cutthroat and bull trout in the lower reaches. Very small water.

Moose Lake: Moose Lake is fished a good deal by locals for small, planted cutthroats that will take a slowly retrieved Hare's Ear nymph (and drys when the wind is not blowing). Few fish are over 10 inches in this deep blue water. There is a campground. Pretty lake in wild country, but the fishing is nothing much.

Moose Creek: This is not the outlet of Moose Lake, but flows to the North Fork a few miles south of the Ford Work Center. A pretty stream running next to a logging road with small native cutthroats and some bull trout. Tough to fish because of the brush.

Mud Lake: Right next to the Coal Creek logging road lies Mud Lake. The only time to fish it is right after ice-out if you can get in. Flashy streamers work well when retrieved with a good deal of zip. Later in the season it gets choked with weeds. Shorelines and the outlet are good for some cutthroats up to 20 inches in this 15-acre pond. Moose occasionally walk across the shallow west end munching aquatic plants as they go.

Nasukoin Lake: Small (7 acres) but fairly deep, Nasukoin is filled with 12-inch cutthroats that are boring to catch on drys after the first half dozen or so. Walk in from where the Moose Creek Road is closed off.

Red Meadow Lake: Small grayling (to 7 inches) abound and there are some nice cutthroats to maybe 16 inches. Try small drys for the grayling, and nymphs worked deep for the cutts. This place is nailed by weekend and out-of-state traffic all summer. I once saw an older lady with pink and blue hair playing "Cocktails for Two" on an organ that was set up outside a motor home at the campground here. Too strange for me. This one is located on Red Meadow Creek Road, 40 miles north of Columbia Falls.

Red Meadow Creek: Parallels Red Meadow Creek Road north of Polebridge, but getting to the water means fighting fireweed and devils club much of the time. The cutthroat fishing isn't worth the effort, but from late July on, some decent bull trout hide beneath the logs and undercut banks. Big streamers work but are tough to fish in the small water. A six-pound fish here is interesting, just ask the resident grizzlies.

Spoon Lake: Ten minutes north of Columbia Falls, off the North Fork Road, lies this 70 acres with some cutthroats. There's better water a bit up the road.

Tepee Creek: Small and brushy Tepee has a freestone bottom. Some good (to 12 inches) cutthroats hold in the pocket water. There's not much of this, though. About 48 miles north of Columia Falls you take the Whale Creek Road to get there.

Tepee Lake: Up by the Ford Work Center, this one is shallow, weedy, surrounded in timber with some nice cutthroats when the winters are not so harsh that the lake freezes out. You can get there from the Tepee Creek Road or the Trail Creek Road north of Polebridge.

Tuchuck Lake: In world-class bear country that is wild and moon-like in appearance, Tuchuck Lake is just a couple of miles south of Canada. It's only 8 acres, but Department of Fish, Wildlife, and Parks biologist Tom Weaver says there are some fair cutthroats in here.

Whale Creek: This stream is closed from the North Fork to Whale Creek Falls, about 10 miles upstream. Some decent cutthroats hold in upper reaches above the falls. It's a fine creek to visit in early September with a camera and polarizing filter. You can spot bull trout to twenty pounds (rarely) holding on the colorful gravels. Their redds are huge and over a foot deep at times. Magic stuff.

Whale Lake: Eight miles or so from the end of the road lies this shallow 20-acre lake. It has some springs that concentrate cutthroats of maybe 12 inches or a shade longer.

Yakinikak Creek: This Trail Creek tributary is small and brushy with some 8-inch or a bit larger cutthroats. I once saw a sow grizzly and her cubs romping away in the upper reaches. Chasing cutthroats on this water is an adrenaline trip.

Other Waters

Cleft Creek: Closed to fishing.

Cyclone Creek: Closed to fishing.

Dead Horse Creek: Closed to fishing.

Hallowat Creek: Closed to fishing.

Hawk Creek: Tiny cutthroats.

Hornet Creek: Closed to fishing.

Ketchikan Creek: Closed to fishing.

Kimmerly Creek: Marginal at best.

Kletomus: Closed to fishing.

Langford Creek: Closed to fishing.

Mathias Creek: Closed to fishing.

Nicola Creek: Closed to fishing.

Ninko Creek: Too small to fish.

Shorty Creek: Brushy and small.

Skookoleel Creek: Closed to fishing.

■ *Special thanks to Pat Clancy and Tom Weaver for their help on the North Fork drainage.*

SOUTH FORK OF THE FLATHEAD RIVER ▪ Twenty years back, the South Fork was too easy. Westslope cutthroat trout of three or four pounds fought to hit a fly on every cast. Then the word spread with vengeance and the river got hammered (this happens to all of us at one time or another) and the fishing edged towards mediocre. This fine, world-class trout stream dancing and rushing through the Bob Marshall Wilderness for 52 miles was about to be trashed from a fly fishing perspective.

People came in on foot to fish the South Fork. They flew in aboard flimsy Cessnas or lurched in on top of jaded pack horses to cast over the sapphire-clear waters. Hundreds of prime fish were derricked from the river, gutted, and grilled in oil over campfires. The population was decimated.

South Fork of the Flathead River
Photo courtesy of Hungry Horse News

The first time I saw this stream was in the early seventies after hiking in from Holland Lake down the Little Salmon River drainage. My first cast took a 20-inch cutthroat. So did the next dozen. In two days on a mile stretch of the South Fork I caught over twenty dozen trout of 15 inches and longer on sophisticated patterns ranging from Sofa Pillows to Renegades to Hornbergs.

People still come to the river each year by the thousands but thanks in part to stricter possession limits, including no trout over 12 inches, the situation has improved. And many outfitters are educating clients about the obvious merits of catch and release. The river is now heading back in that wonderful angling direction but probably receives too much pressure (by backcountry standards anyway) to ever be world class again. All the same, the South Fork ranks with the best and the Bob Marshall is beautiful, unspoiled country. Also, a healthy run of large spawning bull trout moves upriver each season providing sport for fish that may reach twenty pounds. Mountain whitefish are abundant. They are native salmonids deserving of far more respect than they currently receive from anglers. True, they can be a nuisance, especially when nymphing, but they fight (at least a little) and have their place in the natural scheme.

You can reach the river via myriad trails coming in from the Swan and Flathead valleys on the west, from the Middle Fork just south of Glacier on the north, along the Rocky Mountain Front on the east, or through the Spottted Bear Wilderness lying to the south. If you walk you will need at least one week, three being better, to feel the country and explore not only the South Fork, but streams such as the river's headwater, Danaher Creek, or Gordon Creek, or one of the lakes tucked back in the many glacial cirques. And you will want to walk along the 1,000-foot high Chinese Wall or along Big Salmon Lake.

This is the South Fork before it empties into Hungry Horse Reservoir formed by the construction of the Hungry Horse Dam in the fifties. The resevoir is 32 miles long, deep but filling with glacial silt, and the fishing is good at times but declining, as it inevitably does on man-made impoundments. Below the dam for a half-dozen or so miles to the Flathead River the fishing is lousy due to the constant fluctuations in water level caused by power generation regimes. A re-reg dam may change this in coming years, forming a fairly good tailwater fishery, but for now, the water is marginal.

If you like to hike, the river is easily accessible. Just avoid the obvious campsites that have been staked out by outfitters. You'll soon have plenty of company. One trick when hiking along the tributaries is to explore the smaller, marginal paths that break off into the trees. These often lead to hunters' camps that lie unused until fall elk hunting. They offer solitude, comfort, and streamside convenience.

Horse and raft trips, offered by several outfitters, are easy ways to see this country. Floating on your own is possible if you arrange to have your gear flown in, leave the river well above the impassable gorge near Bunker Creek, make a 3-mile portage, and then continue downstream. Life is good but rafts are heavy. Arrangements to tote this gear should be make in advance.

As for the fishing, a five- or six-weight rod of 9 feet is fine. Bring

FLATHEAD RIVER—SOUTH FORK

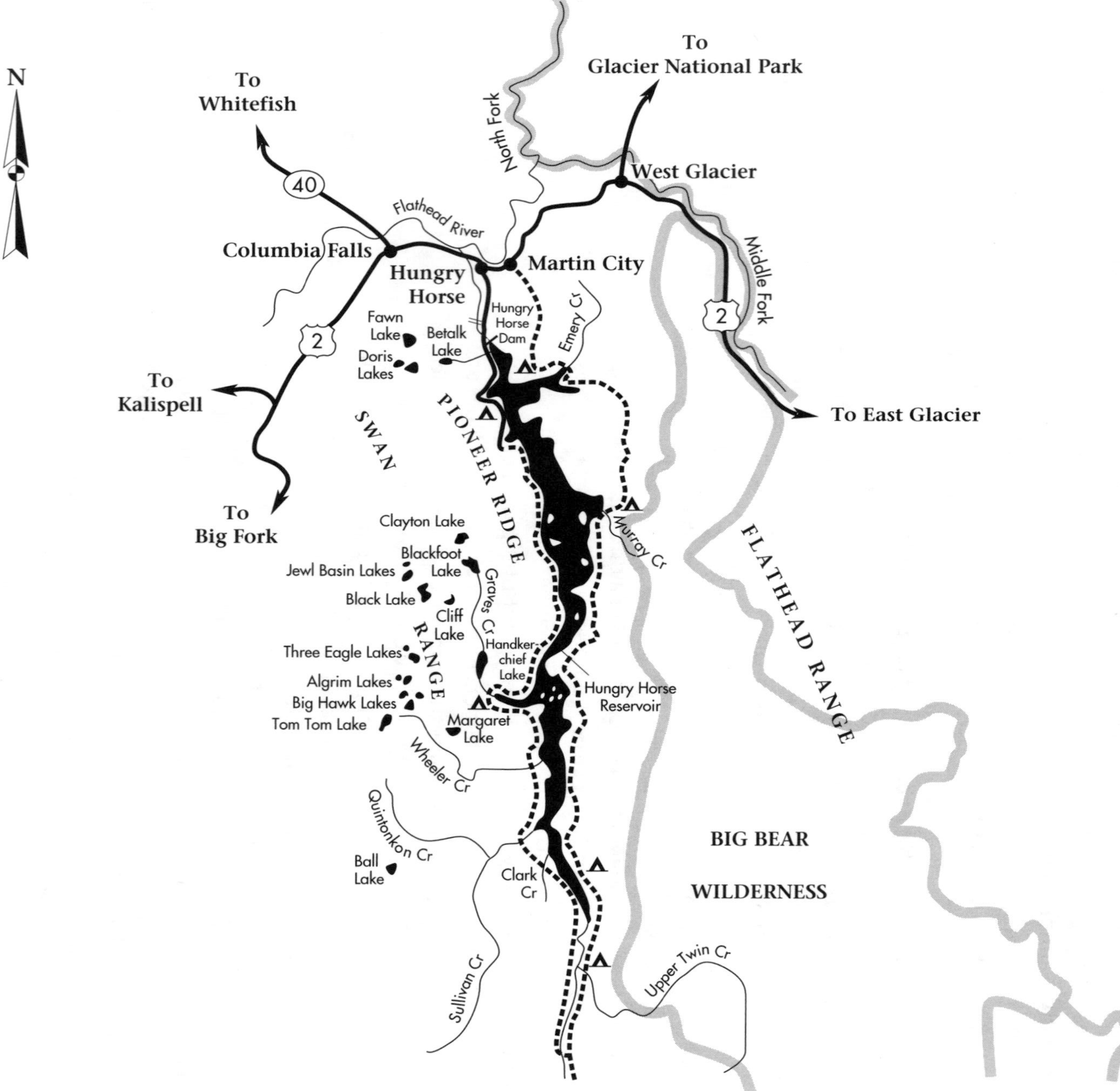

FLATHEAD RIVER—SOUTH FORK

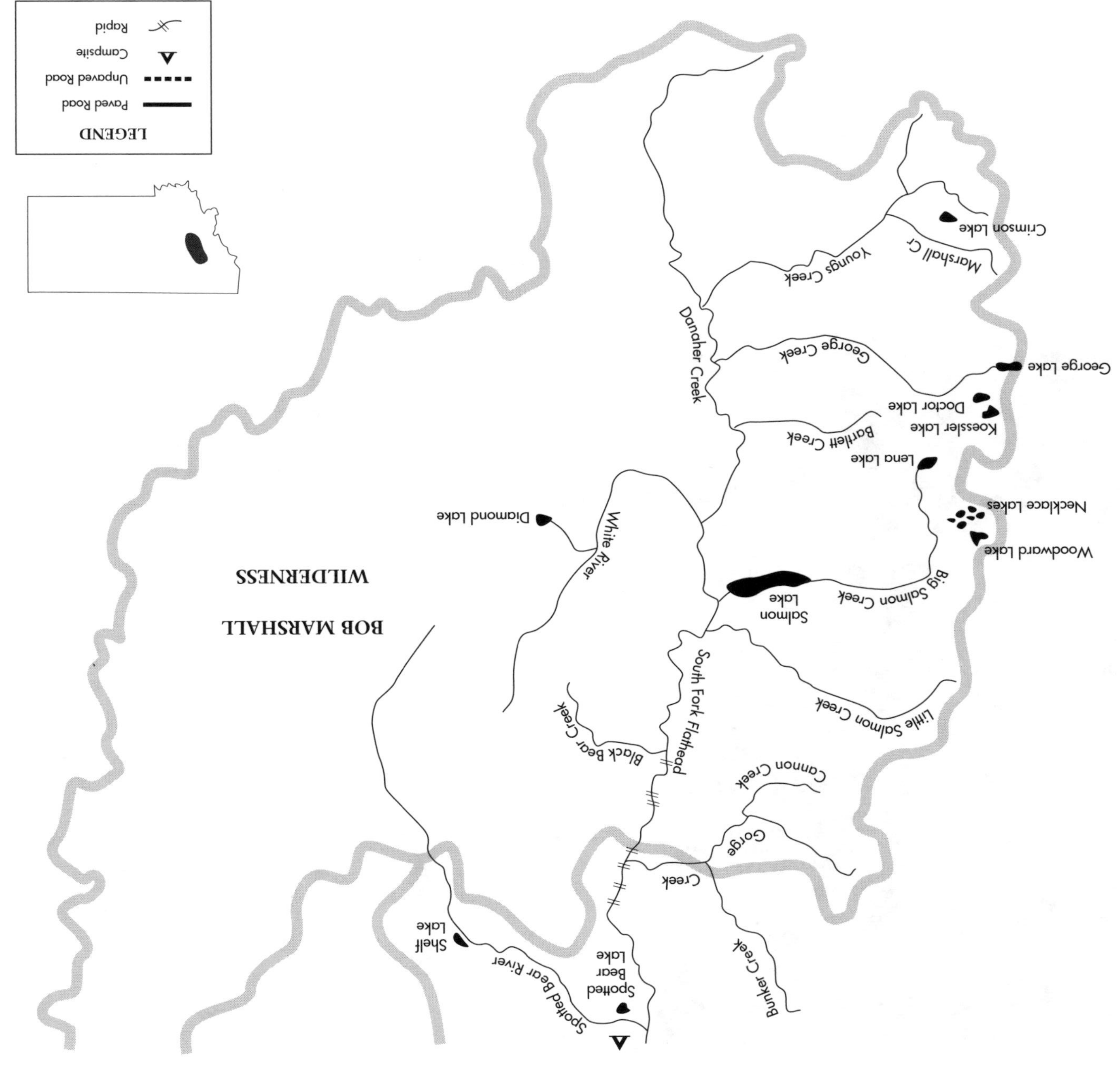

a sink-tip for the lakes. A three-weight of 8 feet is ideal for the tributaries. Fly selection is truly catholic. Sofa Pillows, Royal Wulffs, Humpies, Adams, Bucktail caddis, Hares ear nymphs, Woolly worms, Muddlers, and hoppers border on overkill. The water is cold so bring chest waders and be careful. Runs that look 3 feet deep are often over 10. Fall into the mainstream and you will be in trouble.

The South Fork, like its siblings, the Middle and North forks, is included in the Wild and Scenic Rivers system. The reasons are many and obvious.

Most of the lakes in the South Fork drainage were originally barren, but often have become excellent fisheries following stocking. Some do freeze out but are normally replanted. Trekking into unnamed, alpine lakes is a crapshoot, but fun all the same. On the other hand, fishing every named creek in the drainage would be a severe waste of time. Some of them are a foot wide and some of them hold charming populations of two-inch cutthroat.

Float fishing on the South Fork
Photo courtesy of Hungry Horse News

Fishing Waters in the South Fork Drainage

Ball Lake: Some nice cutthroats live here beyond the end of the Posey Creek Road in the little-fished Quintonkon drainage.

Bartlett Creek: An easy and enjoyable piece of water to work, some nice 10-inch cutthroats hold in small pools and behind boulders along with some spawning bull trout. It's 2 miles above Big Prairie Ranger Station.

Beta Lake: Reached by logging road just above the Hungry Horse Dam, Beta is planted with cutthroat trout. It's fished hard by those who would use bait for nefarious purposes.

Big Hawk Lakes: You can get to Big Hawk Lakes in the Jewel Basin Wilderness by trail from either the Flathead Valley to the west or the Wheeler Creek Road on the South Fork to the east. It's good fishing for 15-inch or larger cutthroats.

Big Salmon Lake: Next to the South Fork, this is the best-known water in the Bob Marshall. Twenty miles above Spotted Bear Ranger Station, it receives a lot of horse and foot traffic. All the same, it's a beautiful lake that has plenty of cruising cutthroats of around 12 inches and big bull trout that will nail a 1/0 red-and-white streamer like a Deceiver that is cast out far from one of the many points along the lake, allowed to sink, and then stripped swiftly and erratically into shore. The bulls are best sought from dusk on. A ten-pound fish in the dark here is entertaining.

Big Salmon Creek: This beautiful stream above Big Salmon Lake is filled with cutthroats in all the right places—logjams, pools, runs, buckets between the current seams. And there are some big bull trout. All of this is below the barrier falls 3½ miles above the lake. Above here the fishing is average for cutthroats. Below the lake the fishing is slightly above average for 12-inch cutthroats. The section below the lake has a fabulous Golden Stone hatch in July. Maybe the lake serves as an enrichment basin, feeding enough nutrients into the short stretch of river between the lake and the main South Fork to create an ideal food base for the carnivorous Golden Stone nymphs. When those nymphs emerge, and the egg-laying females fly back to the river, the trout feed in a frenzy. Any big, straw-colored dry fly works. To impress the trout with your sophistication, show them imitations such as the Yellow Fluttering Stone or the Ginger Flex-Stone in size 6. Do the trout from the lake drop down into the river to feed on this hatch? I've often wondered because suddenly the trout run a larger average size—fish 14 to 16 inches not uncommon.

Black Bear Creek: An average fishing stream (for the wilderness), Black Bear Creek has 8-inch cutthroats and the usual gang of spawning bull trout. It's about five miles of water down to the river and an hour's walk below the Black Bear Guard Station.

Blackfoot Lake: This one is 16 acres in timber 4 miles above the end of the Graves Creek Road. It's home to rainbows, cutthroats, and hybrids to 15 inches.

Black Lake: Another Graves Creek drainage lake which gets hit a bit despite the long hike in. There are some fat cutthroats swimming here.

Bunker Creek: This stream was logged all over the place, but some of the riparian zone was saved, resulting in adequate fishing for small cutthroats and decent spawners in May and June. Bull trout move up here also. Every season hunters get lost and sometimes die in this drainage. The country looks deceptively mild but when a storm cruises in, getting lost does not require any special talent. Flowing from the southwest, Bunker Creek joins the South Fork near the Meadow Creek Trailhead.

Clark Creek: This small, brushy stream has 3- to 7-inch cutthroats and a few bigger early in the year hiding everywhere. A challenge of sorts.

Clayton Lake: Another pretty lake in the Jewel Basin that is large, over 60 acres, and deep, over 100 feet in the middle, with brushy shorelines. It has a decent population of Yellowstone cutthroats averaging around 15 inches and running larger. At ice-out, drys work well, but as the season progresses this action stops. Most people give up. Try a Gold-Ribbed Hares Ear nymph or even a Prince cast well ahead of the easily spotted cruising trout. The old "twitch-and-wait" method will take fish. You can get there via 3 miles of trail from the end of Clayton Creek Road, off the west-side road along Hungry Horse Reservoir.

Cliff Lake: In the Graves Creek drainage, like many higher-elevation lakes, Cliff at 5,500 feet is stocked periodically with cutthroats. The second year following stocking is normally the best with the action declining into the next stocking cycle. Check with the local Department of Fish, Wildlife, and Parks for the stocking schedule of the region's lakes if you like to plan ahead. Take the trail up Graves Creek for 3 miles, then go up the drainage to the west for a mile.

Crimson Lake: You bushwhack a couple of miles up from the Marshall Creek Trail to reach this lake in the Youngs Creek drainage. It used to be decent for westslope cutthroat, but may have frozen out since the last plant in 1988.

Danaher Creek: This beautiful headwater stream of the South Fork wanders across a wide mountain meadow after breaking out of a steep, timbered canyon. There are beaver dams here and there. There is a lot of traffic because the valley provides wilderness for people entering from the Rocky Mountain Front. Lots of cutthroats to maybe 15 inches and a few bull trout and native mountain whitefish. Still this is a fine stream to fish. By trail it is 5 miles above Big Prairie.

Diamond Lake: You've got to want to fish for these cutthroats because there is three miles of bushwhacking after you reach Peggy Creek from the White River Trail. It's located in mountainous terrain between Gladiator and Sphinx mountains.

Doctor Lake: On the eastern side of the Swan Crest, Doctor Lake is usually reached from trails out of Upper Holland Lake. Lots of 12-

A Special Fly for the South Fork of the Flathead River

The South Fork is richer than its cousins, the Middle Fork and the North Fork, but even with more reliable hatches the cutthroats seldom get fussy about flies. The one exception occurs with the Golden Stone hatch during July. The river has a superb population of these big insects, one of the best in the state, and the heavy egg-flying flights of the females can make the fish selective.

STIMULATOR

Hook: curved dry fly hook (Mustad 94831)

Thread: fluorescent fire orange

Tail: light elk or deer hair

Body: fur and antron mixed dubbing—light ginger

Palmer Hackle: ginger

Wing: light elk or deer hair

Head: amber seal fur or goat hair

Hackle: ginger (wound through the head fur)

The Stimulator, a Randall Kaufmann pattern popular all over the West, can be tied in different sizes and colors to match a variety of insects, but the large (size 4, 6), ginger version works spectacularly during the Golden Stone hatch. Even if there are only a few insects around, the fish look for them and the light Stimulator makes a good prospecting fly.

inch cutthroat trout. Overpopulated actually. A good place to keep some fish for an evening meal.

Doris Lakes #1 & #2: Small but decent for average cutthroats, you can reach these lakes by trail from the end of the Beta Lake logging road in lovely cut-over country.

Emery Creek: Small, brushy and, like a dwindling number of streams of this type, it holds lots of 2- to 7-inch pure strain westslope cutthroat trout. While on a electroshocking survey with Fish, Wildlife, and Parks biologist Joe Huston one year I was amazed at the number of trout he and his crew turned up. But Huston said, "Those fish are as safe as a baby in Jesus' arms," referring to the extreme difficulty of catching more than a couple. Emery flows into Hungry Horse Reservoir near its northeast end.

Fawn Lake: Just north of the Doris Lakes, Fawn Lake has about the same quality fishery for cutthroats.

George Lake: Heavily stocked by helicopter (an amazing sight in its own right) with westslope cutthroats. Getting in requires an act of faith and good conditioning. Come in from Upper Holland Lake to Shaw Creek, then George Creek, then bushwhack straight up for 75 miles (really 2) and you are home. If you come before late July bring ice skates.

Gordon Creek: Lots and lots of people hit this stream on the way in to the South Fork from Upper Holland Lake. Still, this is classic, beautiful wilderness water with 8-inch cutthroats and some spawning bull trout that average a few pounds.

Gorge Creek: This stream drains three fairly good fishing lakes—Inspiration, Olor, and Sunburst—near the Swan Crest. A trail follows the creek as it cascades and sparkles its way down a deep, humbling rock gorge until it merges with Bunker Creek 11 miles later. The lower stretches have some cutthroats to 10 inches. Farther up the fish are smaller.

Graves Creek: About a mile of fishable water flows in this stream below Handkerchief Lake that has some 10-inch cutthroats and rainbows and a few grayling. As with all Hungry Horse tributaries, there is usually some fishing for larger spawning cutthroats near the mouth in late spring and early summer. Above the lake the fishing is marginal.

Handkerchief Lake: This water is reached by road just up from the mouth of Aeneas Creek along the Hungry Horse Reservoir. It's often crowded in the summer with small boats and a few float tubes as anglers search for another state-record grayling. There are some cutthroats also and a U. S. Forest Service campground.

Hungry Horse Reservoir: When the dam was completed in the fifties some of the finest wilderness river in the world was covered. Now there is a lake filling inexorably with silt and the fishing for cutthroats and whitefish is often mediocre. The reservoir is reached by paved road south from the town of Hungry Horse (lots of neat curio shops and the like) and followed on both sides by roads that are much longer than Hungry Horse's 34-mile length. They twist and turn around the shoreline. This is still beautiful country and there are campgrounds dotting the shore at places such as Lid Creek, Doris Point, Murray Bay, and on Elk Island. Fishing the outlets early in the season is the only hope for cutthroats and in the fall for whitefish. If the water is drawn down for power generation, in low water years the place looks like a muddy, dusty, fly-infested bathtub and getting down to the water is a bitch. But we all know the BPA and the Army Corps of Engineers has our best interests at heart. Right? Right!

Jewel Lakes, North and South: In the Jewel Basin Wilderness, both lakes are managed for cutthroats and are good fishing for hun-

Hungry Horse Lake
Photo courtesy of Hungry Horse News

gry trout. Lots of hikers and a few grizzlies make use of this area. You get there from the well-marked foothills road west of Kalispell.

Koesseler Lake: Just north of Doctor Lake with no trail, it's now managed for cutthroats which grow well in this deep 45-acre subalpine body of water.

Lena Lake: Reached by the Holbrook Trail just west of the divide, Lena Lake is heavily planted yearly with cutthroats. A nice, off-the-beaten-trail alpine lake.

Little Salmon River: Followed by trail for 15 miles, Little Salmon River meets the South Fork at the Black Bear Guard Station. It's beautiful water for cutthroats to 15 inches and, from late summer into fall, large bull trout—over ten pounds. Some brush and timber make the fishing sporting.

Margaret Lake: Large cutthroats live in this deep, 46-acre lake, an hour's hike from the Forest Creek Road. Regular stocking keeps the numbers up.

Necklace Lakes: These are a half dozen ponds on the Swan Crest about 5 tough miles from Upper Holland Lake. Cutthroat trout do well here and there may be some rainbows left. Nice mosquito country. Bring a head net or you won't fish long.

Pilgrim Lakes: The lower lake is around 30 acres and deep and planted with cutthroats. There are some trout in the little upper lake also. Take Alpine Trail 4 miles from the end of the death-defying Noisy Creek Road on the Flathead Valley side. Good mufflers come here to die.

Quintonkon Creek: Located just west of Hungry Horse Reservoir, this is a stream that has some good early season cutthroat action and late season whitefish angling. Lots of brush and deadfalls and very few fly fishers in the course of a season. Bring the cheap waders for this one.

Shelf Lake: Reached above the Spotted Bear River, Shelf Lake always has a few good cutthroats and a bunch of smaller fish.

Spotted Bear Lake: This lake is muddy, swampy, buggy, and fairly good fishing for cutthroats, some nearing 20 inches. It's not far above the Spotted Bear Ranger Station.

Spotted Bear River: Followed by road and trail for 30 miles then just trail for over 30 miles. Above Dean Falls the fishing is typically for small cutts. Below is excellent fly fishing for cutthroats to 20 inches, big bull trout, and lots of whitefish. There are a lot of people wandering through here both going in and coming out of the wilderness.

Still, it is not difficult to disappear and have some fine fishing all to yourself. Impressive limestone cliffs dominate the skyline.

Three Eagle Lakes, Upper & Lower: Not far from Pilgrim Lakes, these waters are regularly managed for cutthroats that grow large in the deep, cold water. They can be very good fishing or mountain-lake-frustration-city, which means switch to nymphs or to big, gaudy streamer, quickly retrieved.

Tom Tom Lake: Less than 30 minutes from the end of Wheeler Creek Road, Tom Tom Lake has westslope cutthroat trout and maybe a few hybrids from some long-ago Yellowstone cutts.

Upper Twin Creek: Like many of the streams in the South Fork drainage, this one is filled with downed trees and logjams which make ideal habitat for the small cutthroats that live here. Bring a 6½-foot rod.

Pack train in the Bob Marshall Wilderness
Photo courtesy of Hungry Horse News

White River: This stream hits the South Fork, coming in from the east, not far from the Holbrook Guard Station. It's a main thoroughfare, especially for those using the Sun River country, but it is good fishing for cutthroats over a foot long and the usual collection of aggressive spawning bull trout. Above Needle Falls the river often runs nearly dry in late summer, and the cutthroats pack into any cool pool or run remaining. Not my idea of a sporting proposition.

Wildcat Lake: Take the Noisy Creek Road to this lake alongside Alpine Trail. Managed for cutthroats, the trout grow well here and take small drys eagerly. There probably aren't any of the ten-pound-plus monsters left that were here before the road opened up the lake to heavier angling pressure.

Woodward Lake: Sees a bit of pressure and is good fishing for cutthroats that run around a foot long and sometimes larger and fat. Best way in is cross country about 3 miles north from Necklace Lake, through the mosquitoes. You can't miss this one. It's 65 acres. The scenery is worth the bug fight.

Youngs Creek: This is the headwaters of the South Fork at the south end of the wilderness, flowing for 15 miles with some big cutthroats in a few of the beaver ponds and in the larger pools. Some bull trout cruise up here also. It's trail starts 6 miles above Big Prairie.

Other Waters

Addition Creek: Small fish.

Aeneas Creek: Too small.

Aeneas Lake: Barren.

Albino Creek: Too small.

Arres Creek: Too small.

Babcock Creek: Some cutthroats and bull trout.

Basin Creek: Some cutthroats and bull trout.

Big Knife Lakes: Barren.

Blue Lake: Cutthroats.

Boulder Creek: Too small.

Brownstone Creek: Too small.

Bruce Creek: Too small.

Burnt Creek: Cutthroats and bull trout.

Call Creek: Too small.

Camp Creek: Cutthroats and bull trout.

Cannon Creek: Cutthroats ranging up to 10 inches. There's 5 miles of fun water; just start at the mouth of the stream, on the Gorge Creek Trail and hike upstream.

Chasm Creek: Too small.

Clayton Creek: Too small.

Cluster Creek: Too small.

Conner Creek: Too small.

Crater Lake: Cutthroats.

Crimson Creek: Too small.

Damnation Creek: Small cutthroats.

Dean Creek: Cutthroats. Its worth walking up the one and a half miles from the mouth to see the falls.

Delaware Creek: Too small.

Devine Creek: Too small.

Doris Creek: Too small.

Felix Creek: Too small.

Fool Hen Creek: Too small.

Forest Creek: Cutthroats.

George Creek: Cutthroats and bull trout.

Gill Creek: Poor fishing.

Harris Creek: Too small.

Harrison Creek: Cutthroats and bull trout.

Helen Creek: Small cutthroats.

Highrock Creek: Poor fishing.

Hodag Creek: Too small.

Holbrook Creek: Cutthroats and bull trout.

Hungry Creek: Cutthroats and bull trout.

Hungry Horse Creek: Cutthroats.

Jenny Creek: Too small.

Jenny Lake: Cutthroats.

Knieff Creek: Too small.

Lick Creek: Too small.

Lion Lake: Some trout but more perch and pike.

Logan Creek: Small cutthroats.

Lost Jack Creek: Too small.

Lost Johnny Creek: Cutthroats. This is one of the Hungry Horse Reservoir tributaries that gets spawning runs, at least up to the falls 1½ miles from the mouth.

Lost Mare Creek: Too small.

Lower Seven Acres: Cutthroats.

Lower Twin Creek: Cutthroats and bull trout.

Margaret Creek: Cutthroats. This tributary of Hungry Horse Creek is not very big, but with the easy access of a logging road it's popular nevertheless.

Marshall Creek: Cutthroats and bull trout.

McInernie: Cutthroats.

Mid Creek: Cutthroats and bull trout.

Middle Fork Bunker Creek: Cutthroats.

Murray Creek: Cutthroats. They run a bit larger here, 10 to 12 inches, than the other Hungry Horse tributaries.

Nanny Creek: Too small.

North Bigelow: Cutthroats.

North Creek: Too small.

North Fork Helen Creek: Cutthroats.

Otis Creek: Too small.

Paint Creek: Cutthroats.

Pendant Lakes: They are not scheduled for planting, but there may be few hapless souls swimming around in these malarial bogs. Concerning mosquitoes—see Necklace Lakes and multiply by ten.

Posy Creek: Too small.

Prisoner Lake: Cutthroats.

Rapid Creek: Cutthroats and bull trout.

Recluse Lake: Barren.

Riverside Creek: Cutthroats and bull trout.

Ross Creek: Too small.

Sandstone Creek: Too small.

Shaw Creek: Too small.

Silver Tip Creek: Cutthroats. The name refers to Grizzly Bears, and they are still around.

Slide Creek: Cutthroats.

Snow Creek: Cutthroats.

Soldier Creek: Cutthroats.

South Creek: Cutthroats.

South Fork White River: Cutthroats and bull trout.

Spruce Creek: Too small.

Squaw Lake: Cutthroats.

Stadler Creek: Too small.

Tango Creek: Cutthroats.

Tiger Creek: Cutthroats.

Tin Creek: Cutthroats.

Trickle Creek: Cutthroats.

Twin Creek: Cutthroats.

Wheeler Creek: Cutthroats, bull trout, and mountain whitefish. It flows into the west side of Hungry Horse Reservoir. It changes with the seasons: spring brings spawning cutthroats; summer means small, resident cutthroats; fall is bull trout time; and winter offers good whitefish nymphing.

Wildcat Creek: Cutthroats.

Wounded Buck Creek: Cutthroats.

■ *Special thanks to Joe Huston for his help on the South Fork.*

FLATHEAD INDIAN RESERVATION ▪ Imagine owing 1.2 million acres of land in western Montana. Country filled with staggering mountains, dense forests, and rolling grass-covered hills stretching off into the distance. Throw into the mix hundreds of alpine lakes, a few choice rivers, miles of sparkling streams, some valley reservoirs, and a spring creek or two.

For many fly fishers this is a basic "died-and-gone-to-heaven" scenario. Spending the rest of your life chasing native cutthroat trout, browns, rainbows, brookies, bull trout, and even lake trout, along with a collection of very large northern pike and good numbers of largemouth bass, has a certain appeal for some of us.

Float tubing for bass on Kicking Horse Reservoir
Photo by Stan Bradshaw

For the Salish and Kootenai Tribes of the Flathead Indian Reservation, such a fantasy is indeed a reality and they are making the most of the opportunity.

Located about 25 air miles south of Glacier National Park and just north of Missoula, the reservation takes in a large portion of the Mission Mountains, the southern end of Flathead Lake, the majority of the lower Flathead River, and the National Bison Range at Moiese.

Some of the better trout waters like the Jocko River, lower Flathead River, along with the valley lakes, ponds, and creeks are discussed in the appropriate drainage sections. Both Kicking Horse Reservoir and Ninepipe Reservoir are locally renowned for providing quality largemouth bass action. The fish run to five pounds in the latter and occasionally over two pounds in the former (along with a rainbow or two of some size). Leech patterns

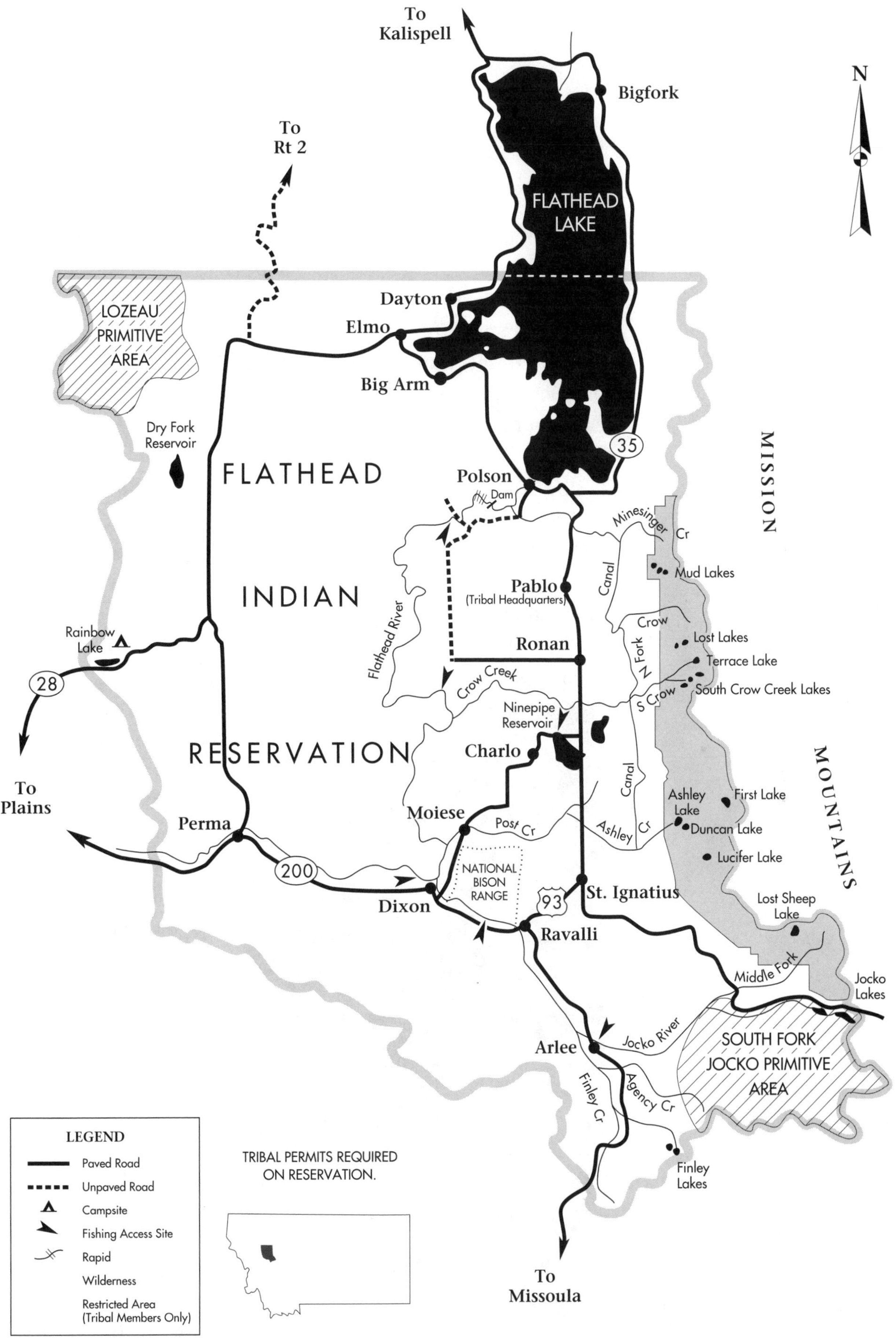
To
Kalispell
Bigfork
N
To
Rt 2
FLATHEAD
LAKE
Dayton
LOZEAU
PRIMITIVE
AREA
Elmo
Big Arm
Dry Fork
Reservoir
35
FLATHEAD
Polson
Dam
MISSION
Minesinger Cr
Mud Lakes
Canal
Pablo
(Tribal Headquarters)
INDIAN
Flathead River
Crow
Lost Lakes
Rainbow
Lake
Ronan
N Fork
Terrace Lake
28
Crow Creek
S Crow
South Crow Creek Lakes
Ninepipe
Reservoir
RESERVATION
Charlo
MOUNTAINS
To
Plains
Canal
Ashley
Lake
First Lake
Moiese
Post Cr
Ashley Cr
Duncan Lake
Perma
Lucifer Lake
NATIONAL
BISON
RANGE
200
Dixon
93
St. Ignatius
Lost Sheep
Lake
Ravalli
Middle Fork
Jocko
Lakes
Jocko River
SOUTH FORK
JOCKO PRIMITIVE
AREA
Arlee
Finley Cr
Agency Cr
LEGEND
Paved Road
Unpaved Road
Campsite
Fishing Access Site
Rapid
Wilderness
Restricted Area
(Tribal Members Only)
TRIBAL PERMITS REQUIRED
ON RESERVATION.
Finley
Lakes
To
Missoula

work well in the shallows and along weed beds at any time and deer hair poppers produce in the evenings in the same locations.

For those willing to backpack up steep (borderline death march in many cases) trails, the Mission Mountains Tribal Wilderness Area offers unspoiled fishing for cutthroat trout in wild, alpine country. Woolly Worms, Hare's Ear nymphs, and Adams are representative of productive patterns in these high-altitude lakes. Some of the best reservation mountain lakes include:

Finley Lakes: Located below Murphy Peak in the Jocko Mountains and reached up the East Fork of Finley Creek by road. Rainbows and cutthroats are in the lower lake and stunted cutthroat in the upper.

First Lake: Really a group of lakes hiding below McDonald Glacier in a beautiful valley. There is no trail and the first time I tried to reach this region coming in from the Swan Valley on the east, I got lost and had to scramble over scree slopes and eventually slide down a tall pine to reach Ice Flow Lake at the head of the drainage. No fish here, but emerald-turquoise water shaded with glacial flour and waterfalls shooting out all over the place. Hollywood could never come close to this scene. Come in from the reservation side, it's longer but easier hiking. Topo maps help, as does a compass and plenty of luck. This is not for the faint of heart. Disappointment Lake at a little over 6,000 feet holds Yellowstone cutthroats, but the area is closed to protect grizzlies

There's a good bet you'll run into mule deer just about anywhere you fish in Montana.
Photo courtesy of USDA–Forest Service

(they have to live someplace) from July 15 through October 1. If the fall is warm, you have maybe a two-week window to get in and out of here, but you will be risking severe snowstorms coming out of nowhere and sending you for a ride on the oblivion express. Life is short—risk it.

Lost (Morigeau) Lakes: In Crow Creek country lying at about 6,000 feet, Upper is 15 acres and Lower 8 acres. Both hold Yellowstone cutthroat of around 10- to 12-inches that are the result of old plantings from airplanes (back when the Fish and Wildlife Service thought all cutthroats were of the same species with only minor differences in color due to environment).

Lucifer Lake: Way up there, sitting below the most spectacular glacial cirque in the southern end of the Missions. A decent trail leads the way to healthy cutthroat fishing. Picture Lake, a quarter-mile farther upcountry, is currently barren—too high and too cold. All of this is fine, remote country that takes more than a few hours of rough hiking to reach.

Mud Lakes: Four lakes with trout lying between 5,500 and 6,500 feet. They are anywhere from 35 to 145 feet deep. The first has brookies and rainbows. The second holds rainbows. The third has cutthroats and maybe a few rainbows. The fourth has good fishing for cutthroats. The Mud Lakes Trailhead has been moved 1 mile north to Minesinger Road.

Fishing tribal waters requires special permits. **See page 207.**

South Crow Creek (and Terrace) Lakes: About 5 miles east of Ronan, near the top of the Missions between 5,900 and 6,500 feet, 30 and 55 acres, up to 100 plus feet deep, and filled with cutthroats that will reach 12 inches. Good fish for this far above the sea. This is spectacular glacial cirque country that is a killer to get into. The "trails" are rough and seem to go straight up. If you've never backpacked and wish to discover how "enjoyable" this masochistic pursuit really is, this is a good place to find out.

Other reservation mountain waters of marginal interest to anglers are Ashley Lake and Creek (day use only due to presence of grizzlies and closed from July 15 through October 1), Crazy Fish Lake (tribal members only), Crow Creek, Duncan Lake (barren), Eagle (tribal members only), Finley Creek, Lost Sheep Lake, Lower Jocko Lake (tribal members only), Meadow Lake (tribal members only), Minesinger Creek, North Fork Crow Creek, South Fork Crow Creek, and Upper Jocko Lake (tribal members only).

While the rest of the state wrangles over stream-access laws, clearcutting in sensitive drainages, irrigation allocations, and fisheries management directions, to mention just a few of the problems, the Confederated Salish and Kootenai Tribes have designed, adopted, and implemented a management plan for their abundant natural resources that is progressive by any management standards. The tribes have far fewer agencies, departments, directorates, and other bureaucracies to contend with, and this streamlined situation has made the implementation of a fisheries management plan on the reservation a relatively straightforward process.

"Yes indeed, this is a wonderful chance for us to improve what is already a great resource, said tribal fisheries manager Joe DosSantos. "In some cases we will be able to restore native populations to historic levels. This is just an exciting project for everyone involved."

Adopted in 1985, the plan first inventoried all waters and fish populations on the reservation. Following this, various population goals were drawn up for specific locations. Reaching these numbers entails habitat improvement, stocking, possession limits, guaranteeing stream flows and, in some cases, closing streams to fishing.

What the Flathead Reservation fisheries management plan means to anglers is that for less than the cost of a tank of gas you can purchase all required tribal permits and then spend a morning wading a small river taking numerous browns of 15 inches or so, enjoy lunch and the drive up the road a piece to catch largemouth bass on deerhair poppers on cast after cast.

The next day you can float the lower Flathead River, working large streamers along weed beds and gravel bars for northern pike exceeding twenty pounds. Then you can hike into the mountains and fish high country lakes for black-backed, crimson-slashed native cutthroat trout. All of this while surrounded by steep glacial cirques, remnant glaciers, and waterfalls shooting out of massive snow fields. If you are in good shape, you can visit lakes that are seldom fished. You will not see other people—only elk, eagles, and maybe grizzlies or goats.

"Our high mountain lakes are really doing well," adds DosSantos. "Some of them do have Yellowstone cutthroat, but we have already replanted 12 lakes with pure-strain westslope cutthroat and our overall goal is to give preference to native species."

"Our philosophy is to manage our land as a complete system and to emphasize recreational fishing is not consistent with those objectives. Basically, if you do successfully operate a system as we are trying to, fish populations will increase as a matter of course. As everyone knows, the concept is not complicated—take care of the land and the fish will take care of themselves."

You must get a tribal recreation permit to fish on the Flathead reservation. The permits are available at the tribal headquarters in Pablo and various western Montana sporting goods outlets. Those interested in further information on Flathead Indian Reservation fishing opportunities may contact Joe DosSantos at Salish and Kootenai Tribes, Box 278, Pablo, MT 59855. Telephone (406) 675-2700, ext. 380.

This fisherman's line disappears in the white water of Crystal Falls. Taken in about 1910.
Photo courtesy of University of Montana Mansfield Library

GLACIER NATIONAL PARK

When people think of Glacier National Park, mind-blowing vistas, the Going-to-the-Sun Road, and grizzly bears leap to mind. Mention fishing and you will draw blank stares and often less-than-tactful chuckles.

The trout fishing in Glacier will never compete with the top-of-the-line action found in Yellowstone, but there are some compelling arguments for the northern park. Chief among them are lack of crowds and relatively untouched angling.

Of the two million or so visitors to Glacier each year, less than one in twenty does anything more than cross the park from east to west. These hordes never fish, or if they do, the action consists of winging a Royal Wulff on to the virtually barren waters of McDonald Creek or maybe flinging a red-and-white spoon into St. Mary Lake. These normally futile endeavors lead to Glacier's reputation as a poor fishing location.

Living less than thirty minutes from Glacier, I have discovered that there is a good deal of quality fishing in the park. Walk just a mile or so from the road and you will be alone, working untouched water in many cases. Walk even farther into the interior and you may be fishing a lake or stream that has not seen a fly cast with serious intent for several years. Big fish swim here—Yellowstone and westslope cutthroat, rainbows, bull trout, lake trout, and brook trout.

The fact that this is prime grizzly habitat is worth mentioning. First of all, I am all in favor of the great bears. The northern Rockies without them would be an empty, shallow place. If a human or two gets eaten every now and then, those are the breaks. The bears are taking a beating, also. There may be as many as two hundred grizzlies in the park and they can be aggressive. In fact many bear experts fear park bears more than their brothers found in national forest and wilderness areas and the larger specimens found in Alaska. Glacier's grizzlies have been exposed to humans for many years and this familiarity and resulting loss of fear of humans make their behavior unpredictable.

Whenever a bear sighting is reported, rangers close appropriate trail(s) for as long as necessary. Whenever you see bears at a distance, leave the area immediately. Make noise when you are hiking, especially when near rushing water. If confronted by a grizzly at close range,

GLACIER CHECKLIST

- **Get Park fishing regulations**
- **Get Park map**
- **Check fishing conditions at your destination**
- **Check for trail closures due to bears**

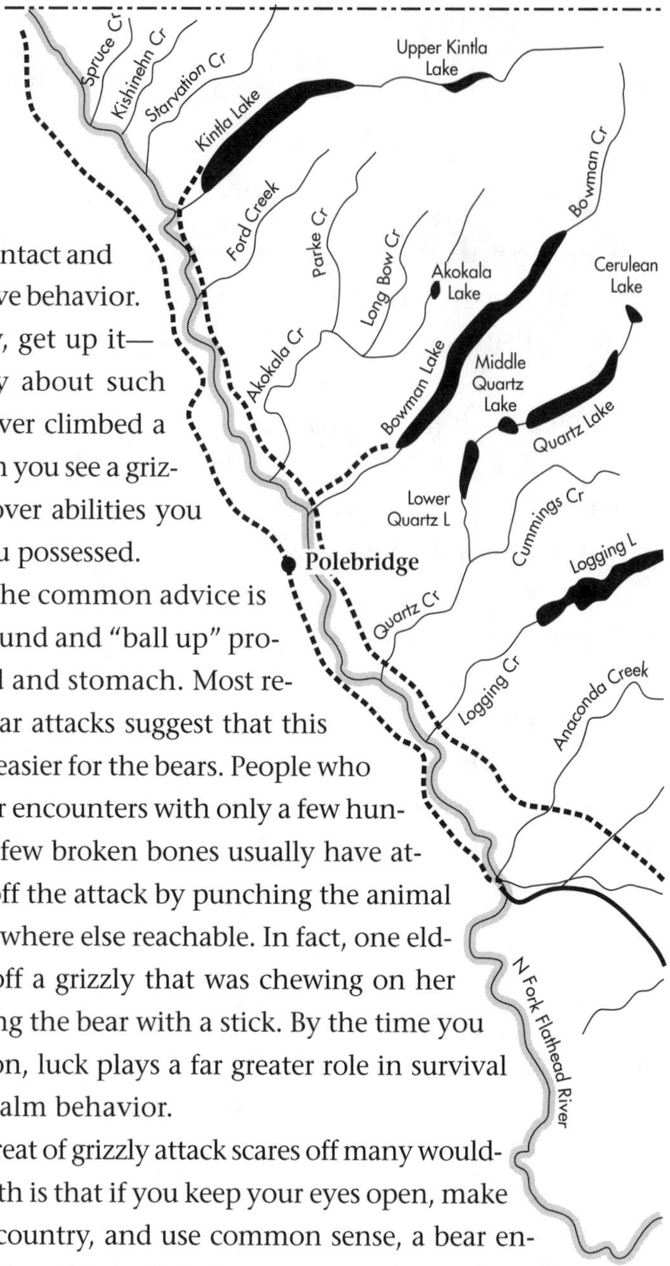

avoid direct eye contact and any other aggressive behavior. If a tree is nearby, get up it—fast. Don't worry about such things as "I've never climbed a tree before." When you see a grizzly, you will discover abilities you never thought you possessed.

If attacked, the common advice is to drop to the ground and "ball up" protecting your head and stomach. Most recent reports of bear attacks suggest that this may make things easier for the bears. People who have survived bear encounters with only a few hundred stitches and few broken bones usually have attempted to fend off the attack by punching the animal in the nose or anywhere else reachable. In fact, one elderly woman ran off a grizzly that was chewing on her husband by beating the bear with a stick. By the time you are in this situation, luck plays a far greater role in survival than advice and calm behavior.

While the threat of grizzly attack scares off many would-be anglers, the truth is that if you keep your eyes open, make noise in the backcountry, and use common sense, a bear encounter is extremely unlikely. Grizzlies want even less to do with humans than we do with them.

On a more relaxed front, be sure and pick up park fishing regulations when entering Glacier and get current information at the ranger station near your destination. Lakes in the high country often freeze out or are closed because of bears. Five minutes of conversation with a ranger can save several hours of futile hiking. Also, most backcountry lakes and trails are not free of snow and ice until July, at the earliest. Campsites must be reserved in advance at St. Mary and Apgar entrances or major ranger stations no more than twenty-four hours in advance on a first-come, first-served basis—sort of a Motel 8 wilderness gig.

Finally, there are times when any pattern will take fish (as is true with all alpine fishing), but a varied selection of nymphs, drys, and

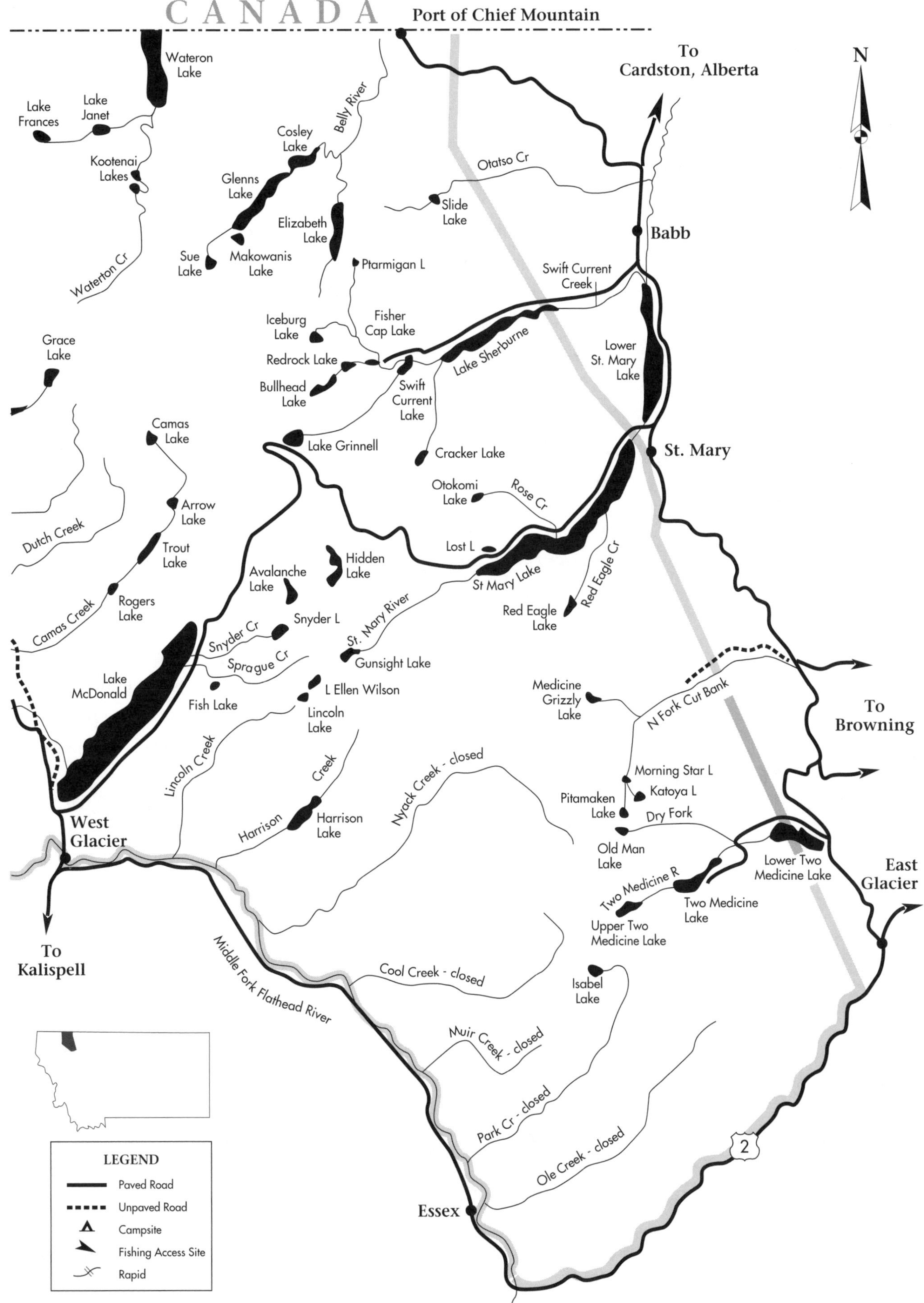
CANADA
Port of Chief Mountain
To
Cardston, Alberta
N
GLACIER NATIONAL PARK
Wateron
Lake
Lake
Frances
Lake
Janet
Kootenai
Lakes
Belly River
Cosley
Lake
Glenns
Lake
Elizabeth
Lake
Sue
Lake
Makowanis
Lake
Waterton Cr
Otatso Cr
Slide
Lake
Babb
Ptarmigan L
Swift Current
Creek
Iceburg
Lake
Fisher
Cap Lake
Redrock Lake
Bullhead
Lake
Swift
Current
Lake
Lake Sherburne
Lower
St. Mary
Lake
Grace
Lake
Camas
Lake
Lake Grinnell
Cracker Lake
St. Mary
Otokomi
Lake
Rose Cr
Arrow
Lake
Dutch Creek
Trout
Lake
Lost L
Hidden
Lake
Avalanche
Lake
St Mary Lake
Red Eagle Cr
Rogers
Lake
Camas Creek
Snyder L
St. Mary River
Red Eagle
Lake
Snyder Cr
Sprague Cr
Gunsight Lake
Lake
McDonald
Fish Lake
L Ellen Wilson
Lincoln
Lake
Medicine
Grizzly
Lake
N Fork Cut Bank
To
Browning
Lincoln Creek
Creek
Nyack Creek - closed
Morning Star L
Katoya L
Pitamaken
Lake
Dry Fork
West
Glacier
Harrison
Harrison
Lake
Old Man
Lake
Lower Two
Medicine Lake
Two Medicine R
Two Medicine
Lake
East
Glacier
Upper Two
Medicine Lake
To
Kalispell
Middle Fork Flathead River
Cool Creek - closed
Isabel
Lake
Muir Creek - closed
Park Cr - closed
2
Ole Creek - closed
Essex
LEGEND
Paved Road
Unpaved Road
Campsite
Fishing Access Site
Rapid

streamers always helps. In other words, if you've got a box of weirdly colored streamers, bring them along. They may save the day. If I were limited to just three patterns, they would be Gold-Ribbed Hare's Ear nymphs, sizes 12–18; Adams, sizes 12–20; and Olive Woolly Worms, sizes 6–10. High country fishing is not sophisticated from a selection standpoint, but it is frequently exasperating.

The Continental Divide splits the fishing in Glacier into eastern and western regions with a third area in the north along the Canadian border.

Eastern Waters

The lakes and streams on the east side of the park are influenced by a drier and much windier climate. Forests are not as thick, tall, or dense. Rivers and streams, as is true in most of the park, have either few trout or populations of very small fish, usually brookies.

POPULAR FLIES
Adams
Elk Hair Caddis
Gold-Ribbed Hare's Ear
Goddard
Olive Woolly Worm
Royal Wulff

Grinnell Lake: This lake sees a good deal of pressure by Glacier standards because it is only 1 mile from the Upper Josephine Lake boat dock which is a mile from Many Glacier. You'll find some fishing for brook trout and the same holds true for Josephine.

Gunsight Lake: Some good-sized rainbows abide here. The lake is 6 miles from Going-to-the-Sun Road.

Hidden Lake: Not far from the Going-to-the-Sun Road near Sun Point, this water is small, but deep, and has trout.

Medicine Grizzly Lake: Plenty of slightly stunted rainbows around a foot long live here. This is an 11-mile round-trip hike from the Cut Bank Campground.

Oldman Lake: This one provides good fishing for cutthroat trout and sees a bit of action despite being 6 miles from Two Medicine

Lake. The last stretch of trail travels through a pleasant, open forest.

Otokomi Lake: Otokomi means "yellow fish" in Blackfeet. The lake has large, cruising cutthroats that are quite spooky, but a nymph, cast well ahead of their perceived cruising pattern and then jerked a few inches when they are about ten feet away, works wonders. This small lake is nestled in a glacial cirque with scree slopes plunging to the shoreline. The trail climbs steadily for 5.5 miles from Rising Sun Campground to an altitude of 6,482 feet.

Catching the rise on Swiftcurrent Lake
Photo courtesy of Hungry Horse News

Ptarmigan Lake: Five miles from Many Glacier, Ptarmigan has fine fishing for brook trout.

Red Eagle Lake: Some large rainbows and some cutthroats swim here. The water is 8 miles from St. Mary. The trail forks at about 5 miles. Take the right-hand path.

Red Rock Lake: This lake offers fair fishing for brook and rainbow trout and lies only 3 miles from Many Glacier.

Upper Two Medicine Lake: Has some fat brook trout (and a few rainbow) that often hit drys near evening. Take the Two Medicine Lake (large water with brook and rainbow trout—fish may be spotted cruising near shore on occasion) tour boat to the head of the lake and then hike 5 miles from 5,164-feet elevation to a little over 5,550. There is a campsite at the head of the lake.

Other Eastern Lakes with Trout

Bullhead: Brook trout.

Cracker: Bull trout.

Fishercap: Brook and rainbow trout.

Iceberg: Barren.

Katoya: Cutthroats, if not frozen out.

Lost: Small brookies.

Morning Star: S1ame as Katoya.

Pitamakan: Same as above.

Saint Mary: Bull trout, cutthroats, lake trout, rainbows, whitefish.

Sherburne: Northern pike, few brookies.

Slide: Cutthroats.

Swiftcurrent: Brook trout, rainbow, kokanee.

Windmaker: Brook and rainbow trout.

Other Eastern Streams with Trout

Cut Bank Creek: Brooks, cutthroats, rainbows.

Dry Fork Creek: Brook trout.

Kennedy Creek: Bull trout, cutthroats, whitefish.

Rose Creek: Bull trout.

Saint Mary River: Cutthroats, rainbows, whitefish.

Swiftcurrent Creek: Brook trout.

Two Medicine River: Brook and cutthroat trout.

Northern Waters

This area offers some of the finest, most remote fishing in Glacier, especially for brook trout and grayling. There is more precipitation here than along the Rocky Mountain Front of the eastern side of the park, resulting in denser forests. This is also some of the best grizzly habitat around, so many areas frequently are closed for lengthy periods. Extreme caution and awareness are advised.

Belly River: An early season stream, the Belly has brook trout, rainbow trout, and grayling. A Goddard or Elk Hair Caddis, Adams, or Royal Wulff will handle the situation. The Blackfeet name for the river, Mokowanisz, refers to the digestive system of a buffalo.

Elizabeth Lake: Nine miles from Chief Mountain Customs Station on the U.S.-Canadian border, Elizabeth offers nice angling for grayling. There are also rainbows and brooks in lesser numbers. One story suggests that legendary mountain man Joe Cosley named the lake for one of Theodore Roosevelt's daughters, who happened to be named Bertha, Lois, and Helen. Spend a few days in the country and you begin to see how things are easily confused. Wild stuff here.

Francis Lake: Francis is good for rainbows. You can get there from the Upper Waterton boat dock in Canada.

Glenn's Lake: Brook, cutthroat, and lake trout and some whitefish live in this lake located 11 miles from Chief Mountain Customs.

Kootenai Lakes: Superb brook trout fishing found in even better bear country means that these lakes are often closed. They are only 2.5 miles from the Upper Waterton boat dock. Lots of mosquitoes. Lots.

Lake Frances
Photo courtesy of Hungry Horse News

Other Northern Waters

Cosley Lake: Brook and lake trout, whitefish.

Janet Lake: Barren.

Mokowanis Lake: Good for brookies.

Sue Lake: Cutthroats if not frozen out.

Waterton Lake: Designer bait fishing water for a bit of everything.

Waterton River: Mainly whitefish.

Western Waters

The western section of Glacier is bordered by the Middle and North Forks of the Flathead River. Each of these rivers has its own section in this guide, but the tributaries located in the park are discussed here. This region is marked by thick pine forest including some red cedar. The fishing in the streams is usually marginal, but migratory movements of bull trout and westslope cutthroat trout can liven things up for a few weeks in July and August. These species are alive with spawning colors at this time and also under a good deal of stress. Play and release them quickly. A number of lakes are quite good.

Akokala (Indian) Creek and Lake: Both are good for small (to 10 inches) westslope cutthroat. The lake is 5.5 steep miles above Bowman Lake. Due to oil exploration many years ago this used to be known as Oil Lake.

Arrow Lake: Located 7.5 miles up Camas Creek (a mile or so above Trout Lake) in prime bear country, Arrow lake has good fishing for cutthroats and some big bull trout.

Avalanche Lake: This is one of the more popular hiking destinations lying in a beautiful waterfall-filled cirque a couple of miles east of Going-to-the-Sun Road. The far end of the lake is not bad for small cutthroat. Don't bother with the creek unless you own an 18-inch, one-weight rod.

Bowman Lake: You can drive to Bowman up the North Fork. A canoe or float tube is best to work the shoreline for bulls, cutts, and whitefish. Not great fishing. The creek can be fun for small fish. Bear vibes are strong here.

Camas Lake and Creek: This tributary to the North Fork is in "bear valley," but the lake has fair fishing for Yellowstone cutts.

Float tubing on Avalanche Lake
Photo courtesy of Hungry Horse News

Ellen Wilson: This excellent brook trout lake is located 9 miles from Lake McDonald or 2.5 miles from Sperry Chalet.

Fish Lake: Just a few minutes through the woods from Going-to-the-Sun Road, this marshy lake offers fair cutthroat fishing. Bring waders unless you like leeches.

Grace Lake: Grace offers good fishing for big westslope cutthroat trout, but the hike is 12 miles from the inside North Fork Road at Logging Creek.

Harrison Lake and Creek: Harrison Lake is most easily reached by floating the Middle Fork and then hiking 4 miles to the lake. Or you can hike 11 miles east from West Glacier for cutthroat and bull trout. Good brookies in beaver ponds along the creek.

Hidden Lake: About 3 miles from Logan Pass, Hidden Lake has some nice Yellowstone cutts that will take a twitched nymph provided it is cast far enough ahead to avoid spooking the fish. The hike out is steep. Offers nice fishing in early September as is true of many Glacier lakes.

Fishing the outlet on Bowman Lake
Photo courtesy of Hungry Horse News

Isabel Lake: It may or may not be worth the 33-mile round-trip for anglers. Conflicting reports (no one fishes here much) suggest populations of cutthroat and brook trout and even bull trout up from the Middle Fork. You get there by hiking up Park Creek, across the river from Essex.

Kintla Lake and Creek: Some cutthroat trout and a few good bull trout live here, and you can drive right in and watch the tame deer and the not-so-tame campers. The lake is big water, requiring a canoe or float tube. Upper Kintla Lake is 8 miles from Kintla in spectacular cirque country. There are good numbers of 15-inch bull trout.

Lincoln Lake: Lincoln lies at the foot of 1,300-foot Beaver Chief Falls and a couple miles south of Gunsite Mountain. The 8-mile trail dead-ends here. Scenic action for cutthroat.

Logging Lake and Creek: With average fishing for small cutts and a few bull trout, the lake is 4 miles above the inner North Fork Road. The creek is closed to fishing between Logging Lake and Grace Lake.

McDonald Lake: Fished more than any other lake in the park, McDonald is lousy action for a little of everything. On occasion a few nice cutts can be seen working near shore along the Going-to-the-Sun Road and they can be fun.

McDonald Creek: Below Apgar, McDonald Creek offers very spotty fishing for a cutthroat trout and a few rainbows (of some size on occasion) on drys. The upper creek is beautiful and almost devoid of fish, but this does not dampen the enthusiasm of thousands of eager anglers who try their luck on the fighting 4-inch cutthroats hanging out here. Except the section from the lake to McDonald Falls is closed to fishing.

Quartz Creek and Quartz, Lower, and Middle Quartz Lakes: These waters have cutthroats and a few bull trout. The lakes are 4 to 6 miles from Bowman Lake.

Trout Lake: This is another "bear valley" lake on Camas Creek that is fly fishing only for cutthroat trout. You get there via a 4-mile trek over the ridge from McDonald Lake.

Other Western Waters

Anaconda Creek: Cutthroats and mountain whitefish.

Cerulean Lake: May have cutthroats if not frozen out.

Coal Creek: Closed to fishing.

Cummings Creek: Cutthroats.

Fish Creek: Closed to fishing.

Ford Creek: Small cutts.

Kishenehn Creek: Bull and cutthroat tout, mountain whitefish.

Longbow Creek: Cutthroats from Akokala.

Muir Creek: Closed to fishing.

Nyack: Closed to fishing.

Ole Creek: Closed to fishing.

Park Creek: Closed to fishing.

Parke Creek: Few cutts.

Rogers Lake: Cutthroats.

Sage Creek: Cutthroats.

Snyder Lake: Cutthroats.

Spruce Creek: Cutthroats and white-fish.

Starvation Creek: Bull and cutthroat trout, whitefish.

There are other waters in Glacier and, because of the nature of high mountain lakes, they may have trout one year and freeze out the next winter. The rangers located throughout the park are reliable sources of up-to-date information. At the main visitor centers, the employees are often too harried by the thundering herd to absorb new data.

Typical action on the Kootenai
Photo by John Holt

THE KOOTENAI

Rumors and the Kootenai River seem to go together these days like fly fishing and trout. You often will hear stories about how strong the river's rainbows are or how big they can grow, but is any of this true? After all, anglers and truth are not always on speaking terms.

Tucked away in the northwest corner of the state and flowing past the logging community of Libby, the Kootenai is not as well known as other waters in Montana. Much of the river was destroyed with the completion of the Libby Dam in 1972. Ninety miles of the river (48 in the United States and 42 in Canada) are buried under many feet of water known as Lake Koocanusa. Much of the remaining 48 miles in Montana now provides a quality tailwater fishery.

The source of all this water—4,000 cfs is the normal flow, but this jumps up to 30,000 cfs during peak power generation periods—are the rugged ice and snow capped peaks of the Canadian Rockies to the north. The Kootenai is the second-largest river in the state next to the Clark Fork.

The rainbows fight well for their size, which averages in the one- to two-pound range for most of the floatable length of river (they may run up to five or more pounds, especially in the spring near the mouths of tributaries such as the Yaak River and Callahan Creek).

In recent years meat fishers (and an occasional fly fisher) have taken rainbows exceeding twenty pounds (with some approaching thirty) out of the Kootenai just below the dam. The trout line up below the power-generating dam and feed on a chum line of chopped-up kokanee salmon, and trout that have passed through the turbines.

This situation could be an interesting fishery for those willing to use Hi-D sinking lines and large streamers. But those using bait and lures are depleting a finite resource and, as Region One fisheries manager Jim Vashro said, "There are only so many of those tremendous fish and even if they are the fast growing Kamloops strain, once they are gone, it will take quite a few years to grow some more."

Most of the rainbows you will catch in the river run between 8 and 12 inches, but they are wide, thick, and silvery. In recent years guide Dave Blackburn has noticed a slight drop in this average. Neither he nor Vashro believe that this is a cause for major concern yet, but regulations have been put into effect to help protect spawning trout.

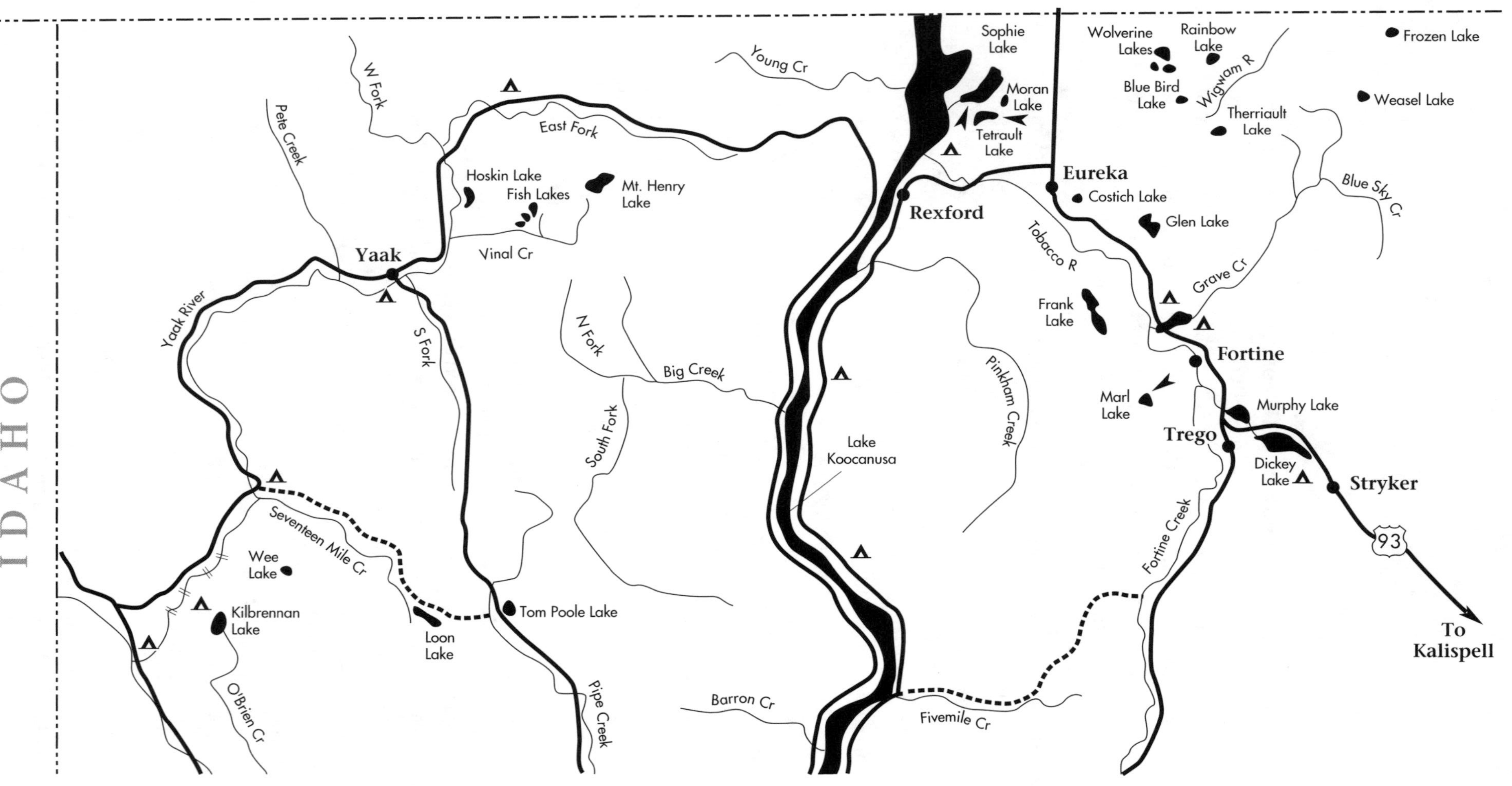

CANADA
IDAHO
Young Cr
Sophie Lake
Moran Lake
Tetrault Lake
Wolverine Lakes
Rainbow Lake
Blue Bird Lake
Wigwam R
Therriault Lake
Frozen Lake
Weasel Lake
Blue Sky Cr
Eureka
Costich Lake
Glen Lake
Rexford
Tobacco R
Grave Cr
Frank Lake
Fortine
Marl Lake
Murphy Lake
Trego
Dickey Lake
Stryker
93
To Kalispell
W Fork
Pete Creek
East Fork
Hoskin Lake
Fish Lakes
Mt. Henry Lake
Vinal Cr
Yaak
Yaak River
S Fork
N Fork
Big Creek
South Fork
Pinkham Creek
Lake Koocanusa
Fortine Creek
Seventeen Mile Cr
Wee Lake
Kilbrennan Lake
Tom Poole Lake
Loon Lake
O'Brien Cr
Pipe Creek
Barron Cr
Fivemile Cr

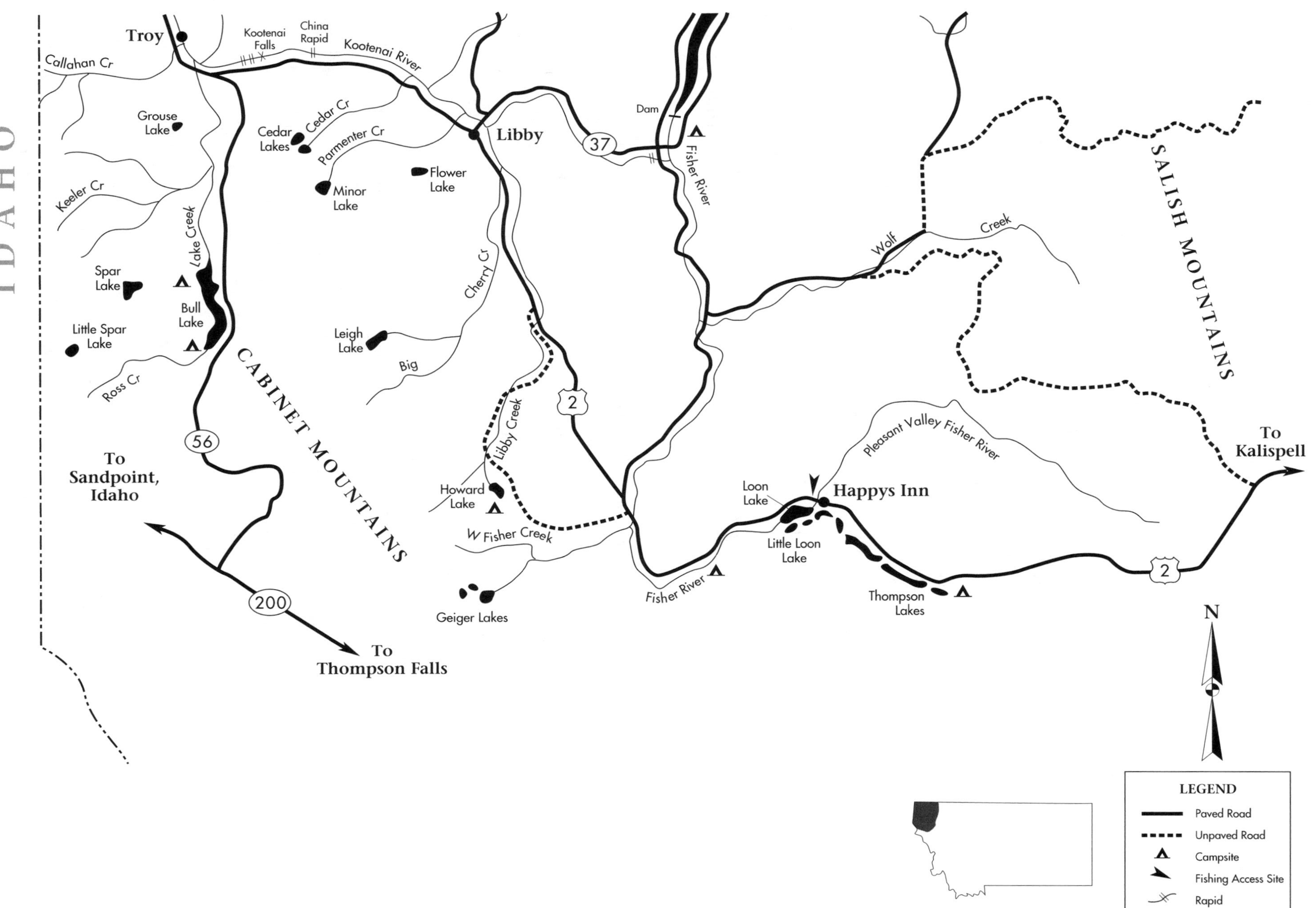

IDAHO
Troy
Callahan Cr
Kootenai Falls
China Rapid
Kootenai River
Grouse Lake
Cedar Lakes
Cedar Cr
Parmenter Cr
Libby
37
Dam
Fisher River
Flower Lake
Minor Lake
Keeler Cr
Lake Creek
Spar Lake
Bull Lake
Little Spar Lake
Ross Cr
Cherry Cr
Leigh Lake
Big
Wolf
Creek
SALISH MOUNTAINS
CABINET MOUNTAINS
56
2
Libby Creek
To Sandpoint, Idaho
Howard Lake
W Fisher Creek
Geiger Lakes
200
To Thompson Falls
Pleasant Valley Fisher River
To Kalispell
Loon Lake
Happys Inn
Little Loon Lake
Fisher River
Thompson Lakes
N
LEGEND
Paved Road
Unpaved Road
Campsite
Fishing Access Site
Rapid
KOOTENAI RIVER

The section of the river from the dam to Libby is paralleled by both Montana Highway 37 and a county road. Access for wader and floaters, while not abundant, is adequate. The same holds true for the stretch between Libby and China Rapids about nine miles downstream. All told, there are about 30 miles of floatable water. This part of the river is open year around and on "warm" winter days you will see anglers working nymphs or even dry flies if a hatch is on. The river is never crowded with either waders or floaters. This is just too far off the beaten track. For the rest of the way to the Idaho border, U.S. 2 is the major source of access.

The first stretch of the river (above Libby) is marked by large riffles, runs, and quiet glides with sections of large bankside boulders. Try working large streamers between the rock formations. Sink-tip lines will help you reach the calmer bottom areas where the big fish hang out. This is a good way to take bull trout. When the trout are rising, cast to the pods of fish in midstream. Weed beds and deep pools are also productive areas.

This is big water and it's easy to get intimidated by the sheer size of it. The best approach here is to cut the river down to fishable size. Experienced anglers work to trout within 30 or 40 feet with accurate, controlled, and calculated casts. Even with the large numbers of slurping trout, sloppy casting can put a damper on the festivities.

Below town the boulders along the banks and out in the current are the best bets (the mouths of creeks are the next best). When floating, look ahead for any "buckets," big patches where the water slows down and the insects concentrate, or even small pockets of calm water along the seams of two different currents. Good fish always hold and feed in these spots. They feel safe here because the surface is broken enough to provide at least a little cover and they take with less discrimination than, say, out in the middle when a hatch is breaking. The trick when floating and fishing this seamy water is to plan the cast well in advance, leaving time to drift the fly right into these prime places.

Even though it's not a wilderness river, timber-covered mountains drop down to the water and the Cabinet Mountains are visible to the southwest. Eagles, deer, and other wildlife are common. This is a peaceful float until a hatch of insects starts popping on the surface.

Then the rainbows turn on and literally hundreds of fish will begin dimpling the smooth river.

There are over 1,400 catchable-size trout per mile and there is sufficient aquatic life to support 3,000 catchable-size trout per mile. So when nature throws the switch, and the heavy feeding begins, the angler with good skills will catch a lot of trout, often to several pounds. And on small drys.

Dave Blackburn describes the daily and yearly hatch cycles as follows, "Sporadic hatches of Iron Duns and Blue-Winged Olives occur year round, as do the midges. Salmon flies hatch from late May to early June. Although the population of these insects is on the rise, there is no intense, concentrated activity.

"Consistent, prolific hatches of mayflies and caddisflies don't start coming off the water until June when the river warms. Blue-Winged Olives, Iron Duns, and Grannom caddis are the main attractions early in the summer, replaced later by Spotted Sedges, Little Sister Sedges, and Pale Morning Duns (which, in spite of the name, linger into the evenings). Late in the summer, heavy swarms of Spotted Sedges and Little Sister Sedges smother the river with their mating flights. Tricos and Spotted Sedges provide the main staple through November.

"Most surface activity occurs in the evenings, when even the largest trout can't pass up food available in such dense concentrations," adds Blackburn.

Trico on aster
Photo by Bob Scammell

While there is some cloudy runoff in April and early May, especially below the Fisher River, the upper 3 miles below the dam are always clear. Early season angling from March through May produces the larger rainbows, as these fish move upstream on their spawning migrations. Nymphs and streamers, both bounced on the bottom, are the most productive flies at this time.

Dry fly action picks up in June and peaks in July and August. Days are long this far north and rises that begin around 7:00 in the evening often last until almost 11:00. Streamers come into play again from September through October. Nymphs hold sway in the winter.

In the summer, when the water level kicks up from a 30,000 cfs release from the dam, the rainbows often move into the newly submerged, grassy banks to pick off terrestrials washed into the river.

A Special Fly for the Kootenai River

If there is an "all-around" mayfly imitation, it is the Parachute Adams. On tough rivers with smooth flows and heavy hatches, a size 16 or 18 works as well as anything until the fish really lock into a selective snit. The fly probably looks like an emerging or a drowned mayfly, and the apparent vulnerability of the fly helps trout overlook deviations in shape, color or size.

PARACHUTE ADAMS

Hook: standard dry fly

Tail: grizzly hackle fibers

Body: gray natural or synthetic fur

Spike: white kip tail hair

Hackle: brown and grizzly mixed

The Parachute Adams is visible enough and buoyant enough to serve well during float fishing. That versatility makes it especially valuable on a boat river like the Kootenai. Anglers there use the Parachute Adams most of the time during non-hatch periods, throwing it out there until the trout demand something different.

Ant, beetle, and grasshopper imitations, cast into the grass, can produce some very hot action—kind of like fishing your unmowed back lawn after an extended rain.

Despite the fact that it is large water, an 8½-foot, five-weight rod for dry fly fishing is ideal for the Kootenai. Bring along a 9-foot, seven-weight rod for large nymphs and streamers. A double-taper floating line and a sink-tip wet line cover the action in the main river. Anyone fishing for the monsters below the dam should bring appropriate equipment—a ten-weight rod, rigged with a Hi-D or lead-core, 30-foot shooting head for throwing 3/0 streamers, wouldn't be out of place.

Cliff Dare, the first guide on the river, has seen changes since the dam was completed, "In the early years, everyone used big dry flies on the Kootenai, size-10 and -12 Renegades and Adams, the same ones they'd use on other local rivers. Now the normal dry fly sizes are 16s and 18s. The nymphs have also become exact imitations, and scud patterns are very popular. Even with streamers, the smart fishermen are using flies that look like kokanee salmon, especially near the dam, and crayfish."

The same types of flies that work on other tough tailwater rivers will catch trout on the Kootenai. During the aquatic insect hatches, emerger patterns are often more effective than dry flies. The smooth stretches of surface develop a thick meniscus, and insects struggle for a disproportionately long time in the film, creating a concentration zone. An imitation half in and half out of the water often works when a true dry fly, sitting completely on the surface, fails on critical fish.

You should come ready to match the major hatches:

- Midges—(especially important during the winter months) in black, red, gray, olive, and brown ranging in size from 26 to 14. Important stages include the pupa, adult, and mating cluster. A Griffith's Gnat is a standard adult imitation on the river.

- Mayflies—the Blue-Winged Olives, Iron Duns, Pale Morning Duns, and Tricos—are abundant enough to lock fish into selective feeding. No-Hackles, in appropriate sizes and colors, match the duns. For the the spent Trico egg-layers, a size-

18 or size-20 Black Clear Wing Spinner is very effective. No single emerger pattern has become the standard on the Kootenai yet, so bring the standards for your home waters.

Pale Morning Dun on bunch berry
Photo by Bob Scammell

▪ Two net-making genera, the Spotted Sedge and the Little Sister Sedge, and the case-making Grannom, are the most important caddisflies. Try an Emergent Sparkle Pupa, in size 16 tan, size 12 brown and yellow, and size 14 black and olive variations, when trout are rolling and jumping during a hatch. The best dry flies are the Henryville and Hemingway Special.

▪ Among the terrestrials, the old Joe's Hopper, often fished wet like a dead-drift nymph, is still popular. Modern flies, such as the Dave's Hopper and Schroeder Hopper, also catch trout. The foam-type ant and beetle patterns can be important at times.

▪ For nymph patterns, try the San Juan Worm—it seems to work on every tailwater river. A good shrimp fly, such as the Big Horn Scud, always seems to interest fish. Bead Head Nymphs, with black beads instead of bright gold, in sizes 18 and 16, have been hot flies on the river in recent seasons.

▪ In the streamer department, a big, foam Edgewater Crayfish that dives and swims on the retrieve, can catch large rainbows. A kokanee fly, with a silver body, white wing, and slim red topping, up to 10 inches long, also attracts the biggest trout. Woolly Buggers, in either olive or black variations, still take plenty of fish on the Kootenai.

This is very big water and those who have never floated this river should hire the services of a reputable guide. China Rapids is hazardous and the Kootenai Falls are a death trip, period. And watch out for standing waves where the Yaak enters the Kootenai. Factor in the wild fluctuations in water levels caused by the operation of the dam and you have the potential for a drift-boat nightmare. This is not difficult water to float after you have been shown the ropes a

Kootenai Falls
Photo courtesy of Mansfield Library, University of Montana

time or two (which is good advice for any new piece of water). If you are wading, be extremely careful even during low water levels. Use chest waders, stream cleats, and perhaps even a wading staff.

Is the Kootenai a destination river? For some it is. Those who have experienced a summer evening filled with clouds of caddflies and dozens of rainbows tend to keep coming back.

Fly Fishing Waters in the Kootenai Drainage

Big Creek: Big Creek enters Lake Koocanusa on the west side, after flowing through rich, thick forest. A short rod and a tight roll cast help here. Some nice spawning cutthroats and rainbows show up in the spring and stay maybe as late as July. Try large attractor drys, like a Wulff or a Double Wing, or flashy streamers. The resident cutts are somewhat smaller.

Blue Sky Creek: A small tributary of Grave Creek south of Eureka, this stream used to be paralleled by an old logging road that is now blocked off. Some nice cutthroats move up in early summer and a few sizeable bull trout run up in late summer. This is tight fishing, interesting because you could end up playing a fish of several pounds in four inches of water. It's something to experience once a season, but for, the sake of the fish, don't make a habit of it.

Bluebird Lake: Bluebird is a few miles up trail from Little Therriault Lake at the end of the Grave Creek Road. It holds some cutthroats and the 3-mile hike is easy and scenic. This is a good place to break in the kids on carrying your gear. It is in treeless mountain country below the crest of the Galton Range. Drys, nymphs, whatever. They all work. You'll pass Paradise Lake on the way. There are sometimes cutthroats swimming here, too. At other times it is barren.

Brimstone Lake: Only a few acres, Brimstone is managed for cutthroat trout with plants on an every-other-year basis. Like most lightly fished cutthroat waters, this one is not difficult to fish. By road, it lies 1 mile south of Fortine on U.S. 93 north of Whitefish.

Bull Lake: South of Troy on Montana 56, 5 miles long, and about a tenth that wide, Bull is managed mainly for that exciting gamefish, the kokanee salmon. I'd rather nymph fish for carp. There are some cutthroats and kamloop rainbows here, along with largemouth bass and northern pike. Perhaps even a bull trout or two. Work the creek inlets like Upham and Payne on the east shore to narrow the water down a touch.

Burke Lake: In Yaak country, Burke Lake lies not too far from the Canadian border. It is "world-class" fishing for an overpopulation of stunted brook trout that race five hundred at a time towards any fly cast upon or into the water. This is entertaining for fifteen or twenty seconds. It's located about two miles north of Hawkins Lake, off the Hawkins Creek Road.

Cad Lake: Cad is a tiny lake, less than 5 acres, lying between Kalispell and Libby. It is planted with Arlee rainbows every other year. By road it's 1½ miles above Horseshoe Lake.

Les Hampton fishes both Cad and nearby Cibid often because, in his words, "They're so close that I can pop a float tube in the water after work for a few hours of evening casting." He says about the Arlee rainbows in these waters, "Each year class will all be pretty much the same. If you find a concentration of 12-inchers, they'll all look and weigh the same. The Arlee strain does fine in still-water environments, developing stocky bodies and short heads if they survive a summer. And they fight hard, seeming to dig for the bottom more than other types of rainbows, but of course they mature early and die after three years. That's their genetic programming. They are insect eaters, and take small flies readily."

Callahan Creek: A marginal fishing stream for rainbow, cutthroat, and bull trout, this tributary of the Kootenai (just east of Troy) is of interest because some big spawning rainbows can be taken on big streamers near the mouth in the spring. As with most of the good things in life, timing is everything and this is usually a function of luck.

Cedar Lakes: Reached by the Cedar Creek trail west of Libby, the upper lake is 54 acres and the lower one is 21. A lot of backpacking traffic strolls into this country due, in part, to the mountain and cirque scenery, and a little bit because of the fishing for 10- to 12-inch trout.

Cedar Lakes below Dome Mountain
Photo courtesy of USDA–Forest Service

Cibid Lake: About three times the size of Cad Lake, Cibid is just a few hundred yards away. Managed for rainbows, it's not bad action for fish running around 10 to 12 inches.

Crystal Lake: Crystal Lake lies right next to U.S. 2 halfway between Kalispell and Libby. Lots of rainbows and kokanee salmon are dumped in here each year. It is large—175 acres—and deep. There are also perch and northern pike and plenty of small boats trolling for salmon. Most people probably know this as the water behind Happy's Inn.

Sam Rowe says, "I fish Crystal a lot because it's full of surprises. I don't bother with the fresh, stocker trout. I'll use a 2/0 streamer, my own imitation of a kokanee, and catch not only pike and bass but also some real nice holdover rainbows. The two- and three-year-old fish in this lake get to be real healthy specimens."

Dickey Lake: Right next to U.S. 93 south of Eureka, this is very large water for this country (nearly 600 acres) and has all kinds of species in it, including kokanee (what else?), cutthroats, rainbows, brookies, largemouth bass, and northern pike, along with motorboats and the like. Summer homes dot the shoreline in this rolling, timbered country. The shallow-water areas at the inlet on the east end have that aqua-blue Caribbean look and local rumor consistently vibrates to the tune of "there are some huge brook trout in that lake." Sinking lines and big streamers in the evenings during the fall may tell the story.

Dickey is so deep that you are pretty much limited to pecking at the edges. Most people make the mistake of positioning a boat thirty or so feet out and casting towards the shore. In areas with sharp drop-offs, which includes the entire north and south shorelines, they are retrieving flies far over the heads of the fish. They'd do a lot better standing on the bank, or putting the boat next to the bank, and either casting out into the lake, so that the fly follows the contours of the bottom upwards, or casting parallel to the shoreline.

East Fisher River: This pretty stream, located 40 miles south of Libby on U.S. 2, is followed by a good road all the way. There's not much water in the summer and the headwaters are being logged to death. In spite of this rainbows, cutthroats, and those ubiquitous brookies hang around waiting for a well-placed dry fly.

East Fork Yaak River: This used to be a beautiful stream but most of the drainage has been logged to oblivion. The little pools and quiet runs are silted up. There is still some good water in the lower stretches where the riparian areas are left alone. Once in the stream, you can pretend you're in a real forest and take some nice rainbows and brookies and a stray cutthroat on general searching flies, such as Elk Hair Caddis, and attractors. It's hard to believe that 20-inch-long trout once swam here. Take the Yaak River Road 4 miles above Upper Ford Ranger Station.

Fish Lakes: Three of these five lakes—North, Middle, and South—are managed for westslope cutthroat trout. The lakes nestle high up in the Cabinet Wilderness, which is not huge as far as Montana wilderness areas go, but contains some beautiful high country and a few hold-out grizzlies. The trail in is steep, but the place receives some pressure in July and August when snow levels drop enough so that people can hike in. These lakes are about 4 miles up Vinal Creek from the Vinal Creek Road.

Fisher River: In spots, this is still a classic Northwest forested stream, but heavy logging in the region has hurt the drainage to the extent that the fishing is now average, at best. During spring runoff, the Fisher is the major contributor of silt to the Kootenai. As a matter of fact, anytime it rains, it runs mud into the river. Some cutthroats, rainbows, brookies, and whitefish are still taken in the stream. U.S. 2 crosses Fisher about 14 miles south of Libby.

Five Mile Creek: Montana 37 crosses this stream as it runs along the east shore of Lake Koocanusa above the dam. It is small water but in early summer some good-sized cutthroats move upstream. You'll also find brook trout here. The cutthroats are part of a Fish, Wildlife, and Parks Department program that plants migratory cutthroats in the reservoir tributaries to establish permanent spawning populations. Since Libby Dam wiped out the upper river and the natural flow of things, this is a good plan with a decent chance of succeeding.

Flower Lakes (and Creek): Both the creek and the artificial impoundments are closed to fishing because they are part of the Libby water supply system. But the natural lakes are open and stocked periodically with cutthroats. Because most people have heard that the system is closed, they are relatively unfished and consequently, a good bet.

Fortine Creek: Access is not always easy but is available from a country road running east from U.S. 93. Resident trout are small, but some of the spawning cutthroats are good sized in early summer.

Frank Lake: Frank is 10 miles south of Eureka off U.S. 93 on poor, rutted road. The closeness to the city, and the fact that it is very good fishing, makes this a popular spot. It's hit hard all year, especially by ice fishers. Its size, over a hundred acres, gives the trout some protection. The Fish, Wildlife, and Parks Department manages it for Eagle Lake rainbows.

Cliff Dare suggests fishing it right at ice-out. He likes a size-6 Gray Stonefly Nymph (a common insect along the wave-washed shoreline of the deeper end). He throws the fly up onto the ice and pulls it off. He doesn't bother retrieving too far away from the ice shelf. If one of the cruising rainbows doesn't take the fly within 5 feet, he casts it back up onto the ice.

Almost three-quarters of Frank Lake is very shallow, never getting much deeper than 10 feet There are two islands at this shallow end and both of them are fish magnets. During June the lake has a fine damsel fly hatch and trout cruise over the weed beds, intercepting the swimming nymphs. A size-6 or size-8 Olive Marabou Damsel, retrieved with a "jerk, jerk, and pause" movement, will take these fish.

With the hot summer weather the best fishing happens in the other quarter of the lake, the deeper 40-foot basin at the north end. The water is clear, and aquatic weeds grow over most of the bottom. A deep presentation with a fast-sinking line is effective here, but you have to experiment to find the right depth. This part of the lake stratifies, and the trout hang at the top of the thermocline, usually around 15 to 20 feet The damsel fly isn't the best fly in this deep water—a size-16 to size-22 String Midge Larva, in olive or red, fools many more trout. The fly has to be inched ever so slowly over the bottom.

Frozen Lake: This lake straddles the United States–Canadian border and, if you pretend real hard, the logged-over country you drive through to reach the trailhead won't remind you of Gary, Indiana. There is a boat launch on the Canadian side and a good number of put-puts smoke up the water in the summer. Just the same, if you are willing to lug a float tube down an old logging road to the lake, you can catch big cutthroats (I've taken a couple over 20 inches) with flashy streamers worked into and along the downed shoreline timber. Some large bull trout also cruise the shoreline. Try a Clouser Minnow, letting it drop down into the openings of the logs (work it like a leadhead jig). To get there go 30 miles up Grave Creek Road, then east to the end of Frozen Lake Road, then hike about a mile into the lake. This lake actually lies in the North Fork of the Flathead drainage but you get there from the Kootenai side.

Glen Lake: Six miles southeast of Eureka, Glen is large (340 acres) and managed for rainbows. It's not much for aesthetics, especially during the midsummer drawdown, but there are some nice fish and lots of anglers and boats and trucks.

The structure of the lake is equally uninspiring. It's a dammed-up bowl, the shore all the way around sloping down steadily to a maximum depth of 38 feet in the center. The way to find trout is to cast parallel to the shore, moving systematically outward into deeper and deeper water until you start getting strikes.

Grave Creek: Grave Creek flows into the Tobacco River (which empties into Lake Koocanusa) from the northeast. A good run of spawning cutthroats moves upstream from late spring until July. Late summer finds the bull trout and mountain whitefish doing the same. This is a wide, swiftly flowing mountain stream with riffles, whitewater, pools, and downed timber. Pretty stuff. Fish attractors like Royal Humpies and Air Heads with short, accurate casts, hitting the pockets.

All of the tributaries play host to at least a couple of nice, spawning trout. When the fish are in the small streams, leave them alone. Working these during spawning is kind of like having your car tipped over while hugging your sweety at the drive-in. Go about eight miles south of Eureka on U.S. 93 to get on Grave Creek.

Grouse Lake: Over by Troy, this lake is a 1-mile walk-in. It's a small, 3-acre spot of water, but it is fertile. It's managed for brook trout, offering good fishing the year after each plant and then declining until the next blip in the planting cycle.

"It's a finicky lake, maybe because there are so many freshwater shrimp in it," remarked Cliff Dare. "One day it'll be easy and the next day it'll be impossible."

Hawkins Lakes: These lakes are not far from the upper reaches of Pete Creek in the Yaak drainage. Upper (2 acres) and Lower (4 acres) are managed for cutthroats and are fairly good for fish running 12 to 14 inches. Both ponds are really weedy. Bring scud imitations. All of this country is going fast (it will grow back but not in our lifetimes), so you'd better fish it now if you like shade. Logging road north from the headwaters of Pete Creek will get you within a half mile of these lakes.

Hoskin Lake: Hit the Forest Service trail 2½ miles north of Yaak. Hoskin is planted with westslope cutthroats every other season and is good fishing for trout in the one-foot range. The Dirty Shame Saloon is nearby and worth a stop if you're dry or in need of a T-shirt. Some time back a couple of the boys got a little buzzed up and blew some fingers off playing with dynamite outside the tavern. My kind of place (really).

Howard Lake: Thirty miles south of Libby on Libby Creek and Howard Creek roads, Howard is planted with Arlee rainbows every year. The paved road and the public campground make this a popular spot. It's good fishing from float tubes (watch out for trollers). Gold Ribbed Hares Ears and Marabou Damsels are effective nymphs. Zonkers, Krystal Buggers, and Rabbit Leeches also work well.

Kilbrennan Lake: This one is popular with people around Troy. Kilbrennan is northwest of the city, roughly 10 miles of gravel roads away. It's a good lake for float tubing for brookies and cutthroats. Much of the bottom is mud, and midge larvae are abundant on this type of substrate. There are weed beds on the west end, with large populations of crayfish (use an Edgewater Foam Crayfish) and bullheads (use a dark Muddler Minnow). Brookies like bright flies, too, especially in the fall, and a Mickey Finn is an effective streamer here.

Lake Creek: "The big flood in the winter of '74–'75 wiped out pools and logjams, and even straightened out sections. This stream is still good, but not as good as it was before the flood," commented Cliff Dare.

"It's best when the spawners are in it. Fish can only come up a quarter mile from the Kootenai before running into generators. Most of the spawners come downstream from Bull Lake. Those rainbows stay in the stream from mid-June to mid-July. They take dry flies well, especially a size-14 and size-16 Parachute Adams and Elk Hair Caddis."

Pollution has diminished the fishery somewhat, also, but there are still rainbow, cutthroat, brook, and bull trout, and battling whitefish. Lake Creek has excellent caddisfly populations, and for an all-around searching nymph pattern nothing beats a Free-Living Caddis Larva. Take the Lake Creek Road turnoff about two miles south of Troy off U.S. 2.

Leigh Creek: The outlet of Leigh Lake and a tributary of Big Cherry Creek, this is a fine little hike-in fishing stream for rainbows and brookies. There's a pretty falls on it and no angler worth his graphite (or bamboo for traditionalists) would pass the big spill basin without trying a few casts.

Leigh Lake: Leigh can be good fishing for brook and rainbow trout (with some trophy specimens over five pounds). The lake lies below Snowshoe Peak in the Cabinet Mountains. It's a good 3-mile trek in nice country that is popular with backpackers. Woolly Worms sometimes take trout when they turn difficult here (or in any other high country lake).

Lake Koocanusa: The result of the completion of Libby Dam in the 1970s, Koocanusa can be good fishing for cutthroats and Kamloop rainbows along the shore, especially by creek mouths, from late spring into summer. There are also lingcod, kokanee, and whitefish, and some bull trout on occasion.

Cliff Dare touts two fishing situations on Koocanusa:

▪ In June fish the windward side. There'll be a mud line a few feet off the shore, and two- to four-pound rainbows and cutthroats cruise along this edge. They'll hit a size-8 Black Ant pattern, fished wet a few inches below the surface.

These guys can get really crabby if you crowd them.
Photo courtesy of USDA–Forest Service

■ Thoughout the spring months you will see large schools of rising fish. The water is alive with dimples. These are small kokanee salmon, not trout, but they can be hooked on a size-18 Adams. They have to be played gently because they have soft mouths. These are not much as a sport fish, but they're excellent eating.

The reservoir's main problem is that the Army Corps of Engineers often draws the water level down over 150 feet during the late summer and early fall for power generation, which is the main purpose of the dam. The Corps has stated that recreation values are 1 percent of the overall operating scheme. When Koocanusa is drawn down this low, huge muddy beaches are exposed, making boat launching next to impossible. Hordes of flies swarm in the air. The place resembles a very large sewer. The Corps doesn't care. Why should you? There are plenty of other places to fish in the region in the summer.

Leon Lake: This is another large lake lying near U.S. 2 between Kalispell and Libby. It's planted with cutthroats and rainbows, which do well in the 87-foot depths, and it is often decent fishing.

Libby Creek: Eight miles east of Libby, this creek goes under U.S. 2 and dumps into the Kootenai. It's good-looking water, but is heavily polluted with mining waste. It does get some rainbow, cutthroat, and bull trout that run up from the river. Fishing is best in the spring, when nymphs, like an Olive Hare's Ear or a small Montana Stone, work well. And there is an extended whitefish season, but you can only use maggots or artificial lures.

Little McGregor Lake: This muddy-bottomed lake near U.S. 2 covers 38 acres and is 30 feet deep. It's average fishing for rainbows and sometimes good fishing for large brook trout. The marshy shoreline dictates the use of float tubes.

Little Spar Lake: This alpine lake up Spar Creek is planted with cutthroats by helicopter. The water is large by high-country standards, over 50 acres, and deep—nearly 100 feet Most people stay down below at Spar, hustling kokanee and lake trout.

Loon Lake: Over 200 acres in area, Loon is full of panfish, trash fish ("Who you callin' trash, boy?"), small- and largemouth bass and some fat rainbows. You should try for the rainbows early in the season, before the water warms up. Work the narrow neck between the two basins thoroughly with poppers for largemouths in late May and June. It's located about 3 miles southwest of Fortine.

Loon Lake: This one is in the Pipe Creek drainage and it is managed for rainbows. There are also a few brookies.

Marl Lake: Not far from Fortine, Marl is over 100 acres and planted with generic rainbows. There are some holdover Kamloop rainbows from an earlier stocking. Ask in town how to find this one. It can be good from a float tube with leech patterns. Take Meadow Creek Road about 3 miles west of Fortine, then go south 1½ miles on rough road.

Moran Lake: About 8 miles northwest of Eureka and a half mile east of Sophie Lake, this water has brookies and rainbows and can be good. Dick McLean fishes it and says, "It's not much over 30 feet anywhere and it's always possible to find the trout. There's a long point near the center of the lake, and off the point there's a flat no more than 10 feet deep. The rainbows cruise that area every evening. My best fly on Moran is a Carey Special."

Mount Henry Lake: There are a number of ways into this lake in the Yaak drainage, all indicated by signs that point to a trailhead. This is still pretty country and you will get wonderful views of the clearcuts once you reach the 8-acre lake. It's managed for cutthroats and it's good fishing most of the time from July until the snow flies in the fall.

Murphy Lake: Just east of U.S. 93 south of Eureka, this lake is overrun with summer campers. You can catch largemouth bass, yellow perch, northern pike, and rainbow trout. You need a boat or a float tube. The southeast shoreline is the most productive.

Pipe Creek: Pipe Creek enters the Kootenai 3 miles west of Libby and is readily accessible, heavily hit, and contains cutthroat, rainbow, and brook trout. As with most creeks in this country, beaver ponds lie about in the swampy, meadowy sections. Brookies of some size often inhabit these. A Bunny Leech underwater or a Mosquito dry fly on the surface turns trouts' heads.

Pleasant Valley Fisher River: Much of this stream is on private land but a number of miles parallel U.S. 2. Most of the rainbow and brook trout in this fishy-looking stretch average around 7 inches, but away from the road near evening, a few larger ones can be taken on drys like a Hairwing Adams or a White Wulff.

Seventeen Mile Creek: The road follows this stream in the Yaak drainage. It offers fair angling for resident cutthroats and rainbows, plus some spawning fish up from the Yaak. During midsummer, when the Yaak gets too warm, brookies come up for the cool water. It's overgrown along the banks.

Sophie Lake: Sophie is over 200 acres of lake about 8 miles northwest of Eureka. It has a population of cutthroats, but is now managed for Kamloop rainbows (the species that lives a long life and grows rapidly). Leeches and damsel nymphs work as imitations, but sometimes a gaudy streamer does even better. During the heat of the day a hopper dropped next to the shore and occasionally twitched will also pull trout a long way.

Spar Lake: Twenty-five miles south of Troy via Iron Creek or Lake Creek Road, nearly 440 acres big, and 200 feet deep, Spar is intensively managed for kokanee salmon. There are also brook trout and some lake trout. The Forest Service manages the campground, picnic area, and boat ramp. It's popular with Troy anglers.

Ten Lakes: Most of these lakes are barren, but Rainbow has cutthroats that get hit hard once the snow leaves this high country just south of the Canadian border. Near the end of Grave Creek Road take Wigwam Creek Road for 3 miles, then hike 2 miles cross country to get there.

Tetrault (Carpenter) Lake: Located 7 miles north of Eureka and covering over 100 acres, Tetrault is planted with 20,000 Arlee rainbows each year. These are quickly nailed by the locals, but some of the survivors reach a nice size and provide challenging float tube action. There are also bluegills and largemouth bass here.

Therriault Lakes (Big and Little): Both have campgrounds and both are always crowded. Lying below a rugged ridge at the end of the Grave Creek Road, each lake has good numbers of small cutthroats. Small nymphs and dry flies fool these fish. You might have the water to yourself in September.

Timber Lake: Eagle Lake rainbows do well in this water. Timber Lake is 5 miles of rough road south of Eureka. It has plenty of food and the trout average a little over a pound. Scud, leech, and damsel imitations work well from a float tube or canoe.

Tobacco River: Access is limited on this Lake Koocanusa tributary, but you can get on it at the county road bridges. The fishing is good with drys for spawning cutthroats early in the season and with streamers for bull trout beginning in late July. The cutts like bushy flies like Wulffs, Trudes, and Humpies. The bull trout like anything big banged in front of them. There are lots of runs and pools in this underfished (by fly fishers anyway) stream. A two-pound cutthroat or five-pound bull trout in this river is an intriguing problem, especially on a three-weight.

Tom Poole Lake: Reached by a couple of hundred yards of trail off the Yaak River road, this lake is planted with westslope cutthroats and is good fishing for fat trout. This is rich water, full of scuds, leeches, and aquatic insects.

Topless Lake: The name is probably politically incorrect these days, but there are some nice rainbows in this small pond lying near Horseshoe Lake.

Michael Duff reported on a week-long trip during July, "The weather was rainy, which probably helped the fishing. The bigger trout were not easy, but every day I'd catch a few in the 17- to 20-inch range. My top fly was a size-16 Olive Serendipity worked in the surface film. A fast retrieve caught smaller fish. A slow retrieve caught those smaller ones, too, but it also took the occasional big one."

Vinal Lake: Go north on Pipe Creek Road out of Libby, then about 5 miles south of Yaak take the Vinal Lake Road northeast. Finally take a short hike on level ground to the lake. Vinal Lake is managed for cutthroat trout on a yearly basis and this 18-acre lake can be good fishing for 12-inchers.

Weasel Lake: This is an easy-to-reach lake in relatively unspoiled country in the Whitefish Range. It used to be a great place to go and catch a dinner of cutthroats. Some government agency in its infinite wisdom built fishing decks around the western shore and a cute little wooden bridge across the creek. The place is now full of tiny (4 inches) cutthroats. Radios blast, children frolic, dogs bark. It's good water turned into a Brady Bunch nightmare. Go 30 miles up Grave Creek Road, then follow the signs.

West Fork Yaak River: The West Fork is an average, at best, fishery for small cutthroats that average maybe 6 inches, except in early spring. This time of year bigger fish move up from the main Yaak and you can find 12-inchers.

Wigwam River: Wigwam flows into Canada not far from the Grave Creek Road. The stream looks like superb fly fishing water, but holds only a few cutthroats until you sneak across the border and work your way downstream several miles. Pools, runs, and logjams hold trout to 15 inches and you won't have any company except for the grizzlies, wolves, and perhaps a caribou or two. This is tough country best saved for those who know their way around the woods (and the wildlife).

Yaak Falls
Photo courtesy of USDA–Forest Service

Wolf Creek: This tributary of the Fisher River looks like fine water early in the year before it shrinks way down. It's followed by paved road most of the way. There is less than average angling for small cutthroat, brook, and some rainbow trout, plus whitefish in the lower reaches.

Wolverine Lakes (Upper and Lower): These lakes are reached by a 2-mile hike up Grave Creek Road in the Ten Lakes area. Cutthroats swim here and the ones that aren't hammered in the early season (July and August after the snow melts some) are good sport in late September. They average a pound or better by that time of year.

Yaak River: Formerly one of the best unknown rivers in the state, logging and increased recreational pressure have hurt this stream a lot. The lower stretch below the impassable (unless you're insane) falls holds some good rainbow, brook, bull, and cutthroat trout up from the Kootenai, plus chunky whitefish. This is bouncing, canyon water and short casts on the deeper creases and pools work best. There are still old-time wet fly fishermen on the Yaak, and they catch their share of trout on western favorites like the Picket Pin and the Western Bee.

The upper river, much slower water, has nice brook and cutthroat trout, and also ferocious whitefish. Use more delicate dry flies and nymphs here. The upper river is floatable, but DO NOT go over the falls. The trip would be painful. Campgrounds and plenty of national forest allow ample opportunity to spend some time in the woods.

Young Creek: Flowing from the west into Lake Koocanusa about 10 miles north of Big Koocanusa Bridge, Young Creek, like most of the reservoir's tributaries, now has good runs of spawning cutthroat and bull trout that can offer exciting action for fish of several pounds in cramped circumstances. The only problem with all of these streams is that when the snowpack is low and the Corps draws down Koocanusa the fish have a bit of trouble crossing the mud flats to reach the forest segments of the creeks. No one said life was easy, did they?

Other Waters

Alkali Lake: No fish.

Alvord Lake: Largemouth bass. This is good yellow perch water, too, the fish ranging up to 14 inches

American Creek: Small trout.

Barbe Lake: Cutthroats.

Barron Creek: Cutthroat and brook trout. A logging road, right off Montana 37, follows the stream. The best stretch is a few miles above the mouth, at the bottom of the canyon section.

Basin Creek: Too small.

Bear Creek: Cutthroats and bull trout.

Bar Lakes: Cutthroats.

Beetle Creek: Too small.

Betts Lake: Poor access.

Big Cherry Creek: A tributary of Libby Creek with brook, cutthroat, and rainbow trout. Skip the lower miles—the channel still suffers from past mining activity. Hit it in the middle and upper sections.

Blacktail Creek: Too small.

Blue Bird Creek: Too small.

Blue (Green) Lake: Brook trout.

Bobtail Creek: Small trout.

Bootjack Lake: Private.

Boulder Creek: Cutthroats. This stream dumps into the Kootenai near Rexford.

Boulder Lakes: Cutthroats in these lakes up Boulder Creek. The big one is 20 acres and the little one is 4 acres. The smaller pond is actually better, fish hiding in the tangles of drowned logs.

Brimstone (Ant) Creek: Too small.

Bristow Creek: Too small.

Burnt Creek: Brook and cutthroat trout.

Cable Creek: Too small.

Camp Creek: Too small.

Caribou Creek: Too small.

Cedar Creek: Small fish; brookies, cutts, and rainbows.

Clarence Creek: Too small.

Clay Creek: Too small.

Cody Lakes: Brook and cutthroat trout. These are three small lakes up Cody Creek. It's only a 2-mile walk in from the end of the road and the middle and lower lakes have enough nice trout to make the trip worthwhile.

Contact Creek: Too small.

Copper Creek: Too small.

Costich Lake: Brookies, rainbows, and largemouth bass. This lake, close to Eureka, is better suited to bass than anything else. They hit streamers that imitate small trout really well.

Cripple Horse Creek: Few fish.

Crystal Lake: Private.

Curley Creek: Small fish.

Cyclone Creek: Too small.

Dahl Lake: Poor access. Poor fishing.

Dahl Lake Fork of Pleasant Valley Creek: Brook trout.

Davis Creek: Too small.

Deep Creek: Brook, bull, cutthroat, and rainbow trout.

Deep Lake: Private.

Divide Creek: Too small.

Dodge Creek: Small fish.

Double Lake: Brook trout.

Double N Lake: Private.

Dudley Creek: Too small.

Dudley Slough: Private land.

Dunn Creek: Too small.

East Fork Pipe Creek: Cutthroats and rainbows.

Edna Creek: Too small.

Elk Creek: Too small.

Fairway Lake: Cutthroats.

Falls Creek: Too small for most anglers, especially in the upper reaches. On the lower sections there's enough water in the early season on this spring-fed stream for fast fishing for rainbows, cutts, and brookies. In the fall brookies come up out of Lake Creek to spawn.

Falls Creek Lakes: Cutthroats.

Flattail Creek: Too small.

Fourth of July Creek: Too small.

French Creek: Too small.

Garver Creek: Too small.

Geiger Lakes: Cutthroats, rainbows, and hybrids. Popular lakes with horse packers because of the good trail that starts near the West Fisher Guard Station.

Good Creek: Too small.

Granite Creek: Rainbows.

Granite Lake: Cutthroats.

Grimms Meadows Lakes: Private.

Grob Lake: No trout. Plenty of sunfish for the kids.

Hanging Valley Lakes: Rainbows.

Hawkins Creek: Cutthroats.

Hellroaring Creek: Small trout.

Hidden Lake: Cutthroats.

Horseshoe Lake: Rainbows, largemouth bass, and smallmouth bass.

Howard Creek: Rainbows.

Hudson Lake: Private.

Indian Lake: Too small.

Island Lake: Largemouth bass.

Ivan Creek: Too small.

Jackson Creek: Brookies.

Jumbo Lakes: Brookies. No jumbos here, just a bunch of 8- to 10-inch fish in 5 acres of beaver ponds near Hidden Lake.

Keeler Creek: It has bull, cutthroat, rainbow, and brook trout (especially brookies). Keeler is in timbered, brushy country. Some good deep holes make this fun "poking around" water.

Kilbrennan Creek: Brookies.

Klatawa Lake: Barren.

LaFoe Lake: Cutthroats.

Lake Creek (Swamp Creek): Too small and brushy for most fly fishermen.

Lake Creek (West Fisher River): Too small.

Lavon Lake: Rainbows. It is only 17 acres, but it is more than 90-feet deep. Bring a real fast sinking line.

Lick Lake: Cutthroats.

Lime Creek: Too small.

Little Cherry Creek: Too small.

Little Creek: Too small.

Little Loon Lake: Rainbows, largemouth bass, and smallmouth bass. Some of those largemouths run up to six pounds, and in this shallow, 10-acre lake they never get too far from the surface.

Little North Fork Big Creek: Rainbows.

Long Lake: Alkaline.

Loon Creek: Brook and rainbow trout.

Loon Lake (Fortine): Cutthroats and brookies. The shoreline is so marshy that a float tube gives a fly fisherman a real advantage here.

Lost Fork Creek: Cutthroats.

Lost Lake (Eureka): Brookies.

Lost Lake (U.S. 2): Brookies.

Louis Lake: Cutthroats and rainbows.

Lower Bramlet Lake: Rainbows to 14 inches It is only a 1½-mile walk in from the end of the Bramlet Creek Road.

Martin Lake (Fortine): Brookies.

Martin Lake (Big Cherry Creek): Brookies, cutthroats, and rainbows.

Mary Rennels Lake: Private.

McGinnis Creek: There are 6- to 7-inch brookies in this tributary of the Yaak. In the spring, with fish that overwintered here, there are lots of them.

McGuire Creek: Too small.

Meadows Creek (Yaak): Too small.

Meadows Creek (Fortine): Brookies.

Milnor Lake: Largemouth bass and northern pike (a few). It covers roughly 30 acres and is 60 feet deep, with areas of springs. The shallows get weedy in midsummer—bring weedless Dahlberg Divers for subsurface work.

Minor Lake: Cutthroats. A deep, cirque lake of roughly 30 acres up the Parmenter Creek trail. It gets busy in midsummer, but right after ice-out you can have some nice cutthroats, over 20 inches, all to yourself.

Mud Lake: Brook trout.

Murphy Creek: Brook and rainbow trout.

Myson Lake: Cutthroats.

North Fork Big Creek: Too small.

North Fork Callahan Creek: Cutthroats and rainbows.

Phillip Lake: Private fee fishing lake at the mouth of Windy Creek (a tributary of the Yaak).

Phillips Creek: Too small.

Phill's Lake: Cutthroats.

Pine Creek: Brookies.

Pinkham Creek: Brookies, cutthroats, and rainbows. There is a falls 4 miles upstream. There are more fish above the falls, but they are mostly small (10 inches is a trophy). The lower water has a few nice fish.

Pleasant Valley Creek: Brookies and rainbows.

Poorman Creek: Rainbows.

Quartz Creek: Too small.

Rainbow Lake: Rainbows and largemouth bass.

Ramsey Creek: Bull and rainbow trout.

Rattlebone Lake: Largemouth bass. Drive up to the head of Cripple Creek to reach Rattlebone. The bass fishing peaks in early July here, especially the surface action with poppers.

Red Top Creek: Small fish.

Rich Creek: Too small.

Robin Creek: Too small.

Rock Lake: Alkaline.

Ross Creek: Brook and cutthroat trout. Ross feeds into Bull Lake, and the first mile above the lake is the best fishing.

Round Lake: Brookies.

St. Clair Creek: Brookies and cutthroats.

St. Clair Lake: Cutthroats.

Savage Lake: Brookies, largemouth bass, yellow perch, and sunfish—all sharing a 108-acre lake watched over by summer cottages.

School House Lake: No gamefish. It is overrun with sunnies, which makes it a place for plunking small poppers. It's only 4 miles out of Troy, up the Lake Creek Road. It's the ideal spot for taking kids to learn how to fly fish.

Schrieber Creek: Brookies.

Schrieber Lake: Brookies.

Shannon Lake: Small brookies. It is only a half-mile hike. Shannon is at the foot of Cabinet Range, west of Troy and right off U.S. 2.

Silver Butte Fisher River: Small fish.

Sky Lakes: Cutthroats.

Slee Lake: Private.

Snowshoe Creek: Too small.

South Fork Big Creek: Cutthroats.

South Fork Callahan Creek: Too small.

South Fork Meadow Creek: Too small.

South Fork Yaak River: Brookies, cutthroats, and rainbows. The best fishing, for someone willing to hike, is in the steep canyon above the mouth.

South Fork Young Creek: Too small.

Spread Creek: Brook, cutthroat, and rainbow trout.

Stahl Creek: Too small.

Standard Creek: Brookies.

Standard Lakes: Brookies and cutthroats.

Star Creek: Bull and rainbow trout. Like many of the small tributaries of the Kootenai, this one has been heavily logged. As a result, silty runoff has created a delta of mud at the mouth. Spawning fish from the river cannot get up into the stream as easily now.

Sullivan Creek: Cutthroats. There is actually a short tailwater section below the Rexford water supply dam that has fine hatches of net-making caddisflies, mainly a size-14 brown-winged and yellow-bodied Spotted Sedge. On July evenings the angler can have a ball here with a Dancing Caddis or Elk Hair Caddis dry fly.

Summit Creek: Too small.

Sutton Creek: Brook, bull, cutthroat, and rainbow trout.

Swamp Creek (Fortine): Small fish.

Swamp Creek (U.S. 2): Brookies, cutthroats, and rainbows.

Therriault Creek: Cutthroats and rainbows.

Throops Lake: Private.

Trail Creek: Too small.

Vimy Lakes: Rainbows.

Vinal Creek: Cutthroats and brookies.

Weasal Creek: Tiny cutthroats.

Wee Lake: At 15 acres, it is small (thus the name), but it's deep and holds nice 16- to 22-inch fish. The problem is getting to it. Go to the Sylvanite Ranger Station for starters, drive up the Seventeen Mile Creek Road to the Hemlock Creek Road and at the end of that road trek cross country for a mile to Wee Lake.

West Fisher River: Brookies, cutthroats, and rainbows.

West Fork Quartz Creek: Too small.

Williams Creek: Small cutthroats, and bull trout.

Windy Creek: Too small.

■ *Special thanks to Dave Blackburn, Cliff Dare, Michael Duff, Les Hampton, Dick McLean, Sam Rowe and Jim Vashro for their help on the Kootenai drainage.*

Swan River
Photo by Paul Porte

T H E S W A N

If rivers were conscious entities capable of speech, the Swan River would say something like, "You've clearcut my drainages and you've scalped my mountainsides, but I still have trout and I always will."

The Swan has endured an incredible amount of logging, both on Forest Service and private land (much of the latter owned by Plum Creek). There has even been some illegal cutting in the Mission Mountain Wilderness area. Still, there are cutthroat, rainbow, brook, and bull trout in the river.

The size and numbers of the rainbows are rebounding slowly. The improvements are due mostly to the healing of some old clearcuts (hopefully the high water of 1993 blew out some silt from the riverbed) and new catch regulations implemented in the late 1980s. A 1991 census recorded nearly twenty rainbows over 12 inches per 1,000 feet in the Salmon Prairie to Piper Creek stretch (compared to less than six per 1,000 feet in a 1982 count).

The Swan is a stronghold of the endangered bull trout. Biologists in 1993 counted 432 spawning redds—three times more redds than they found in the entire Flathead River drainage. The populations are still threatened by overfishing, siltation in the spawning tributaries from excessive clearcutting, and hybridization with another char, the eastern brook trout, but the state is implementing corrective measures to spur a bull trout recovery.

And, with the help of state fisheries biologists such as Scott Rumsey, populations of cutthroat trout are improving. Rumsey and his crew are currently stocking selected tributaries with thousands of westslope cutthroats in hopes of reestablishing historical populations. The initial results of this work offer some encouragement.

The Swan is a stronghold of the endangered bull trout.

Headwater tributaries to Lindbergh Lake—The river heads in the snowfields of the Mission Mountains. It has its beginnings in wild waters such Gray Wolf Lake and Crystal Lake. The streams in this country cascade in a shower of perpetual whitewater, falling towards the valley floor at over 400 feet per mile before leveling out at Lindbergh Lake.

Mouth of Lindbergh Lake to Swan Lake—After a day of fishing the Swan, one of Marv Bielski's clients asked him, "If this is where you send your friends, where do you send your enemies?"

The Swan doesn't have great numbers of trout. The population of small fish is fair, at best. There are enough rainbows, cutthroats, brookies, and whitefish to provide steady action on a generous day, but even if it had hordes of trout, the Swan would be a tough river to work with a fly in many places.

Most of the private land is posted. You can get in the stream at numerous logging roads, at bridges (at Piper Creek), or at state sites (at Cold Creek and Fatty Creek). But once you reach the water you still have to fight the brush. Piles of snags and fallen trees break up the stream, forming deep pools that give way to long runs of turquoise water. The swift current cuts under rocky banks. It is hard to wade very far between the high water marks until well into the summer.

Spring runoff makes the Swan tough and dangerous to fish at all until late June at the earliest. The current is deceptive and you have to be careful when wading, especially above the snag piles. Being swept underneath one of these—even if you survived—would not be enjoyable. Those same snag piles and the fallen trees make floating for anyone who doesn't know the river intimately extremely dangerous all year.

As the water level starts dropping in late June decent rainbows and cutthroats can be taken during the day on nymphs worked through, along, and around cover and undercut banks. Good patterns include Marv's Stone (#8 to #4), Hare's Ear (#14 to #10), and Tear Drop (#18 to #12). The key is to get the drifting fly deep, down to the eye-level of the fish.

The river doesn't have huge numbers of any one mayfly, just a smattering of various species, but the heavy caddis hatches spark good dry fly fishing. The Swan supports high populations of net-spinning Spotted Sedge, Little Sister Sedge, and case-making Grannom. On any evening through midsummer the insects draw the fish out from the cover into feeding lanes. A good fly that matches color and size, including the popular Spent Partridge Caddis for the adult or the Emergent Sparkle Pupa for the actively hatching bugs, can fool most of the trout.

As summer progresses the terrestrials become important on this overgrown water. Hopper patterns, especially a Joe's Hopper fished

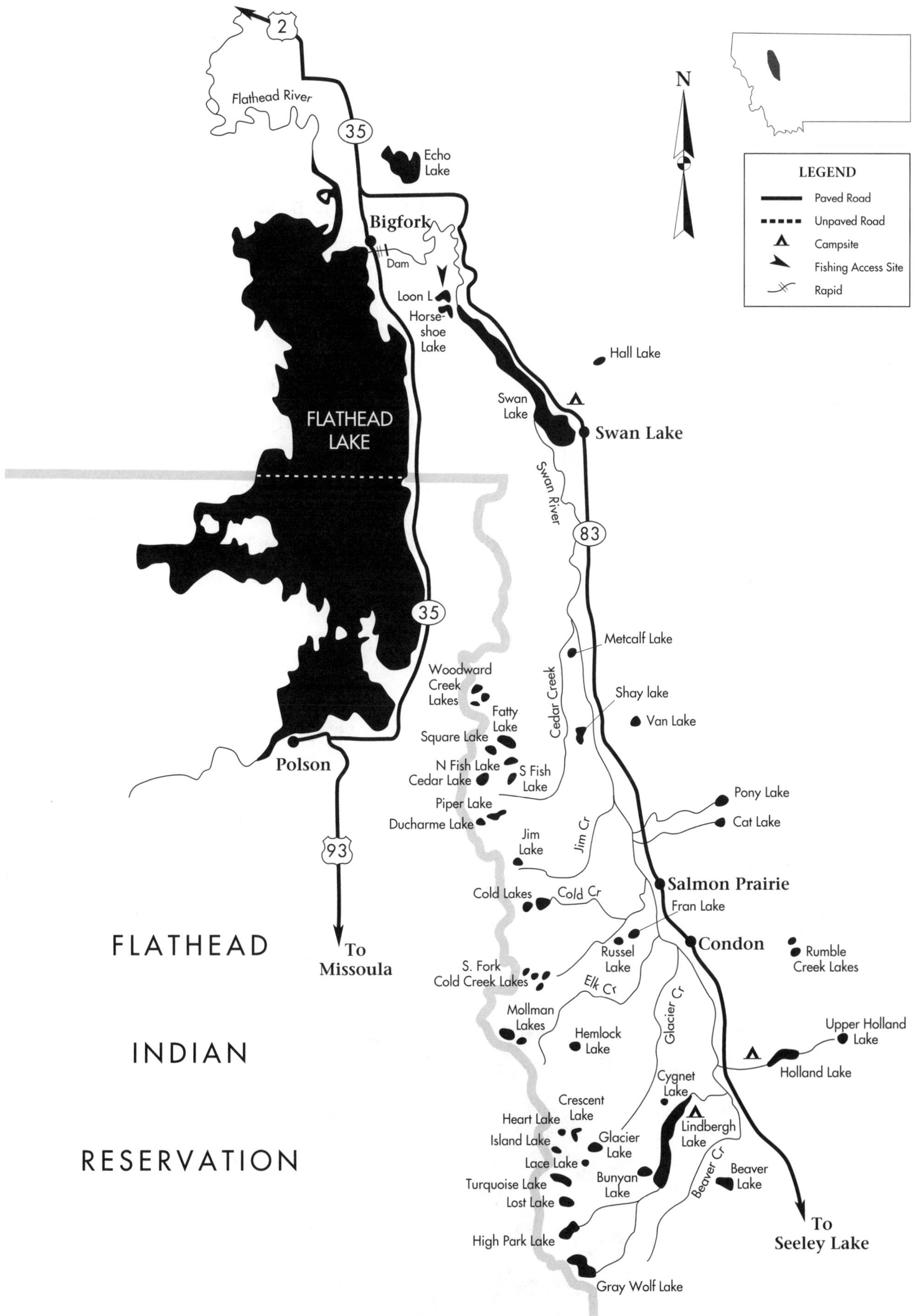

2
Flathead River
35
Echo Lake
N
LEGEND
Paved Road
Unpaved Road
Campsite
Fishing Access Site
Rapid
Bigfork
Dam
Loon L.
Horse-shoe Lake
Hall Lake
Swan Lake
Swan Lake
FLATHEAD LAKE
Swan River
83
35
Metcalf Lake
Woodward Creek Lakes
Cedar Creek
Shay lake
Van Lake
Fatty Lake
Square Lake
Polson
N Fish Lake
S Fish Lake
Cedar Lake
Piper Lake
Pony Lake
Cat Lake
Ducharme Lake
Jim Cr
Jim Lake
93
Salmon Prairie
Cold Lakes
Cold Cr
Fran Lake
FLATHEAD
To Missoula
Russel Lake
Condon
Rumble Creek Lakes
S. Fork Cold Creek Lakes
Elk Cr
Glacier Cr
Mollman Lakes
Hemlock Lake
Upper Holland Lake
INDIAN
Holland Lake
Cygnet Lake
Crescent Lake
Heart Lake
Lindbergh Lake
Island Lake
Glacier Lake
RESERVATION
Lace Lake
Beaver Cr
Beaver Lake
Bunyan Lake
Turquoise Lake
Lost Lake
To Seeley Lake
High Park Lake
Gray Wolf Lake

A Special Fly for the Swan River

When a fly fisherman comes to Montana, his box should contain both general and specific patterns. There is one hatch, the Giant Orange Sedge (or October Caddis), that is important enough to demand at least a rough imitation. There don't have to be a lot of these caddisflies around to get the trout hunting the surface. On the Swan, as well as on Rock Creek, the Bitterroot, and the big Blackfoot, the fall fishing often means big, orange dry flies.

ORANGE BUCKTAIL CADDIS

Hook: standard dry fly (size 8)

Tail: natural,brown deer hair

Body: orange natural or synthetic seal fur

Palmer Hackle: brown

Wing: natural brown deer hair

Hackle: brown

The name October Caddis comes from Oregon (where, lo and behold, the insect does appear in October), but in Montana the bug starts hatching as early as the first week of September. The adults live a long time, as much as two months, and trout get trained to watch for the afternoon and evening egg-laying activity of the big females.

wet, are consistent. The spruce moth can trigger spectacular surface activity when it is abundant. The evergreen forests of the Swan River corridor provide excellent habitat for the spruce moth, rivaling Rock Creek and the Thompson River as the place to be for the fanatics who chase this bug around the western half of the state. Ants and beetles are other important terrestrials.

One hatch worth chasing in early September on the Swan is the Giant Orange Sedge. This size-8 caddisfly is abundant enough to bring the best fish to the surface, the occasional 15- to 20-inch trout appearing from slots that only seemed to hold 10-inchers before the evening hatch. An Orange Bucktail Caddis and a Brown and Orange Emergent Sparkle Pupa are standard matches for the insect.

The favorite attractors on the Swan are not the most garish ones. More subtle patterns, such as the Irresistable, the Humpy, and the Stimulator do better for the rainbows. Even the fly sizes should be on the small side, the #16 to #12 range working better than the #10 to #6 range.

In its upper reaches, the river offers a mix of brook, rainbow, and cutthrout trout. As the Swan grows in size, the brook trout give way to the other two species and the overall size of the fish increases somewhat, averaging perhaps a foot, although there are trout considerably larger. Currently the water from Piper Creek down to Swan Lake is under catch-and-release management.

Bull trout are related to brook trout and look quite similar. During spawning their coloring intensifies, enhancing this resemblance. The fish in the Swan run a few pounds smaller on average than those in the Flathead drainage (the average taken in the region is around eight pounds), but they are strong fighters that take a streamer with a characteristic roll up towards the surface before heading downstream in a determined and often unstoppable

run. The flash of their bright, pink bellies (in the Flathead the color tends towards orange) is unmistakable.

There is a predictable run of bull trout moving up each year from Swan Lake into the many snowmelt and spring-fed tributaries of the upper river. The bull trout wait below stream outlets for water temperatures to drop down to the 40-degree range that will trigger the dash up-creek to spawning gravels. Unfortunately, due to low numbers, the Montana Department of Fish, Wildlife, and Parks has closed the season on bulls until further notice.

The fish are found in fast, gravelly runs below spawning tributaries as late as early September. Biologist Tom Weaver likes to probe beneath and along logs lying in the river, areas that bull trout use for cover during their journeys upstream. When the bulls are present, there won't be any other species of trout feeding out in the open. Cutthroats or rainbows taking caddis in midstream runs are a dead giveaway that the large chars have bolted from the river and are now far up the tributaries building redds.

Too many anglers still try to snag bull trout when they are concentrated below tributaries. Meat-fishing poachers have been known to drive trucks along shallow runs, herding the fish into nets. Catching these swine has become the goal of the Department of Fish, Wildlife, and Parks.

Swan Lake to the Pacific Power and Light Diversion Dam— Below Swan Lake access is offered by Montana 83, Montana 209, and lesser, gravel roads. During the summer the warm water coming off the top of Swan Lake is so warm that it hurts the trout population of this section. The water is slower too, especially near the diversion dam, and it isn't nearly as interesting to fly fish. This section does hold large pike in the eddies and backwaters, and they will hit big streamers.

Diversion Dam to Flathead Lake—Below this obstruction the river provides superb white water kayaking and competitions are held every year. There are trout here, but the water is difficult to work from the bank. Unwary boaters drown on occasion.

The Swan River is not the best fishing river in Montana. Far from it. And it does not run through the most scenic land anymore, either. But it is a river that I love, an underdog flowing steadily against corporate greed and government malfeasance. It is still classic-looking trout water. And there are still trout in it. An angler will not be bothered much by other fishermen, either waders or floaters. Perhaps the river will keep improving if the timber industry ever backs off.

Fishing Waters in the Swan Drainage

Beaver Lake: Reached by a logging road near the head of the Swan drainage, this 26-acre lake is managed for cutthroats and the fish are plentiful in the 10- to 14-inch range. Ice-out happens early on Beaver, which is at only 4,000 feet, and it's a good place to get a jump on the high-country lake season. A float tube makes casting easier due to the timbered shore.

Birch Lake: A cirque lake in the Swan Range, Birch is reached via the smooth-sailing Noisy Creek Road and then a stiff hour's climb to the shore. The cutthroats in 105-feet-deep Birch average about foot in

Bunyan Lake
Photo by Stan Bradshaw

length. A fair number of hikers enjoying the wonders of the Jewel Basin pass by here.

Bunyan Lake: Nine acres, with a shallow bay and a deep center basin, Bunyan looks like a bass lake, with lots of downed timber, but it is fair fishing for dark-backed cutthroats up to 13 inches. Go to Lindbergh Lake, where there is a well-marked turnoff to Bunyan, and drive up 8 miles of Forest Service road.

In late May and early June there are Long-Horn Sedges flitting around and the trout slash and jump for them all day. The fish are chumps for any skittering imitation, such as a size-14 Dark Ginger Dancing Caddis. The best retrieve is a steady, two-handed "run," the rod tucked under the arm and the fly pulled in hand over hand.

Cat Lake: Situated just below Union Peak and 1 mile above Pony Lake, Cat is only 14 acres, but it's over 50 feet deep. There isn't much use fishing anything but the edges. There are cutthroats up to 14 inches once you get here, but this is not easy country to move around in.

Cedar Creek: The upper 8 miles are followed by trail (all the way to Cedar Lake); the lower 3 miles are followed by logging road. Cedar is good cutthroat and brook trout water, and it usually has a few bull trout up from the river.

Cold Lakes: Pretty country to hike into, access is by a mile of good trail starting at the end of the Cold Creek Road. The two lakes are each about 80 acres and very deep. Like most of the higher elevation lakes in the Missions, they are not fishable until well into the summer. Snow and ice make hiking tough and the waters are sometimes still frozen over until July. Both lakes hold good numbers of cutthroats up to 16 inches

Crescent Lake: Crescent was planted with goldens years ago, but there are few (if any) of these left. The trail is a steep mile or so of switchbacks from the end of Kraft Creek Road. Crescent is now stocked periodically with cutthroats and fishing is nice in September following the plant. Dry flies, especially generic types such as the Adams or the Black Gnat, produce as the fish cruise back and forth in groups along the shore and across the inlet.

Fatty Lake: Go to the top of the Fatty Creek Road and then hoof up a poor trail that follows the creek for a mile and a half to this 21-acre lake. The shoreline is swampy and brushy, and there is mud in the shallows. This makes Fatty a spot for the float tube or a canoe. The fishing is fast and furious on a good day for regularly planted cutthroats that average 12 inches and a few rainbows that are 18 to 20 inches

Marv Bielski notes, "You usually see a lot of fish rising here. And they're not fussy about the fly."

Fran Lake: Located in timbered and logged country on the Swan Range side of the river, Fran is reached via logging roads near Condon. The lake is small but good for rainbows and cutthroats up to 15 inches There are also a few Kamloop rainbows cruising here and these fish (a wonderful strain of stillwater trout originally from British Columbia) grow bigger and fatter than the other residents.

Glacier Creek: This ice-cold, sapphire-blue stream, the outlet of Glacier Lake, looks wonderful for trout, but except for some swampy,

Fishing Glacier Creek in spring high water
Photo by Stan Bradshaw

meadow stretches in the middle it's not too hot. That middle section (also known as Glacier Slough) is worth fishing from July to September with ant, beetle, caterpillar, and grasshopper imitations. The fish there are more plentiful and a bit larger (up to 12 inches instead of 10 inches). In the creek section just below Glacier Lake there are some good trout, too—cutthroat, rainbow, brook, and the occasional maurauding bull trout. This is beautiful forest where it hasn't been logged, but the pristine areas shrink yearly in this country. (See Notlimah Lake, also.)

Glacier Lake: Reached by a 30-minute walk on the trail at the end of the Kraft Creek Road, this 103-acre lake sits in scenic country (overrun with hikers in the summer) and is good fishing by wading or float tubing (if you drag one in) for cutthroats averaging 10 inches The exciting aspect of Glacier Lake is that there are a few fish that grow out of the "cookie-cutter" mold of the planters and get much larger.

Here are a few records of those exceptions:

- Phillip May—a 19-inch cutt on June 24th in the morning on a size-10 Black Woolly Bugger.
- Michael Beatty—a 21-inch cutt on July 5th in the evening on a size-12 Devil Bug (skated across the top).
- Tom Poole—a 19½-inch cutt on August 1st in the evening on a size-16 Twist Nymph.

Glacier Lake
Photo by Paul Porte

Gray Wolf Lake: Reached by a steep, 9-mile climb from the end of Beaver Creek Road, this lake sits below a glacier (telling the wise man something about the climate up there). The ground around 300-acre Gray Wolf is mostly rock slope and boulders. With nothing to slow down the wind the lake surface is typically churned to a froth. Gray Wolf is extremely temperamental for 10- to 20-inch cutthroats, but the fish cruise the shorelines on occasion. Try a Hare's Ear nymph worked parallel to the bank.

Hall Lake: The hike in is only 5 miles from scenic downtown Swan Lake, but it is a 3,000-foot climb up to this 12-acre, deep water. Hall Lake is planted heavily with cutthroats. The average fish is 12 inches, but a good trout runs 15 inches.

Heart (or Hart) Lake: The middle lake in the Island-Heart-Crescent chain, it's the best of the three. Unfortunately they have all been hurt by overfishing. Goldens were planted in the 1960s, but except for some bright cutthroats that apparently had licentious relationships with their California cousins, there are none of those goldens left here. The fishing ranges from poor to fair for 12- to 16-inch cutthroats.

Hemlock Lake: Not far up the Kraft Creek Road (there are signs). It is about a 4-mile hike into this 30-acre lake. Hemlock is not as wild or scenic as the higher-up stuff in the Missions, but there is a nice population of 10- to 13-inch cutthroats here.

High Park Lake: This is another high-elevation, way-back, big-water, quite-windy-most-of-the-time lake in the Missions. To get there go to Lindbergh Lake, hike 2½ miles to Crystal Lake, and then hike another 2 miles to High Park. It is not easy to get to, but the fishing is often solid during the calm morning hours for 10- to 15-inch cutthroats. They hit all manner of flies well (out of loneliness, if for no other reason). This is good country in the fall if winter doesn't sneak up out of nowhere. Then you are in trouble.

Holland Lake: A summer-home lake replete with a nice log lodge, it is pretty water, with too many boats in the summer. But there are some very nice trout here. The best fly fishing months are early and late in the year. Rainbow, cutthroat, and bull trout, along with kokanee salmon and lots of whitefish, are found here. The cutthroats especially seem to like dry flies, and they'll cruise the shoreline all day looking for something to eat (except in the summer when watercraft make this life-threatening). There are public and private campgrounds here also. This is one of the "gateways" to the Bob Marshall Wilderness.

Horseshoe Lake: Smallmouth bass (and very fat sunfish) live here. If this lake was in the Ozarks, it would attract hordes of eager bass anglers. It is 9 miles east of Bigfork. Lots of people fish for the one- to four-pound smallmouths found here, but few anglers really seem to understand the habits of this species. You can use a float tube or boat to cover the main basin (which never gets deeper than 15 feet). The smallmouths in Horseshoe feed as much on insects as they do on minnows and crayfish. They gorge on damselfly nymphs, and they rise to *Callibaetis* mayflies. The south shoreline, with dense beds of lily pads, is a consistent area for active fish. The water is clear and a leader tapered to 3X, and sometimes 4X, is often the secret to fooling the smallmouths.

Island Lake: Even with a map this is a difficult lake to find. The trail fades away to nothing a mile or so above Heart Lake. Most of the time you end up bushwacking through steep, brushy, wet country. It's a tough go in alpine country. Island has a few small goldens (to 10 inches?), remnants of a 1960s plant. The fish are finicky and the best bet is to cast a small Olive Woolly Worm, let the thing sink, and then give it a few twitches.

Jim Creek: This creek drains out of the Jim Lake complex. The private holdings have been raped by logging, destroying not only the aesthetics of the area but also the bull trout population of the west fork of the stream.

Jim Lake: This used to be fantastic, timbered country full of grouse, elk, bear, deer, woodpeckers, and fish until Plum Creek ravaged the timber on its holdings (and left an eyesore for years to come). There is an ongoing management program in the basin for cutthroats, but the clearcuts spoil the fun. Thanks, Plum Creek. You guys are great.

You can drive right into the first lake, which used to be wonderful for cutts (as did several of the upper waters). North of Condon take the Cold Lake Road west and follow the signs. Above the first lake there are maybe a dozen more, along with ponds and bogs, in the Mission Mountain Wilderness. All of them have cutthroats up to 12 inches.

Lace Lake: Lies just below Turquoise Lake in the Missions (and is connected by a small stream). There are lots of fat, dark-sided cutthroats up to 15 inches in 18½-acre Lace. It is much easier pickings than Turquoise.

There are lots of shallow-water depressions in this country that pretend to be lakes, but instead are just barren potholes. Two of those, Jewell and Lagoon, are especially easy to confuse with Lace. An angler's instinct plays an important part in avoiding "lakes" like these, but when in doubt an hour of observation will usually save a lot of casting.

Lindbergh Lake: On the valley floor, across the river from Holland Lake, this 725-acre lake is so deep (125 feet) that it would be tough fishing with flies even if it had great populations of trout. It is managed for cutthroats and kokanee, but they have to compete with hordes of squawfish and suckers. Trollers, working up and down the 4-mile lake, do fair for the kokanee salmon. No one catches many cutthroats.

Lindbergh Lake and the Swan Range
Photo by Stan Bradshaw

Loon Lake: Drive the 1½-mile gravel road off the Swan Lake highway to reach the public fishing access. Loon has planter trout, mostly rainbows, in the cooler sections, but it is an especially fine place for warm-water fly fishing, featuring both smallmouths (to three pounds) and largemouths (to five pounds). The 44-acre lake is mostly deep water (50 feet maximum), except on one end.

John Chisolm says about the bass, "The entire shoreline can be good wherever there's structure. There are fallen trees and a few docks spaced around the lake. The north end is shallower, with bays and weeds. The pre-spawn period usually runs from the third week of May until mid-June. The magic water temperature for the best top-water action is 58 degrees. Once the shallows get into the 60s the bass are looking up."

Proven flies that John recommends include the Edgewater foam patterns—especially the Edgewater Pencil Popper, Edgewater Super Cray, and Edgewater Rat—and the Dahlberg Super Shad Diver. A Leech (black or chartreuse) developed specifically for bass by Doug Brewer and John Chisolm, and a selection of Woolly Buggers in black, olive, brown, and burnt orange completes a good basic selection for bass. All of these patterns can be carried in sizes 4 to 2/0.

Chester, Inuk, and friend
Photo by Stan Bradshaw

Lost (or East) Lake: This large, deep lake is back in the Missions between Turquoise and High Park lakes. More people come here each year for slow fishing (nonexistent many times) for large cutthroat trout. The fish top three pounds, as big as they get in this country, but you pay the price on the hike in.

Dale Triplett has caught as many big fish in Lost as anyone. "I don't get excited about it until the first hard frost of September. That brings the fish into the shallows for the last feeding binge and they get a bit more sociable."

Metcalf Lake: One of the premier trophy trout waters in the state, Metcalf is currently under special regulations—one trout daily in possession with a 22-inch minimum length; artificial flies and lures only. It is a 13-acre, lowland lake 14 miles south of Swan Lake. There are no real inlets, but there are underwater springs at the north end. This is the best area during June and July to find rising rainbows, the fish sometimes leaping to take adult damsels in the mornings. Either adult damsel imitations on the the surface or damsel nymph imitations on the bottom (especially the Floating Damsel Nymph worked with a fast-sinking line so that it swims just over the weed tops) are effective around the springs for trout up to 26 inches. Metcalf warms up too much in August during hot summers, pushing the fishing into a brief slump. The trout start feeding heavily again in the fall.

Mollman Lakes: These two lakes and a pothole lie way back in the Missions. A trail comes up the North Fork of Elk Creek, but it wanders around some. All of these waters are managed for cutthroats, which average 12 inches but occasionally top 16 inches. The difference in elevation between the two lakes may be the height of a bar stool. Don't overlook that little pond below the lower lake—it can be good at times.

North Fish Lake: One of those spots for anglers who dislike crowds. It is not easy to find, but take a good map and a compass and work up the North Fork of Cedar Creek. The cutthroats planted in North Fish do very well.

Notlimah Lake: Sometimes confused with the Glacier Sloughs. This 1¼-mile "wide-spot" is several hundred swampy yards farther upstream. There are cutthroat and brook trout here up to roughly 12 inches

Pony Lake: A 17-acre lake on the flanks of the Swan Range. Marv Bielski writes, "Go east on Road #9769 (2 miles south of Piper Creek Road) and follow the signs. It's a good 2- to 3-mile hike to Pony. The cutts will average 12 inches. Bring a float tube."

Rumble Creek Lakes: These two lakes (27 acres and 11 acres) hold out high up on the flanks of Holland Peak in the Swans. They are good for cutthroats ranging up to 14 inches, especially just after ice-out (Surprise!). They are a bit tough to reach because there is no trail. The Rumble Creek drainage is not the easiest route in. Go to the Cooney Lookout, hike the main ridge until the lakes are in sight, and then head cross-country.

Russ Lake: One of three lakes (also see Fran Lake), Russ lies in the Swan River bottomlands. They are easy to reach by a logging road (across from the Condon Ranger District building). Russ, at 10 acres, is the the uppermost and largest of the three. It's fine fishing for cutthroats and rainbows, with good numbers of trout up to 15 inches

Shay Lake: Rainbows and grayling inhabit this deep, 20-acre lake not far off the Fatty Creek logging road. The grayling are an oddity in this area, and that alone makes it worth a visit. The rainbow fishing is good for 8- to 14-inchers.

Marv Bielski warns, "You need nerve to drive to it. It is a horrendous road."

South Fish Lake: Sits in the Cedar Creek drainage (right next to North Fish Lake). It is managed for cutthroats, and the poor things die of loneliness up here.

South Fork Cold Creek Lakes: This long string of thirteen lakes, as small as 3 acres and as large as 20 acres, chains through rough, buggy, and swampy country. Not all of these lakes have fish, but all of the larger ones do. The better ones harbor good populations of 10- to 15-inch rainbows. The hike to the first lake, starting from the South Fork Road, is only a mile, but this country is still not overrun with people carrying fly rods.

South Woodward Creek Lakes: Reached by decrepit logging road, these lakes are managed for cutthroats. There's not a lot of pressure here, but much of the land is owned by Plum Creek, so you better fish these soon before they are logged to oblivion.

Square Lake: Good for 10- to 16-inch cutthroats, Square Lake is up in the Fatty Creek drainage in country so rough, with no real trail, that reaching it is a much greater challenge than fishing it.

Swan Lake: Thousands of acres, a mile wide and ten long, and deep. This is a tough piece of water for the fly fisher unless you happen to be out when things are calm and some cutthroats or rainbows are rising (a rare occurrence). The best places to fish it blind are off the river mouth or along the flats on the south end (and this is also the prime area for bass and pike). Swan holds bull trout that run up the river in the spring and summer. Most people fish by trolling here.

There is a large wildlife refuge at the southern end of the lake; a campground, a restaurant, and summer homes are scattered along the rest of the east and north shoreline. Montana 83 runs the length of the east side of the lake.

Turquoise Lake: More big water high up in the southern end of the Missions. The few trout I've seen here have been either 12 inches or several pounds and neither cared much for my offerings. A lot of people come in here (although anglers generally concentrate on Lace Lake right below it). The entire drainage is pretty, but crowded in the summer.

Upper Holland Lake: Go to Holland Lake to hit the trailhead for the 2½-mile hike to Upper Holland. This lake sits way up near the Swan Crest. It has spooky cutthroat trout that grow long and snakey. These can be caught by the stealthy angler, but even in choppy water a 16-foot leader tapered to at least 6X is a necessity. And don't go big on the flies—size 16 is about the maximum in my experience. There is a campground on the east shore.

Van Lake: Accessible by 2 miles of logging road off the Swan River Road, signs lead the way. Van is managed for rainbows and is fair to good for 12-inchers. It is especially good in the spring. A boat or a float tube is essential equipment; trees and bushes crowding the water all the way around the lake make shoreline casting difficult.

Other Waters

Barber Creek: Too small.

Beaver Creek: Brook trout. It enters the Swan River a few miles below Lindbergh Lake. The best water, paralleled by a logging road, is in the bottom 4 miles.

Bethel Creek: Too small.

Bond Creek: Too small.

Buck Creek: Cutthroats and brook trout.

Carney Creek: Too small.

Cat Creek: Too small.

Cedar Lake: Cutthroats of 6 to 14 inches. Go to the end of the Fatty Creek Road to hit the 4-mile trail.

Cilly Creek: Too small.

Cold Creek: Cutthroat, brook, and bull trout.

Condon Creek: Cutthroat and brook trout.

Cooley Creek: Too small.

Cooney Creek: Cutthroat and brook trout.

Crazy Horse Creek: Too small.

Crystal Lake: Cutthroats.

Deer Creek: Brook trout and beaver dams (on the lower end of this inlet stream of Mud Lake) go together.

Dog Creek: Cutthroat and brook trout.

Ducharme (or Upper Piper) Lake: Reportedly good for cutthroats up to 18 inches It is not even named on the topo maps, but go to Piper Lake (a real tough 9-mile hike to start with) and then walk a quarter mile up to Ducharme. (I sent a friend out to check on this lake and he hasn't talked to me since.)

Elk Creek: Closed.

Elk Lake: There never seems to be a lot of fish in this 200-acre lake in the Elk Creek headwaters, but the ones that are here run good size. A normal day usually produces a couple over 18 inches.

Gilbert Creek: Too small.

Goat Creek: Closed.

Groom Creek: Cutthroat and bull trout. Not bad fishing for little cutts that are fun to catch (and release), but it is tough work busting brush.

Hall Creek: Too small.

Holland Creek: Poor fishing below Holland Lake for rainbows and brooks. Upstream, between Holland and Upper Holland, there is a waterfall. Above the falls there are cutthroats in the few pools and pockets.

Johnson Creek: Brook trout.

Kelly Reservoir: Private.

Kraft Creek: Too small.

Lily Lake: Cutthroats.

Lion Creek: Closed. A genetic study by state biologists on the "bull trout" of this Swan River tributary revealed that eleven of the twenty-five fish collected were actually hybrids between brook trout and bull trout—and that in this drainage, at least, hybridization was a threat to bull trout survival.

Meadow Lake: Rainbows and cutthroats.

Moore Lake: Barren.

Mud Lake: Largemouth bass, northern pike, yellow perch (some real nice ones), and brook trout. The name comes from the soft, boggy bottom, which means that it's not much for wading.

North Fork Cold Creek: Bull and cutthroat trout.

North Fork Lost Creek: Bull and cutthroat trout.

Pierce Lake: Poor for cutthroat and rainbow trout.

Piper Creek: Bull and cutthroat trout.

Piper Lake: Pretty cutthroats. Go up the Piper Creek Road to hit the trailhead. A 9-mile hike keeps the crowds away from this 80-acre lake, but for the hardcore, high-country angler this is a beautiful trip. The trout average 10 to 13 inches, but there are a few that are bigger.

Pony Creek: Cutthroats.

Rainbow Lake: Barren.

Red Butte Creek: Cutthroats.

Rumble Creek: Cutthroat and brook trout.

Simpson Creek: Cutthroats.

Sixmile: Too small.

Skylark Lake: Cutthroats.

Smith Creek: Cutthroat and brook trout. It flows through boggy meadows and the beavers build some nice ponds on Smith Creek.

Soup Creek: Cutthroat, brook, and bull trout.

South Fork Cold Creek: Cutthroats.

South Fork Lost Creek: Cutthroat and bull trout.

Squeezer Lake: Planted with cutthroats by helicopter (does this tell you something?). It is way back near the Swan Crest and tough to get to, but Squeezer is good fishing for the fanatic hiker.

Squeezer Creek: Closed.

Stoner Lake: Yellow perch.

Trinkus Lake: Cutthroats. Be careful. There are actually two lakes here and the upper one freezes out. Go out of Swan Lake up the Bond Creek trail for six miles to reach Trinkus. The fishing is fair for 8- to 14-inch trout.

Whelp Lake: Cutthroats.

Wolf Creek: Too small.

Woodward Creek: Cutthroat and bull trout.

Yew Creek: Too small.

■ *Special thanks to Marv Bielski, John Chisolm, Scott Rumsey, Dale Triplett, and Tom Weaver for their help on the Swan River drainage.*

TRAVEL IN MONTANA

Negotiating your way around Montana is easy. Routes from interstate highways all the way down to some gravel roads are marked on the state road map. Adequate signs make navigation a straightforward proposition.

Gravel roads are accorded the status of main thoroughfares in much of the state, but once you leave the unmarked systems you enter the exciting world of "Where in the hell are we?" Topographic maps help and so does asking directions. Montanans, for the most part, are friendly and helpful. They are used to misguided souls, so they know how to give good directions. You just have to know how to listen. If you run out of gas, they will normally offer you a gallon or two and frequently seem offended at the concept of payment. This is still honest country. May it always be so.

For those new to the state, a little pretravel preparation will make the adventure run quite smoothly.

First, contact Travel Montana at 800-541-1447 (or write to them at Capitol Station, Helena, MT 59620) and ask for a travel package that will include the current Travel Planner, Vacation Guide (full of stuff that is not very exciting for anglers but may amuse others), and a state highway map.

The Travel Planner has comprehensive listings of motels and hotels, bed and breakfast inns, ranches, resorts, hostels and hot springs, licensed outfitters, and private and public campgrounds. Further information includes local chamber of commerce contacts. If you know what area of Montana you will be visiting, contacting the appropriate chamber(s) will result in even more detailed information.

Next, call the Montana Department of Fish, Wildlife, and Parks (FWP) at 406-444-2535 (or write to them at Capitol Station, Helena, MT 59620) and request their fishing guide, state parks guide, and fishing regulations. They will give you a sampling of places to go, campgrounds, fishing access sites.

The Travel Planner, highway map, FWP materials, and this fishing guide offer a lot of information—more that enough to plan an extensive fishing vacation. The only way to fine-tune your trip, would be to hire a guide.

When you purchase your fishing license (for out-of-staters around $40) be sure and pick up a copy of the current fishing regulations (or get it in advance from FWP).

As for driving, if you do the speed limit (as we all should) you will be passed like you are standing still, especially in eastern Montana where speed limits often appear to be treated more as suggestions than laws. Do not despair. You can still traverse the state in about fourteen hours at 55 miles per hour. During spring and fall, all-weather tires or four-wheel-drive are good ideas for the mountain passes. And when the highway department states that a certain pass is closed due to rough weather, believe it. You will be risking your life on a grand scale if you ignore the warnings. And keeping your gas tank topped up is prudent. Off the main roads stations often close early or do not open some days. The boys at the local Cenex like to go fishing, too.

REAL AND PERCEIVED DANGERS

Marauding, red-eyed bears lusting for a taste of human flesh and eighteen-foot-long rattlesnakes as thick as your hip with six-inch fangs dripping milky venom are the deluded creations of Hollywood and not the stuff of everyday Montana reality.

Yes, bears do attack us and snakes do bite us, but these rare encounters are even more rarely fatal. Far more dangerous are threats from lightning, wind, and cold.

Lightning kills more people each year than rap concerts, and a fly fisher waving a graphite rod is a superb conductor of this static electricity. When heavy electrical weather looks imminent, get off the water, look for low ground, discard your rod, and wait for the storm to pass. Undercut banks, caves, and isolated trees are not safe locations. Nor are overturned aluminum boats. When lightning shows up, always think invisible. Try and become the lowest-profile object in the immediate area.

The combination of cold, wind, and moisture can quickly lead to a deadly condition known as hypothermia, a condition in which the body's core temperature drops low enough to cause blood to rush from the extremities to the vital organs. Numbness in the toes and fingers progressing into the arms and legs is an obvious symptom as are shaky fingers. Shivering is another early warning sign. The real danger is the loss of reasoning (in many of us this may be extremely difficult to detect) and the ability to make rational decisions. Paddling around in an ice-cold lake in a float tube is an easy way to become hypothermic, and if early warnings are not heeded, an angler could just stop moving and die. If you start to get cold, get to shelter —tent, car, cabin, etc.— and get warm and dry. Don't try to tough it out. Pay attention to your fishing partners. If they show any signs of hypothermia, get them off the water, to shelter, and warm them up.

Insects are another problem. Mosquitoes, black flies, and deer flies can make life hell. Repellent works well against the first two and a .28-gauge handles the third. Taking B-complex vitamins each day for a couple of weeks also works. Afterwards the body secretes a compound that insects find offensive. Ticks are another matter and Lyme disease and Rocky Mountain spotted fever can cause acute illness or death. Tick patrol at the end of each day during tick season is mandatory. Be sure and remove the head. This may require tweezers.

Most spider bites are locally painful but not life threatening. Treat with cold compresses and perhaps aspirin. If the victim exhibits nausea, vomiting, or diarrhea followed by weakness and disorientation, a systemic reaction is underway and you need to get immediate treatment by a doctor unless you are capable of injecting a syringe of epinephrine (synthetic version of adrenaline). An antihistamine such as Benadryl can help prevent further reaction to histamine and rebound effect.

Rattlesnakes really do try to stay out of our way. The most common places to encounter these gentle reptiles is in rock piles, cliffs and walls, and the dry grasses of eastern Montana. The sound of a rattle will turn even the most graceful among us into a world-class spastic whirling from toe to toe in a desperate attempt to reverse direction.

If bitten, one or two puncture marks will be visible. If venom has been injected swelling and pain will be immediate. Transport the victim as quickly as possible for antivenin treatment. Pain may be severe, but the victim can usually walk to transportation. Splint the affected part if possible. Remove any constricting items such as rings and clothing from the bitten extremity before swelling makes it difficult. The sooner a person reaches medical help the better. Bites are rarely fatal in healthy adults, but the symptoms can be awful.

Most medical experts agree that traditional field treatments, such as tourniquets, pressure dressings, ice packs, and "cut and suck" snakebite kits, are ineffective and often dangerous. Treatment in the field is a waste of time.

The almighty Montana sun can cook your brains and fry your hide in a hurry. Wear a hat, sunglasses, and plenty of sunscreen. Drink cool liquids constantly. A gallon of water per person is the minimum and a cooler full of ice and preferred beverages is a godsend. If dizziness, weakness, or a rapid pulse occur, seek shelter. If you stop sweating and get flushed, cool down fast. You may have heat stroke.

Another problem, especially in the back country, is avalanches. Even in July tons and tons of snow and ice remain on steep rock walls and packed into bowls. Avoid crossing these areas of exposure. A peaceful looking snow bowl with well-defined cornices is an invitation to disaster. If you absolutely must cross such an area, do it one at a time. If caught in an avalanche try and swim with the flow and, as the avalanche starts to slow and the snow starts to pile up, ball up and get one hand in front of your face to create an air pocket and thrust the other hand as high as possible (if it ends up above the snow you'll be easier to find).

Wading swift rivers can also be deadly. Losing your footing can mean being swept under a logjam or into midstream boulders. On slippery, freestone streams, wear stream cleats and even carry a wading staff. Always look ahead and choose footing carefully. Caution is definitely the better part of valor here.

As for bears and other wild animals (re-read the first part of the section on Glacier National Park), make noise to alert animals of your presence. Keep your eyes open and always leave an area immediately whenever a bear or bison or moose is spotted. Yelling, eye contact, and bluffing often provoke attacks and are last resort (like when a charging grizzly is ten feet away) measures. Most big game animals avoid humans like the plague. Attacks are almost always a result of moving into an animal's territory unannounced or threatening its food supply, such as a buried carcass.

The number of anglers injured or killed by these real and perceived dangers is insignificant compared to those that suffer at the hands of car crashes and heart attacks. So do not fear the natural world, just give it a good deal of respect.

SUGGESTED GEAR

Successfully fishing in Montana does not require truck loads of equipment, although most fly fishers are collectors, hoarders, and gadget freaks, often foregoing the monthly house payment in favor of purchasing a new rod. Most experienced anglers have their own preferences, but for those who have never fished Montana or are new to the pursuit, the following, while subjective, is representative of tackle and related gear needed to enjoy fishing in the state.

Rods: If you bring just one pick a five- or six-weight. These have enough strength to handle some wind and big water and still fish smaller streams halfway decently. If you bring two, an ideal combination would be a 9-foot, seven-weight and an 8-foot, four-weight. The seven-weight will fight the wind that blows crazily along the Rocky Mountain Front and out onto the plains and also will work well nymphing and fishing heavy streamers. The four-weight will fish smaller rivers and streams along with quiet ponds quite nicely. Others might include a two-weight for spring creeks, a five-weight for medium rivers, and an eight-weight for the hurricane conditions often found around places like the Blackfeet Indian Reservation.

Reels: While the current cliché is that reels are now much more than a contrivance for holding line, the need for disk drag is almost nonexistent. So if you cannot afford one, do not despair. The chances that a trout will smoke your reel are unlikely. On the other hand, purchase the best equipment you can afford. It can't hurt.

Lines: Use either double-taper or weight-forward lines and match them to your rods or go maybe one step up in weight (say a seven-weight line for a six-weight rod) to cheat the wind a bit. Definitely bring at least a 6-foot sink-tip for nymphing, streamers, and lake action. A 10-foot sink-tip is nice, too. Stick with floaters for two-weights and three-weights. A little weight above the fly works fine. Optional lines would include intermediate and fast-sinking lines for working deep in lakes. Shooting heads are nice and will give you a few more feet, but this is trout, not tarpon, fishing we're talking about. Backing of twelve pounds is adequate.

Patterns and Leaders: A few suggestions are: Blue-Winged Olives, Tricos, Pale Morning Duns in emergers, duns, and spinners; Stonefly Nymph, Pheasant Tail Nymph, Hare's Ear Nymph, Zug Bug, Sheep Creek, Scud, Kaufmann's Damsel Nymph, LaFontaine Antron, Prince Nymph, Partridge & Peacock; Muddler Minnow, Woolly Bugger, Zonker, Spruce Fly, Marabou Leech, Elk Hair Caddis, Royal Wulff, Adams, Humpy, Goddard Caddis, Royal Trude, Hopper, Sofa Pillow, Girdle Bug, and Bitch Creek. A fair investment to be sure, but also a pretty good all-around selection for the rest of the country.

Whatever you have, bring, but be sure and stop at the nearest fly shop or sporting goods store to stock up on a few recommended patterns. The days of proprietors selling you everything in the store are pretty much over. You can buy with confidence in Montana.

Nine-foot leaders tapering to 3x or 4x are basic tools. You can add tippet material for finer work or cut the leaders back for heavy-water nymphing. Or, best of all, you can tie your own.

Clothing: Even in summer bring clothes for cold weather. Snow and sleet, especially in the high country, is a twelve-month-a-year situation. Rain gear is a must as is a hat to protect you from the sun. Boots are helpful. For fall, winter, and spring fishing be prepared for anything weather-wise. This can be very cold country.

Miscellaneous accouterments: Obviously bring your vest. Hip and chest waders will give you added versatility and comfort. If bringing only one pair, bring chest waders. Stream cleats are great for freestone streams. You need sunglasses and sunscreen as well as insect repellent. A small camera for trophy photographs is handy. If you have room bring a landing net, float tube and fins, and a fly tying kit.

BASS

There is an area in western Montana, stretching over a hundred miles, of prime largemouth bass habitat. Few people come to the state to fish for these bass, and most residents ignore the warm-water opportunities here. All this helps explain why the bass fishing is very good.

The best bass fishing is found in the warmest region of the state, the "banana belt," curving along the shoreline of Flathead Lake. The huge expanse of the lake creates not only a more moderate climate but also a much wetter one. As a result there are waters in this northwest rim that are too warm for trout, but the bass (and pike) fishing is excellent by almost any standards. There aren't any monsters—a ten-pound largemouth would be a miracle—but there are fine populations of one- to four-pound fish in the ponds and lakes.

The waters radiate out from Kalispell. There is a shallow duck pond (closed to fishing) at Woodland Park right in the city. One spring the ducklings were disappearing. Every day there were fewer and fewer of them. The state fisheries people came in and electro- shocked and netted out the water, recovering largemouths over five pounds, as well as even larger catfish.

Flathead Lake itself offers good warm-water fishing in the Polson Bay area. Ninepipes Reservoir and Kicking Horse Reservoir, on the Flathead Indian Reservation, are premier bass fisheries. There is a series of natural glacial potholes along the Creston road, on the way to Bigfork, and many of these ponds grow nice largemouths. The Thompson Lakes (Lower, Middle, and Upper), in the Clark Fork drainage, are consistent for one- to two-pound bass, with some bigger ones. Echo Lake and Lake Mary Ronan are examples of larger bodies of water, where it pays to know the habitat (good places for all the electronic toys of the most serious bass anglers). There are bass lakes in the Swan drainage, too, including Horseshoe Lake, which has smallmouth in it.

Seasons for Bass Fishing—

The best way to calculate bass moods and movements is to break the season down into the classic angling phases: pre-spawn, spawn, post-spawn, summer, and fall.

In Montana the water temperature doesn't edge into the fifties until May or even early June. When it does the bass enter the most fickle of all angling phases—the pre-spawn. The fish are like teenagers, all excited about the possibility of a date but not exactly sure when it's going to happen. The changeable Montana weather of late spring doesn't help, either. After three or four warm days the fish are hanging in or near the shallows, hitting bottom flies (especially a Clouser Minnow) nicely. But then a cold northern blast hits the state, frequently with snow, and the fish go immediately into a deep sulk. The key to this period is a series of bluebird days and warmer-than-average nights, not just one or two.

The water in most Montana bass lakes is fairly clear, not the algae-laden soup of lakes in warmer climates, and once the bass start to spawn the nests are easy to spot. They appear as light-colored circles on the bottom, swept clean of gravel and debris. There is a brief period when both the females and males hover over the eggs, but the females, often the biggest fish, leave after a few days. At first the males are skittish, and they flush into deeper water at the sight of the boat or even the splash of a bulky fly. They get bolder once the eggs hatch and there are clusters of fry to protect from predators. Flies that mimic those predators, such as the Tilting Sunny, trigger hard strikes.

Fish in the post-spawn phase are often exhausted from the rigors of guarding the nests. They slip into deeper water and lay quietly on the bottom, not even feeding, for a few days. Fortunately, not all of the fish are in this comatose state at exactly the same time. Some, on a slightly different schedule, are are already on the post-spawn feeding spree. No minnow is safe, not even their own fry, and any crawfish or leech is a target. In many lakes the damselfly hatch coincides with the post-spawn gorging, and smaller bass, up to a pound or so, feed heavily on damsel nymphs.

There are no summer dog days on Montana bass lakes. The water rarely gets too warm for the fish. Once the water temperatures reach the mid-sixties the bass feed steadily, cramming as much growth into the short season as possible. By late June they really start hitting surface poppers well. The clear water and bright summer sun keep the bass wary during midday, but dawn and dusk are great times for cork poppers and deer hair bugs through August.

Sometime in September the fall feeding frenzy begins. The one- to four-pound bass gather in schools and sweep into the coves, herding baitfish against the shore. At Ninepipes they may concentrate on bullheads. At Lake Mary Ronan they may prey on sunfish. The bass can get a bit choosy about the size and color of the matching fly, but once the angler finds the right streamer or floating minnow, the fishing is often spectacular. A Dahlberg Diver, with a strip-and-pause retrieve that leaves a good bubble stream, always seems to excite maurauding school bass.

Shoreline vegetation is the best calendar for marking the changes in the bass fishing seasons. The opening of buds, and sprouting of new leaves, signals the pre-spawn. The flowering of fruit trees coincides with the spawn. Dropping flower petals mark the beginning of summer. The first yellowing of leaves, after the first frost, starts the fall season.

The major adjustment visiting fly fishermen have to make for Montana bass waters involves delicacy. Largemouth bass habitat in other areas can have much heavier weed growth and murkier water. The lakes in Montana often demand a quiet approach, the boat positioned thirty feet from the shore instead of fifteen, and a subtle presentation, the leader tippet testing six pounds instead of twelve pounds. There is one general rule that applies to largemouths everywhere—bigger flies catch bigger bass—but the angler should drop that big fly well beyond the target instead of dropping it on the head of the fish.

STREAM ACCESS IN MONTANA
contributed by Stan Bradshaw

Imagine that you're floating one of Montana's blue-ribbon trout streams, like the Beaverhead. It's a perfect day for fishing, cool, slightly overcast, and bugs are up on the surface. Even better, you're in your brand new customized fishing raft with all the latest doodads. As you come around a bend, a low bridge looms up. Low, but not too low to clear. But, as you start under it, and too late to respond, you spot the strands of barbed wire, hidden in the shadows of the bridge, strung taut across the entire river at raft height. Before you can react, your boat is swept into it, the tubes are torn, and the boat sinks. Within seconds, you and most of your fishing gear are strewn downstream. Question: Do you have any recourse against the jerk who strung the barbed wire?

Or imagine another day on Little Piddly Creek. It's a small creek, too small for floating, but, with runs, riffles, and undercut banks, a good small stream fishery. You get on the creek where it goes under a state highway, and wade upstream, staying in the water all the way. A half mile upstream from the highway, a pickup roars across an adjacent hay meadow, pulls up opposite where you are fishing, and a big beefy fellow jumps out, veins popping out of his neck, and proceeds to read you the riot act for trespassing and tells you that you have to get the hell off the creek. Question: Just what are your rights to fish the Little Piddly?

Both of these hypotheticals occur, in one form or the other, each year in Montana. Prior to 1984, the answers to these questions were anybody's guess. In 1984, two Montana Supreme Court rulings went a long way toward answering these questions. In 1985, legislation enacted to clarify the court rulings further defined the rights of recreationists to use Montana's rivers and streams. At the end of this chapter, we'll revisit those examples and apply the current law to them to provide some answers.

In the early 1980s, a coalition of recreationists and sportsmen's groups, the Montana Coalition for Stream Access, filed lawsuits against landowners on two rivers, the Beaverhead and the Dearborn, to establish the right of recreationists to use them. While there were some differences in the historic uses of these two rivers (the Dearborn had been used to float logs to market; the Beaverhead had not), the issue was the same in both cases—whether recreationists had the right to float, wade, and fish on these rivers. The Supreme Court decided both cases within months of each other, and the basic ruling was the same in each.

The court said that any surface waters capable of recreational use may be used by the public regardless of who owns the streambed, and regardless of whether the river is navigable. This ruling marked a dramatic departure from the law in most other states. With the exception of Wyoming, in every other state the right of public use hinges on whether a waterway is navigable by some kind of craft ("navigable" is one of those chameleon terms in the law that changes meaning according to how it's used, so take care to know in your home state what the term means). After 1984, in Montana, if a stream held some recreational value, landowners could not keep recreationists out of the stream.

The court, and later the legislature, placed some limits on this right of access, however. First, the law limits your right to use a stream to the land between the "ordinary high water marks." What is the ordinary high water mark? It is:

> The line that water impresses on land by covering it for sufficient periods to cause physical characteristics that distinguish the area below the line from the area above it. Characteristics of the area below the line include, when appropriate, but are not limited to deprivation of the soil of substantially all terrestrial vegetation and destruction of its agricultural vegetative value.

The legislature was careful to caution that a floodplain is not considered to be within a stream's ordinary high water mark. Is that clear as mud now?

Actually, the ordinary high water mark is pretty clear most of the time. If you stay below any visible shoreline vegetation, you're probably okay. Otherwise, if you are in doubt about where the mark is, err to the narrowest possible interpretation. Better to narrow your range of movement some than to risk a trespass charge.

The second major limitation to public use is that it does not include a right to cross private lands. You can enter a waterway at some point of public access, such as a highway right-of-way or a fishing access site, but a landowner may post his land against trespass (more about trespass below) above the ordinary high water mark.

The statute also allows landowners to petition the Fish, Wildlife, and Parks Commission to close or restrict waters to public use if the stream does not support any recreational use, public use is damaging the banks and land adjacent to the stream, the public use is damaging the landowner's property under or next to the stream, or if the public use is causing other environmental damage. In the year after passage of the law, there was a spate of closure petitions. Most of these were denied. Only two, one on Nelson Spring Creek, and one on a part of the Musselshell River, were granted.

On Nelson Spring Creek, the commission simply prohibited wading in the stream during cutthroat spawning (June 15 to September 15) to protect spawning beds. Since the landowner on this stream charges a fee, this has the practical effect of keeping uninvited people off the stream during that period.

On the Musselshell, the Fish, Wildlife, and Parks Commission closed the river to public use through the landowner's bison pasture for safety reasons. In both cases, the closures are marked by signs.

An Infestation of Orange

Anywhere you go in Montana, you are likely to be struck by the profusion of fluorescent-orange-topped fenceposts. Those orange monuments are the moral equivalent of trespassing signs in Montana. No, it doesn't really mean that we Montanans can't read. It's simply an offshoot of the stream-access battles of the mid-eighties. One concession to landowners was the simplification of a previously obscure posting requirement by allowing the use of fluorescent orange paint to signify that land is posted, and describing what constitutes adequate posting (a landowner simply has to post his land at gates going into his land and on stream banks where they pass into his land).

Orange paint aside, however, Montana law requires some specific notice that land is closed to trespass before you can be cited for criminal trespass (The one exception to this is big-game hunting—if you plan to hunt big game on private land, you need the landowner's permission even if the land is not posted). This notice can be made by use of signs, orange paint, or even verbally ("Get the hell off my land" will do), but the burden is nonetheless on the landowner to notify you that you are not welcome on his land. If you pass onto land that is not posted and you haven't otherwise been notified that you are not welcome, you can go above the ordinary high water mark. Use this right judiciously, however; landowners have been quite rightly outraged by careless recreationists who have abused the land, and in some instances have simply closed their land off to public use.

When the legislature first amended the law to allow orange paint for posting, word quickly circulated that anyone who posted their land with orange paint couldn't let anybody—even their relatives—on it. Wrong. Just because land is posted does not mean that you can't ask permission. The orange paint simply means that you cannot use the land without express permission (On the other hand, if the landowner posts a sign that says "No trespassing, don't ask," you can take that as a hint about the value of asking permission). If you're not sure about whether you can cross private land to get to a reach of stream, find the landowner and ask permission. The worst you can get from the landowner is a "no."

Now back to those hypothetical problems.

As to the jerk whose barbed wire destroyed your raft, a number of possibilities exist. First, it is not illegal to run boundary fences or stock fences across rivers and streams. But Montana law does make it a criminal misdemeanor to impede navigation on a public stream (Section 45-8-111 MCA). This carries with it a possible fine of $500 and possible jail time. Not exactly a capital crime, but a clear statement of public policy against this kind of shenanigan. The trick here may be in determining whether the fence is a legitimate boundary or stock fence, or whether it is a spite fence. As a practical matter, the criminal statute has rarely, if ever, been used in Montana, perhaps because most people, including county attorneys (who would have to prosecute any violations under it) are unaware of it.

A second possibility would be a civil suit. While civil liability in a case like this always requires close scrutiny of the specific facts, the law generally does not countenance the deliberate placement of hazards such as this. In fact, the stream access statute says that a landowner is liable to a recreationist only for "willful or wanton misconduct"—basically intentional acts. If this happens to you, and you and your camera survive it, get pictures—not only of the damage, but also shots of the hazard from every angle, especially the upstream side.

A couple of other observations about this situation are in order. First, if you are able to see the hazard before you get to it, Montana law allows you to leave the ordinary high water marks and portage around it "in the least intrusive manner possible." This does not mean that you can leave the river at the slightest excuse and call it a "portage," but where an obstacle makes the river genuinely unpassable, you may get out and go around it. Curiously, the legislature has specifically allowed you to portage around artificial obstacles, but is silent as to natural obstacles. So if you come to a waterfall or some other natural obstacle and the adjacent land is posted, you are on your own.

Hypothetical number two: The answer to this one is simple. As long as you keep inside the ordinary high water mark, you may lawfully fish Little Piddly. Whether you want to brave the wrath of a big brute who seems dangerously close to commiting mayhem is a judgment call that you have to make.

But let's embellish the facts a little.

What if, when you got out of your car on the state highway, you could see no orange paint or other indications of "no trespassing" on the land adjacent to the creek? Then, you could cross the field to get to the creek, at least *until* the landowner came out and yelled at you and told you to get off. At that point, you either have to leave his land or stay inside the ordinary high water mark.

Despite the variations described above, staying legal under Montana's stream access law is not all that difficult. Likewise, staying on an amicable footing with landowners and your fellow anglers is fairly easy. If you follow the basic rules below, you should have no trouble using our rivers and streams with a minimum of hassle. Just use a little common sense and courtesy.

Rules of the River

1. If in doubt about your right to get onto a given stream, ask permission.

2. Make sure you know the current regulations for the water you are fishing.

3. Don't litter. If you see litter, pick it up and take it out. Leave the river cleaner than you found it.

4. If you take a dog, keep it under control. If you can't control it, leave it home. If you want it to survive your trip, don't let it harass livestock.

5. If you are camping, don't leave a trace.

6. Take extreme care with fire. If things feel dry to you, don't build one.

7. If there are other anglers on the stream, give them a wide berth.

8. If you're crossing private land, leave all gates as you find them, and leave all fences intact.

HATCH CHARTS FOR WESTERN MONTANA

Fly fishermen have basically three choices with insect hatches: Ignore them, accept them, or hunt them. The hatch charts are designed to help all of these strategies (even "ignoring them" works best when it isn't practiced in ignorance). These charts are not complete. The expanse of the state, with its diverse terrestrial and aquatic environments, makes that impossible. The charts identify the major insect hatches, the ones heavy enough to trigger consistent and often selective trout feeding. The dates for these hatches, covering a number of waters, are broad, too, but the references in the write-ups to individual rivers or lakes give more specific time periods.

The waters mentioned in the hatch chart are rivers unless otherwised noted.

CADDISFLIES	JAN	FEB	MAR	APR	MAY	JUNE	JULY	AUG	SEPT	OCT	NOV	DEC
Grannom *Brachycentrus* sp. size 12–16, wings=dark gray to almost black, body= medium to very dark green The early Grannom (*B.occidentalis*) is also known as the Mother's Day hatch. The summer Grannon is *B. americanus*. Bitterroot, Kootenai, Little Blackfoot, lower Clark Fork, Swan, Thompson				•	• •		•	• • • •	• •			
Green Sedge *Ryacophila* sp. size 12–16, wings=mottled brown or gray, body=bright green There are many important species hatching throughout the summer months on fast-water streams and rivers. Blackfoot, Rock Creek				•	• • • •	• • • •	• • • •	• • • •	• • • •	• •		
Traveller Sedge *Banksiola crotchi* size 6–10, wings=tan to brown, body=tan to brown Appears on lakes two to three weeks after ice-out. Brown's Lake, Georgetown Lake				•	• • • •	• • • •	• • • •	• • •				
Great Grey Spotted Sedge *Arctopsyche grandis* size 8–10, wings=mottled dark gray, body=green Rock Creek					•	• • • •	• • • •	•				
Spotted Sedge *Hydropsyche* sp. size 12–14, wings= spotted brown, body=dirty yellow Major species include *H. vera, H. oslari, H. occidentalis,* and *H. Cockerelli.* Bitterroot, Lolo Creek, Kootenai, Rock Creek, Swan, Thompson, upper Clark Fork, West Fork Bitterroot						• •	• • • •	• • • •	• • • •	• • •		
Little Sister Sedge *Cheumatopsyche campyla* size 16–18, wings=tan, body=ginger Bitterroot, lower Clark Fork, Kootenai, Swan, upper Clark Fork						•	• • • •	• • • •	• • •			
Long-Horn Sedge *Oecetis avara* size 12–14, wings=ginger, body=ginger Bunyan Lake							• • •	• • •				
Giant Orange Sedge *Dicosmoecus* sp. size 8, wings=mottled dark brown, body=burnt orange Also known as October Caddis, which is misleading because it is more important during September in Montana. Bitterroot, Blackfoot, Rock Creek, Swan, West Fork Bitterroot									• • • •	• • •		

CRANE FLIES	JAN	FEB	MAR	APR	MAY	JUNE	JULY	AUG	SEPT	OCT	NOV	DEC
Orange Crane Fly *Tipula* sp. size 6–10, wings=light veined, body=orange Upper Clark Fork							• • •	• • • •	•			

DAMSELFLIES	JAN	FEB	MAR	APR	MAY	JUNE	JULY	AUG	SEPT	OCT	NOV	DEC
Various species size 8–12, wings=clear in most species, body=bright blue or green in most common species. (Often hatch at the same time as mosquitoes.) Lakes: Brown's, Burnt Fork, Echo, Frank, Georgetown, Gleason, Horseshoe, Hubbart Reservoir, Medicine, Metcalf, Moore, Willow, Woods						••	••••	••••	••			

MAYFLIES	JAN	FEB	MAR	APR	MAY	JUNE	JULY	AUG	SEPT	OCT	NOV	DEC
Blue-Winged Olive *Baetis parvus and Baetis tricaudatus* size 16, wings=slate gray, body=olive Also called Iron Dun on some Montana rivers Bitterroot Irrigation Ditch, Bitterroot, Blackfoot, Kootenai, Little Blackfoot, lower Clark Fork, Rock Creek, Thompson, upper Clark Fork			••••	••			••••		•	••••	•	
Red Quill *Rhithrogena morrisoni* size 14, wings=medium gray, body=light reddish brown Also known as Western March Brown lower Clark Fork			•	••••	•							
Green Drake *Drunella grandis* size 6–8, wings=gray, body=dark olive Formerly was genus *Ephemerella* Bitterroot, Thompson, upper Clark Fork, West Fork Bitterroot					•	••••	•••					
Brown Drake *Ephemera simulans* size 10–12, wings=brown, body=yellowish brown Bitterroot, Thompson, upper Clark Fork, West Fork Bitterroot					•	••••	•••					
Light Cahill *Cinygma dimicki* size 12–14, wings=cream, body=cream Also known as Western Light Cahill lower Clark Fork						••	•••					
Gray Drake *Siphlonurus occidentalis* size 10–12, wings=medium gray, body=gray Bitterroot Irrigation Ditch, Bitterroot, lower Clark Fork, Thompson							•••	•••				
Ginger Quill *Heptagenia simplicoides* size 12–14, wings=ginger, body=ginger Lolo Creek, lower Clark Fork							•••	•••				
Callibaetis *Callibaetis americanus* size 14–16, wings=gray, body=gray Blackfoot, Cottonwood Lakes, Elk Lake, Georgetown Lake, Horseshoe Lake, Job Corps Ponds							••	••••	••••	•		
Pale Morning Dun *Ephemerella infrequens* and *Ephemerella inermis* size 14–18, wings=pale gray, body=pale yellow Bitterroot, Blackfoot, Kootenai, lower Clark Fork, Rock Creek, upper Clark Fork								••	••••	•••		
Trico *Tricorythodes minutus* size 18–20, wings=dark gray, body=very dark olive (appears black) Bitterroot Irrigation Ditch, Bitterroot, Blackfoot, Georgetown Lake, Kootenai, lower Clark Fork, Rock Creek, Thompson, upper Clark Fork								••	•••			
Blue-Winged Red Quill *Rhithrogena undulata* size 16, wings=brownish gray, body=reddish brown Also known as Small Western Red Quill Bitterroot, West Fork Bitterroot								•	••			
Slate-Winged Mahogany Dun *Paraleptophlebia bicornuta* size 12–14, wings=dark gray, body=blackish brown lower Clark Fork									••	••		

STONEFLIES	JAN	FEB	MAR	APR	MAY	JUNE	JULY	AUG	SEPT	OCT	NOV	DEC
Winter Stone	••••	•••										
Capnia sp. — size 16–18, wings=dark veined, body=very dark olive (appears black)												
Little Blackfoot												
Skwala			•••	•••								
Skwala parallela — size 10–12, wings=dark veined, body=olive												
Bitterroot, lower Clark Fork, West Fork Bitterroot												
Brown Stone			•	••••	•							
Nemoura sp. — size 10–14, wings=dark veined, body=brown												
lower Clark Fork												
Salmon Fly						•••	••					
Pteronarcys californica — size 4–6, wings=dark veined, body=dark orange												
Bitterroot, Blackfoot, lower Clark Fork, Rock Creek, Thompson, upper Clark Fork												
Little Olive Stone						•••	••••	••				
Alloperla sp. — size 14–16, wings=dark veined, body=bright olive												
Blackfoot												
Golden Stone						•••	••••	••				
Calineuria californica — size 6–8, wings=ginger veined, body=golden												
Big Salmon, Bitterroot, Blackfoot, Clearwater, Rock Creek, upper Clark Fork, West Fork Bitterroot												
Yellow Sally							••	••••	••••	•		
Isoperla sp. — size 14–16, wings=yellow veined, body=bright yellow												
Nez Perce Fork, West Fork Bitterroot												

TWO-WINGED FLIES	JAN	FEB	MAR	APR	MAY	JUNE	JULY	AUG	SEPT	OCT	NOV	DEC
Midges	••••	••••	••••	••••	••••	••••	••••	••••	••••	••••	••••	••••
Diptera — sizes 14–28, midges come in most colors												
Various species												
Hatch everywhere and all year												
Midges are especially important on rivers during the winter months and on high mountain lakes all summer.												

INDEX OF WATERS

M

N

O

P

Q

R

S

Design & Layout
Q Communications Group
Helena, Montana
Composed in
Stone Serif & Futura
Printed on Joy White Offset (acid-free) by
Thomson-Shore, Inc.
Dexter, Michigan

Find Yourself in Montana

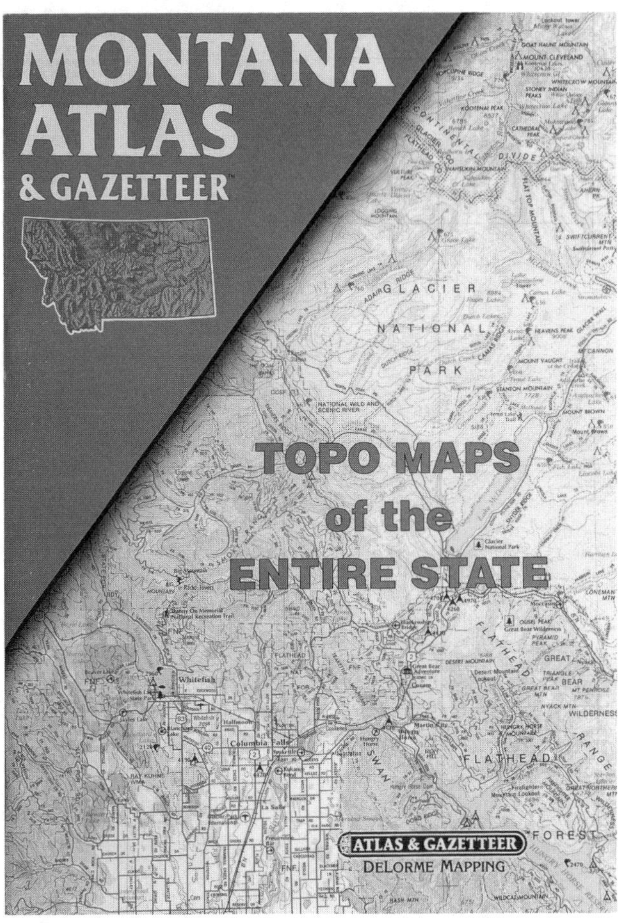

Montana Atlas & Gazetteer

In this atlas the entire state fits into 74 quadrangle maps that you will find indispensible while traveling and fishing in Montana. The maps cover everything from major highways to back roads; from national forests and parks to state fishing access sites; from major rivers, lakes, and reservoirs to high mountain lakes and streams; from towns to campgrounds. It will get you there and bring you back.

11 x 15⅝ inches, 96 pages

$14.95 (please add $3.00 for postage)
For additional atlases to the same address add just $.50 each. VISA and MasterCard accepted.

Described in the introduction to the *Montana Fly Fishing Guides* by John Holt.

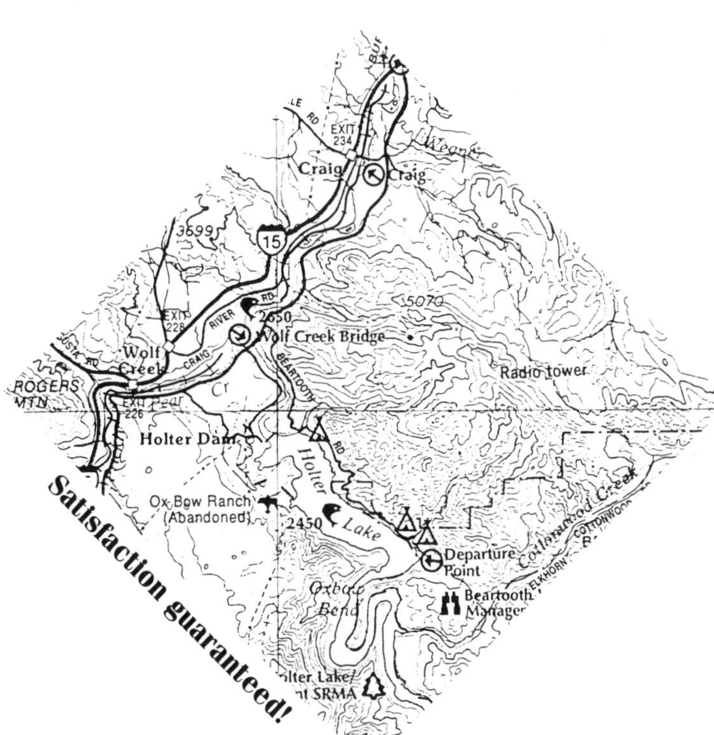

To order, call or write:

The Book Mailer
P. O. Box 1273H
Helena, Montana 59624
(406) 443-1888

(Wyoming and Idaho atlases also available for $14.95 each plus postage)

Ask about the Cordes/LaFontaine Pocket Guide how-to series on fly fishing. Includes basic fly fishing, dry fly fishing, fly fishing with nymphs, fly fishing on lakes, fly casting, fly tying, and other fishing topics.

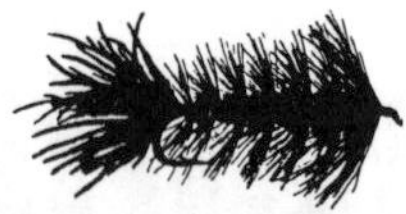

Other Greycliff Titles

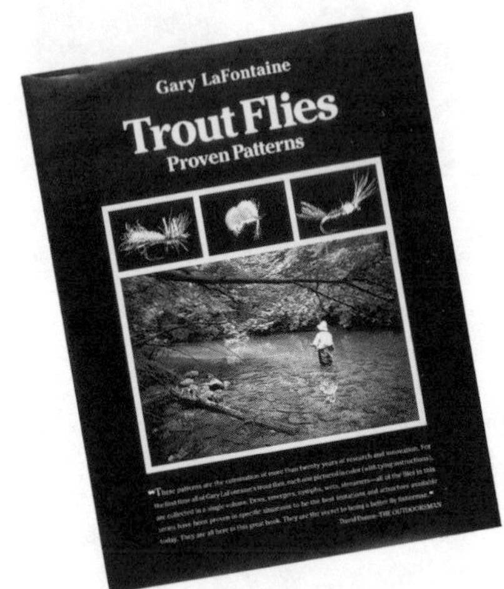

Trout Flies: Proven Patterns by Gary LaFontaine

"Straightforward, yet witty; pragmatic, yet impassioned—this is the best book on fly fishing I've read in years."
—John Holt, author of *Montana Fly Fishing Guide*

Trout Flies presents the most carefully tested series of proven fish-takers available to fly fishermen. Sixty-two of them, including nationally acclaimed patterns such as the Emergent Sparkle Pupa and completely new innovations like the Twist Nymph. This is not just another recipe book—it abounds with fine observations on the habitat, the fish, and the techniques. It gives anglers the best of modern flies and all the information they need to fool fish consistently with these exciting patterns.

Hardcover, 8½ x 11 inches, 280 pages, 62 flies—each with b/w & color photos, description, illustrated tying steps, recipe, and entry from Gary's fishing log, ISBN 0-9626663-1-9, $39.95

The Dry Fly, New Angles by Gary LaFontaine

"*The Dry Fly* offers some of the best reflective analyses of trout behavior and dry-fly form and function in print."
—John Randolph, *Fly Fisherman*

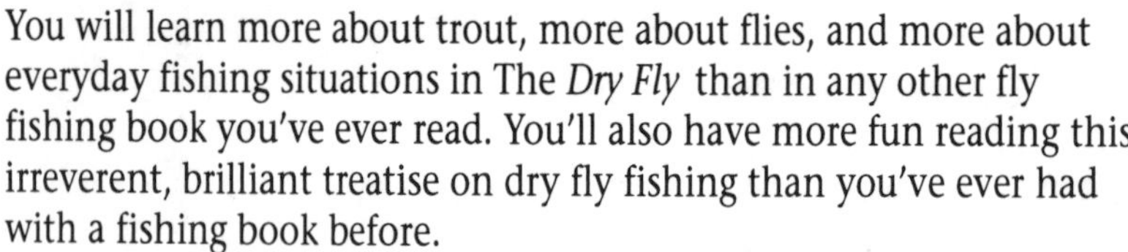

You will learn more about trout, more about flies, and more about everyday fishing situations in The *Dry Fly* than in any other fly fishing book you've ever read. You'll also have more fun reading this irreverent, brilliant treatise on dry fly fishing than you've ever had with a fishing book before.

Hardcover, 8½ x 11 inches, 308 pages, 150 illustrations, more than 50 b/w photos, 4 pages of color plates, ISBN 0-9626663-0-0, $39.95

River Rap Audio Series—Gary LaFontaine interviews the experts on fly fishing the best rivers. Imagine fishing the **Madison** with Craig Mathews, the **Henry's Fork** with Mike Lawson, the **Upper Yellowstone in the Park** with Bob Jacklin, and **Montana's Upper Yellowstone** with John Bailey. Each packs a lifetime of fly fishing insights on his river into a 90-minute audio cassette. Reviewer Ron Markum ran out of superlatives to describe the audios and ended commenting, "I do know that last summer was the finest of my fly fishing life because of them."

Each river is on its own 90-minute audio tape that comes with a 6-page booklet including map of the river, fly pattern list, and hatch chart. $13.95 each

To order, call or write:

The Book Mailer
P. O. Box 1273H
Helena, Montana 59624
(406) 443-1888

Please add $3.00 for postage. For additional titles to the same address add $.50 each. Visa and MasterCard accepted.

Satisfaction guaranteed!